Allan Janik

Assembling Reminders

Studies in the Genesis of Wittgenstein's
Concept of Philosophy

Santérus
Academic Press
Sweden

www.santerus.se

All rights reserved. No part of this publication may be reproduced, stored in a retrieval system, or transmitted, in any form or by any means, electronic, mechanical, photocopying, recording, or otherwise, without the prior written permission of the publisher, except in the case of brief quotations embodied in critical articles and reviews.

© 2006 Allan Janik and Santérus Academic Press Sweden
ISBN: 978-91-7335-000-6
Layout: Santérus Academic Press Sweden
Cover: Sven Bylander and Santérus Academic Press
The picture on the cover is a sketch of Wittgenstein by Michael Drobil.
Santérus Academic Press Sweden is an imprint of
Santérus Förlag, Stockholm, Sweden
academicpress@santerus.se
www.santerus.se
Printed by BOD, Germany 2012

To the Memory of Marcel Faust

Contents

1. PREFACE: Wittgenstein on Being Influenced • 11

2. LUDWIG BOLTZMANN: Reason Overshoots the Mark • 23

3. HEINRICH HERTZ: Alternative Representations • 45

4. ARTHUR SCHOPENHAUER: The Opaque Self • 73

5. GOTTLOB FREGE: The Quest for Objectivity • 97

6. BERTRAND RUSSELL: Loaded Questions • 123

7. KARL KRAUS: Style as Strategy • 145

8. ADOLF LOOS: Craftsmanship • 163

9. OTTO WEININGER: The Problem of Limits • 183

10. OSWALD SPENGLER: The Physiognomical Turn • 205

Wittgenstein's Works

I refer to Wittgenstein's works parenthetically in the text as follows. Ludwig Wittgenstein,
PI with paragraph number = *Philosophical Investigations*, trans., G. E. M. Anscombe (Oxford: Basil Blackwell 1958).
BBB with page number = *The Blue and Brown Books*, ed. Rush Rhees (New York: Harper's 1956).
BEE with ms and page number = Wittgenstein's *Nachlass* Bergen Electronic Edition (Oxford: Oxford University Press 2000).
C+V with page number = *Culture and Value*, ed. G. H. von Wright in collaboration with Heikki Nyman, revised by Alois Pichler and trans. Peter Winch (2nd ed. with revised translation; Oxford: Blackwell 1998).
E with letter number = Paul Engelmann, *Letters from Ludwig Wittgenstein with a Memoir*, trans., L. Furtmüller (Oxford: Basil Blackwell 1967).
F with letter number = *Briefe an Ludwig von Ficker*, ed. G. H. von Wright (»Brenner Studien« Vol. 1; Salzburg: Otto Müller, 1969).
Fr with letter number = »Gottlob Frege: Briefe an Ludwig Wittgenstein«, eds. Allan Janik & C. P. Berger, *Grazer Philosophische Studien*, Vol. 33/34 (1989), 3–33.

ICE: Wittgenstein Gesamtbriefwechsel (New York: InteLex Electronic Publishers 2004).

GT with date = *Geheime Tagebücher*, ed. W. Baum (Vienna: Turia & Kant 1992).

K with page number = *Denkbewegungen* [The Koder Notebook], ed. Ilse Somavilla (Innsbruck: Haymon 1996).

L+C with page number = *Lectures and Conversations on Aesthetics, Psychology and Religious Belief*, ed. C. Barrett (Oxford: Blackwell 1966).

N with page number = *Notebooks 1914-16*, trans. G.E.M. Anscombe (Oxford: Basil Blackwell 1961).

O with letter number = *Letters to C.K. Ogden*, ed, G.H. von Wright (Oxford: Blackwell 1973).

OC with paragraph number = *On Certainty*, trans. G.E.M. Anscombe & Denis Paul (New York: Harper's 1969).

OCL with section and paragraph number = *Remarks on Color*, ed. G.E.M. Anscombe (Berkeley and Los Angeles: University of California Press 1978).

R, K, M with letter number = respectively to *Letters to Russell, Keynes and Moore*, ed. G.H. von Wright (2nd ed. rev.; Ithaca, Cornell University Press 1974).

T with proposition number = *Tractatus Logico-Philosophicus*, trans., D.F: Pears and B.F. McGuinness (London: Routledge & Kegan Paul 1961).

WV with page number = *Wörterbuch für Volksschulen* (Vienna: Hölder-Pichler-Tempsky 1977).

WWK with page number = *Wittgenstein und der Wiener Kreis shorthand notes by F. Waismann*, ed. B.F. McGuinness (Oxford: Basil Blackwell 1967).

Z with paragraph number = *Zettel*, trans, G.E.M Anscombe (Oxford: Blackwell 1967).

PREFACE

Wittgenstein on Being Influenced:

Reflections on MS 154 V 15, 1931

PERHAPS THE MOST ASTONISHING claim that Ludwig Wittgenstein ever made was that he was basically an unoriginal thinker who merely reproduced the ideas of others with a vengeance in his philosophical »work of clarification« (C+V, 16). Foes as well as friends of his way of philosophizing for the most part find this statement simply absurd. Whatever Wittgenstein was, he was certainly a highly original thinker; however perverse one might consider his novel way of doing philosophy. Why, then, should he have so considered himself? Why do we have so much difficulty seeing what was more than obvious to him? The answer lies in the fact that friends and foes alike have not taken his own remarks about himself seriously enough to investigate meticulously the ways in which his ten precursors, Boltzmann, Hertz, Schopenhauer, Frege, Russell, Kraus, Loos, Weininger, Spengler, Sraffa, might have led him to develop his »work of clarification« as he did. The purpose of this study is to initiate systematic study of 9 of those figures and their influence upon him (at the time of this writing virtually nothing is known about how the Cambridge economist Piero Sraffa might have influenced him).

The point of departure must be a close reading of the frequently cited but seldom analyzed text in which Wittgenstein's list of influences occurs. It runs as follows:

I think there is some truth in the idea that I think only reproductively. I don't believe that I have ever *invented* a line of thinking, I have always taken one over from someone else. I have simply straightaway seized upon it with enthusiasm for my work of clarification. That is how Boltzmann, Hertz, Schopenhauer, Frege, Russell, Kraus, Loos, Weininger, Spengler, Sraffa have influenced me. Can one take the case of Breuer and Freud as an example of Jewish reproductiveness? – What I invent are new *comparisons*.

When I modeled the head for Drobil too the stimulus was essentially a work of Drobil's and my contribution once again was really clarification. What I do think essential is carrying out the work of clarification with *courage*: otherwise it just becomes a clever game.

The Jew must see to it that in a literal sense »all things are as nothing to him«. But this is particularly hard for him, since in a sense he has nothing that is particularly his. It is much harder to accept poverty willingly when you *have* to be poor than when you might also be rich.

It might be said (rightly or wrongly) that the Jewish mind does not have the power to produce even the tiniest flower or blade of grass; its way it rather to make a drawing of the flower or blade of grass that has grown in the soil of another's mind and to put it into a comprehensive picture. We aren't pointing to a fault when we say this and everything is all right as long as what is being done is quite clear. In is only when the nature of a Jewish work is confused with a non-Jewish work that there is any danger, especially when the author of the Jewish work falls into the confusion him-

self, as he easily may. (»Doesn't He look as proud as though he had produced the milk himself?«)
It is typical of a Jewish mind [like mine] to understand someone else's work better than he understands it himself.

Wittgenstein, MS 154 v 15, 1931
(C+V, 16–17)

This is surely one of the most tantalizing texts that a philosophical genius – Wittgenstein is surely entitled to the term, if anybody ever was – ever wrote about himself. It is astonishing in the light of the frequency with which the list of influences as well as the idea that Wittgenstein was a reproductive, because Jewish, thinker, is quoted that it has not yet been the subject of a close reading; for the text is more complicated than has generally been recognized. Let us consider it in detail with a view to getting straight about precisely what Wittgenstein wanted to say about himself and, above all, his philosophy.

The first point to be made about that text is that it can be read as a statement about his lack of originality, his »Judaism«, the origins of his ideas or any combination of them. Yet, to restrict it to merely those themes, as most commentators do, is to oversimplify the text drastically. What is really at stake here is in fact something very important about the origins of Wittgenstein's conception of philosophy. The themes of Judaism, reproductivity and even the idea that Wittgenstein produced the definitive list of »influences« in the conventional sense upon his thought are all secondary and, in a sense that he in fact specifies himself, misleading. It remains to be seen how that is so.

Wittgenstein begins by agreeing with himself: he is a reproductive thinker. The point of stressing that he begins by agreeing with himself is to emphasize that he has already been mulling over the notion that he is merely a reproductive thinker for some time. It is not a mere aperçu.

The idea that he was merely a reproductive thinker, which seems to satisfy him so much, has hardly ever been taken seriously coming, as it does, from one of the 20th century's most original minds. After all, Martin Heidegger, his only real competition among philosophers for that title (apart perhaps from the much neglected Ludwik Fleck), did everything to play up the »inspired« nature of his philosophical insights in his darkly oracular mode of presentation both when lecturing and in print.

Even more unnerving is the idea that Wittgenstein's »reproductive«, unoriginal character is connected with his being Jewish. This has understandably been a red flag in many quarters. Have not Jewish intellectuals been at the forefront of intellectual and artistic creativity from Einstein, Husserl, Proust and Chagall down to today? However, making that objection misses Wittgenstein's point massively for his seeming modesty (verging on the pathological in the eyes of many) is anything but that. As it turns out »reproductive« Jews like him have a way of understanding other people – and here it is clear that he means the profoundly creative – *better than they do themselves*. Indeed, the swing of the pendulum from the beginning to the end of the text could hardly be wider. It seems as if he has moved from self-hatred to megalomania but that too is exaggerated.

His example of the relationship of the reproductive to the innovative mind, however, is highly instructive. It is that of the relationship between Freud and Breuer, whereby Breuer made the breakthrough to understanding the repressed causes of hysterical behavior but it was Freud who developed his insight into the mechanisms of unconscious motivation and produced a therapy for the disorders that are caused by repression that we now know as psychoanalysis. This was certainly one of the reasons why Wittgenstein could identify his work in philosophy as Freudian: like Freud, Wittgenstein took up – his word is »seized upon« – insights from others but developed them boldly *à outrance* to attain depths that the innovator himself was incapable of sounding. However, his case is yet more complicated than Freud's; for, whereas Freud had but a single inventive predecessor, Wittgenstein had ten.

The more one looks at the passage as a whole, the closer one comes to recognizing that Wittgenstein's understanding of »Jewish« as related to the kind of cultivation that enabled the great (assimilated) Jewish patrons of the arts in places like Vienna and Berlin around 1900 (including the Wittgensteins) to recognize and appreciate talented young innovators in the arts.[1] Such aesthetic cultivation requires 1) *insight* into the worthwhile character of an artistic innovation, 2) which by its very nature as innovation, is, in a sense, *incomprehensible* to the traditionally-minded, be they artists or connoisseurs, as well as 3) the *ability to persuade* the traditionally-minded that it is possible to practice painting or poetry in a radically new, but nevertheless intelligible, way. Such competencies made the sponsors fin de siècle salons into cultural leaders and motors for intellectual change: without being directly involved in the creative process their reception of novelty was itself highly creative. It is hardly surprising that there should be a parallel to Wittgenstein's self-understanding. This would be one way of understanding what it is to take an isolated phenomenon and paint it a part of a comprehensive picture. It is certainly an adequate description of what Freud did with Breuer's insight (the infamous Anna O. was Breuer's case study, not Freud's) into the repressed character of hysterical behavior. Whether Wittgenstein also thought of Hertz's relationship to Maxwell in this context is an open question but the model seems to fit there as well. In any case, it is in this most creative sense that Wittgenstein was »reproductive«. However, we should not be misled by the passive mode of expression: being receptive to influence in this sense is anything but a passive matter. The reference to the Jew »having nothing of his own« would in this context, in fact, refer to receptivity as a condition for understanding someone better than he did himself. Gradually the sense of Wittgenstein's text becomes comprehensible.

Moreover, it has scarcely been noted in the literature that what Wittgenstein's remarks about taste from 1947 (*C+V*, 68–69) are directly related to those about being Jewish and reproductive in the notorious seemingly pathetic passages from 1931. The observations on taste are highly useful for determining exactly what he was driving at in terming himself reproductive since he considers having taste as antithetical to being original. Whereas the genuinely creative person is wild and gripping in what he does the person of taste is sensitive in his receptivity to originality. He is especially sensitive to the appropriate form of re-presenting established forms (or ideas) in a modern context: he translates older forms into a new language adjusting them, refining them, polishing them and making them acceptable to a new age. His effect is to charm his reader but he is tempted to do so on the basis of mere cleverness and/or tricks. This boils down to asserting that the reproductive philosopher develops rhetorical strategies for convincing his reader of what the truly innovative wild thinkers have thought. To that end he develops various stylistic tactics for refining their insights. In the course of doing so he is capable of seeing things implicit in their thought that they were themselves not aware of. In effect, Wittgenstein asserts that he is reproductive with respect to insight but innovative with respect to the form of presentation of philosophical thoughts, which itself is a certain kind of creative activity:

recollecting their wild thoughts in tranquility allows him to see aspects of their views that were obscure to them.

In any case, it is no less important to consider *exactly* what Wittgenstein is claiming when he maintains that he was *influenced* by the 10 figures he mentions. It is frequently assumed that he is referring to his philosophical development in general; whereas what he explicitly refers to is his »work of clarification«. As to his understanding of the word, Wittgenstein's discussion of his relation to Drobil provides a little (but not much) help here. The professional sculptor's work was a kind of paradigm that Wittgenstein adjusted to his own purposes by stripping it down to its essentials. We can get a bit clearer by considering a case from Wittgenstein's better understood work in architecture that forms a strict parallel to the example of his »clarifying« activity as a sculptor. Paul Wijdeveld insists that what is distinctively Wittgensteinian in the austere elegance of Palais Stonborough was less the result of his desire to create a new aesthetic form than of a desire »to clarify the roots of traditional monumental architecture«[2] This was a matter of showing the basis of the achievement of, say, a Fischer von Erlach, of helping people to understand what was fundamental to his achievement by stripping it down to its essentials such that what was indeed fundamental could be unequivocally seen at a glance. But to return to the main point at issue here, what do these considerations from art and architecture imply about his »work of clarification« *in philosophy*? In fact, the reference appears to have more to do with his *philosophical method* than it does with the substance of his philosophical views. Thus Wittgenstein emphasizes that he takes his contribution to philosophy to be the introduction of new comparisons, which would indicate that the ten figures on his list showed him the way to a method rather than specific solutions to problems.

In addition, the fact that he was writing in 1931 indicates

that Wittgenstein was referring to his mature philosophical method as it would ultimately be expressed in the so-called »philosophy chapter« of the *Philosophical Investigations*, i.e., Paragraphs 89–133 in part I of that book. However, since the list is also chronological it is not entirely false to see it as recording something important about Wittgenstein's philosophical development as well. Finally, we should also note that what Wittgenstein wants to call our attention to in mentioning Boltzmann, Hertz, Schopenhauer, Frege, Russell, Kraus, Loos, Weininger, Spengler and Sraffa is something in the work of each of them that the figure in question himself *did not see*. At the beginning of the 21st century it is easy to overlook the fact that at the time Wittgenstein encountered these figures the *philosophical* achievements of Boltzmann, Hertz and Frege, for example, were only known to a select few (the former remain so for the most part). Even today it is anything but simple to imagine that the likes of Weininger and Spengler, let alone Kraus and Loos have something profound to tell us about how to deal with the problems of *analytical philosophy*. This is all in aid of saying that an investigation into how the 10 influenced Wittgenstein cannot merely be a matter of looking into their writings or exploring their achievements, rather it must be an investigation into how their work led Wittgenstein to insights *implicit* in it that they themselves did *not* see. The nine studies that make up *Assembling Reminders* are an effort to do that.

The essays collected here draw heavily upon the history of ideas with a view to getting straight about exactly where, on Wittgenstein's own account, what is most difficult to grasp in his way of approaching philosophical problems comes from and how that fits into philosophy today. They take their point of departure in what Wittgenstein said about being influenced by the ten figures listed above. In the first version of his list, as Alois Pichler indicates in the notes to the second German edition of *Culture and Value*, it is composed of only Frege, Russell, Spengler and Sraffa. This seems to indicate that his main philosophical impulses came from them. Adding Boltzmann, Hertz and Schopenhauer thus appears to give us a clue concerning the kinds of considerations that made first Frege and then the others important for him. In some sense the slant he got on Frege and Russell from the earlier three would appear then to have led him to the others. It is certainly highly significant that the list originally began with Frege, as the studies below bear out.

»Influence« covers a multitude of sins. So we should be clear from the start about what counts as philosophically interesting with respect to that concept. Inasmuch as the notion of »influence« has a philosophically significant meaning, it refers to the way in which one thinker takes over a concept from another such that his or her own problems can be viewed in a fresh new way. What was previously puzzling becomes manageable. To be influenced in this sense is to develop a concept of one's own on the basis of a suggestion made by another such that one is capable of »seeing things together« in a new and profitably way, i.e., asking new questions and/or representing hitherto anomalous phenomena. In short, if we are to consider influence at all in the history of philosophy, it should be absolutely central matter and not a mechanical push-pull phenomenon.

It is clear from Wittgenstein's list that he means to say something similar about what he took to be his most important philosophical achievement, his new method of making philosophical problems »dissolve« by introducing strikingly new comparisons, when he speaks of having been »influenced« by the ten figures mentioned. The very fact that he *fails* to mention any number of thinkers with whom he was intensely preoccupied his whole life long such as Kierkegaard, St. Augustine,

Tolstoy, Freud, William James or Lichtenberg or important contemporaries like Frank Ramsey, to name but a few, should not pass unobserved. The crucial thing is that these figures, who may have »influenced« him in the less interesting, conventional sense, seem not to have had an impact upon his philosophical method, his peculiar approach to philosophical problems. Moreover, we know that in Wittgenstein's case what was strikingly provocative was more important than what was true when it came to stimulating his thoughts as the case of Weininger demonstrates. Thus he could write to Moore on the 23rd of August 1931 that; »it isn't necessary or rather possible to agree with him but the greatness lies in that with which we disagree.« (*M*, 17) This singular regard for the fascinating at the expense of the true is diametrically opposed to the »scientific conception of the world« as Otto Neurath termed the program of the Vienna Circle. It is one of the important things that must be explained in Wittgenstein's thought.

It is by no means the only thing we need to learn: despite the availability of the complete *Nachlass* in the form of the Bergen Electronic Edition (*BEE*) and the Brenner Archives' edition of his complete correspondence *(ICE)*, the most important questions about whence Wittgenstein came and whither his philosophy leads remain matters of speculation. These studies are bold conjectures that aim at helping us to explain the genesis of his thought. They make no claim to completeness. They should illuminate precisely those aspects of Wittgenstein philosophical background that seem to militate against identifying him with scientific empiricism and analytical philosophy but also with any other conventional type of philosophy. In fact the deepest affinities of the later Wittgenstein are with a rehabilitated Aristotelian practical philosophy, a defense of »impure reason«, which requires *inter alia* Wittgensteinian insights. However, that is material for a study in itself. The

PREFACE: WITTGENSTEIN ON BEING INFLUENCED

aim here is to sketch his points of departure within a neglected strain in the philosophy of science as well as his ways of bringing insights from outside the tradition of positivism and analytical philosophy to bear upon the central problems that analytical philosophers face. This book should contribute to the ongoing discussions of the origins and meaning of Wittgenstein's philosophy by focusing discussion sharply upon what Wittgenstein has said about himself.

My debts are numerous. They are for the most part identified in the notes. However, a special word of thanks is due to Brian McGuinness, who more or less suggested the whole project with the assertion that Wittgenstein tells you what is important as background to his thought. He has also provided encouragement and corrective insight for which I am very grateful. The errors that remain are my own.

Unless otherwise specified, all translations are my own. I have occasionally modified the standard translations.

Allan Janik
Innsbruck, March 2006

CHAPTER 1

Ludwig Boltzmann: Reason Overshoots the Mark

»Philosophy gets on my nerves«[3]
Boltzmann, Notes for a lecture on natural philosophy

IN 1931 WHEN WITTGENSTEIN came to make the final version of the list of figures who had influenced him, Ludwig Boltzmann was at the head of that list.[4] Informed commentators such as G. H. von Wright and Brian McGuinness assume that this list is chronological. This ought to mean that in his own eyes the deepest strain in Wittgenstein's view of philosophy as he saw it at the beginning of what is conventionally termed his *later* period came from Boltzmann. Yet, the question of how Boltzmann had an impact on what was to become the method of *Philosophical Investigations* remains little discussed in the voluminous literature on Wittgenstein. We forget at our peril that Wittgenstein's list relates to not merely to influences upon his philosophical development generally but specifically the figures who molded his »work of clarification« as he understood it in 1931. It is easy enough to find loose (and thus not particularly interesting) analogies between, say, Boltzmann's advocacy of the utility of mental pictures or models, as would say today, in physical theory and the so-called »picture theory« of the proposition in the *Tractatus* but his work seems light years away from the later Wittgenstein – or so it *seems*. In fact, it is precisely the *analogical* character of the most fundamental mode of human knowing that is at the very heart of both Wittgenstein's mature philosophy[5] and Boltzmann's theory of knowledge. In any case, it is precisely the relationship between Boltzmann's view of philosophy and Wittgenstein's mature concept of philosophical method that requires elucidation if we are to take Wittgenstein himself seriously.

Brian McGuinness has pointed out that Boltzmann's »influence« upon Wittgenstein is not likely to bear upon his work in physics, which the teenaged Wittgenstein was not intellectually equipped to appreciate, but with the philosophical views that came to preoccupy him increasingly in the period from the mid-1890s until his death in 1906.[6] It should not pass unnoticed that this seemingly innocent assertion actually informs us that Wittgenstein did not come to philosophy from physics or engineering but began as a teenage philosopher of science, who, like Boltzmann himself, also happened to be interested in aeronautics. Indeed, it seems that Wittgenstein's choosing a career in philosophy was not build upon but an alternative to his early work in aeronautical engineering (which does not preclude his having learned things of value for his philosophizing in the course of his training as an engineer).[7] With that in mind we propose to take a look at Boltzmann's *Popular Writings* (*Populäre Schriften*)[8] with a view to establishing the historical background to the well-known views on philosophy that we find in the *Philosophical Investigations*.

The center of Boltzmann's epistemology is the notion that we come to know nature in the basis of the »pictures« (*Bilder*) that we form, i.e., by speculating in the form of making models or analogies which would guide us in our search for scientific explanations. Thus he considers Christopher Columbus (alongside Michael Faraday, usually considered to be a brilliant experimentalist and J. Robert Mayer, who first formulated the Law of Conservation of Energy) as an outstanding »theorist«

on the basis of the way his bold new picture of the world radically advanced knowledge. These »subjective« models do not and cannot correspond to nature in a 1 to 1 basis but anticipate the contours of a terrain that the scientist, like Columbus, proposes to explore with the utmost exactitude. Our »subjective« ideal of clarity and precision cannot in and of itself rule out vagueness in our concepts *a-priori* precisely because they cannot have a 1 to 1 correspondence with what they would map. Furthermore those ideals do not imply that we are always in a position to define crucial concepts precisely. »Species« (30; 47) and »number« (137; 319) are two, among many, crucial concepts that science profitably employs but cannot define. Clarity for Boltzmann will not be in the first instance a matter of defining concepts exactly but of the conceptual coherence and suggestive power of models in guiding us in our search of knowledge. Thus Boltzmann urges scientists to formulate bold conjectures in the form of mathematical models to guide our inquiries into nature along a sure path. These models will be useful to the extent that they are completely clear; their mathematical structure insures complete clarity. For that reason Boltzmann admonishes scientists not to bring experience into the process to early (108; 262); for it may turn out to be counterproductive with respect to the clarity of our concepts. Herein lies the main difference between Columbus and the modern scientist. Boltzmann emphasizes the role of ingenuity and imagination in our efforts to understand recalcitrant nature, citing the example of Maxwell (and anticipating Wittgenstein and others who would question whether the successful scientist should be termed a »discoverer« or an »inventor«). Subsequent experience shows the value of our models inasmuch as it contradicts or confirms what we have claimed is true. Unlike Mach, but like Popper, Boltzmann is a curious kind of realist. The speculative of character our theories and the arbitrary elements in our models does not disturb Boltzmann because he sees the activity of being involved in the theoretical enterprise in a similar way to, say, Imre Lakatos or Stephen Toulmin later, i.e., as a collective, Socratic, self-critical one: »its very defects are grounded in its own nature and it is theory itself that uncovers its own errors« (36; 79).

He goes so far as to insist that the empirical correctness and conceptual clarity of our models is so deeply anchored in the very nature of the theoretical process itself that it was superfluous for his highly-esteemed colleague Hertz to make correctness and clarity explicit demands upon our models of nature (58; 164: it is highly significant that Boltzmann makes no mention whatsoever of the third Hertzian property of models, their »appropriateness«, here). He further emphasizes that it is of the nature of theory as subjective analogy that it always be underdetermined as we would say. Beyond that, he scandalized many of his contemporaries (and anticipated Bohr's approach to quantum mechanics) by insisting that there could well be a number of »true« theories that could account for a given phenomenon. The aim is not to »explain« nature on the basis of, say, some causal agency behind it but to describe natural phenomena as comprehensively as possible on the basis of fallible analyses that reduce complex natural processes to simple components which are qualitatively identical with those processes.

Yet, he was not unaware of the controversies surrounding such a novel, constructivist view of knowledge. From Mach onwards the possibility of producing genuine knowledge of nature on the basis of mathematical models was confronted with the question of how we could be certain that the clear and distinct models we make for ourselves of natural phenomena in fact refer to something in the world external to us. From the point of view of the subject, the clarity of our ideas, like

1. LUDWIG BOLTZMANN ...

the intensity of our experiences, is no simple guarantee that our ideas and experiences correspond to anything. This was especially vexing for Boltzmann as an advocate of the theory of atoms at a time when they could not be observed. How could he establish that they were anything more than figments of his imagination?[9] In the light of this problem it should not be surprising that Boltzmann takes what he termed the philosopher's »confusion« (*Verwirrung*), i.e., solipsism in the face of the »unverifiability« of atoms, seriously indeed as part of his project to defend the use of models. The subjective origins of the theoretical enterprise is emphasized by Boltzmann to the extent that he will indeed refer to the solitary theorist as a kind of solipsist, spinning out ideas that are either adapted to empirical reality or rejected by it. The evolutionist flair of his remarks is completely deliberate; for Boltzmann was an enthusiastic Darwinist. Thus the evolutionary perspective is also very important for him on confrontation with that very »confusion«. The problem of solipsism on his view, then, has two aspects: one bearing upon the existence of the external world and another bearing upon the existence of other minds (both of which would turn out to be major preoccupations of Bertrand Russell later). With respect to the first Boltzmann claimed that the very resistance that the world makes to our conceptions in fact turns out to be a source confirming their objectivity. The world collides as it were with the solipsist when he fails to take the proper course of action thus jolting him out of his reveries and »selecting« the objective kernel by separating it from the arbitrary subjective husk of his representations of it (150; 336) in a manner that fully anticipates Popper and evolutionary epistemology.

As for what has become known as the Problem of Other Minds, i.e., the sensations of others, Boltzmann argues that the sensations of the other are known by analogy with our own (not a mechanical but a psychological one Boltzmann is quick to point out, 60; 167). In this context Boltzmann makes a remark that anticipates both Carnap's project in the *Logical Construction of the World* and sketches succinctly the contrary position to Wittgenstein's celebrated rejection of private language in the *Philosophical Investigations* (*PI*, I, 258): »Our own world picture would be ideally perfect if for each of our sensations we had a sign and furthermore a rule by which to construct from these signs the occurrence of all our future sensations...« (59; 166). Be that as it may, since the other pulls her hand out of the fire in the same agitated way that I do, I infer that she has the same experience of being burned that I do. However, with respect to other minds the need to adopt the common language that we all must learn implies that I must describe the sensations of others in the same way that I describe my own. In such matters certainty is linked to common judgment.

It should be noted that in the course of developing his arguments against solipsism Boltzmann employs a clever thought experiment involving a machine that »looked like a human body and behaved like one«. He concludes in a behaviorist vein that »nobody could prove that it was less aware of itself than a human« (73; 183–4). Both the theme and the strategy for dealing with it on the basis of a thought experiment (although not the substance of the issue) are highly reminiscent of what we have subsequently become familiar with through knowledge of Wittgenstein's later philosophy. They are typical of Boltzmann. Clearly, the common concern with solipsism, manifesting itself in Boltzmann as a need to refute it and in Wittgenstein as a need both to indicate why it forces itself upon the reflective mind but, nevertheless, is philosophically absurd, runs deeply through both Wittgenstein and Boltzmann. As far as Wittgenstein is concerned, it has been clear since David Pears published his two volume study, *The False Prison*, in 1987–88 that all of his philosophizing is intimately linked to a lifelong concern with solipsism.[10] So, it is hardly absurd to suggest that this concern is itself linked to the views of his first mentor even if Wittgenstein would vigorously object to the idea that we know other minds *per analogiam* as Boltzmann claimed (*PI*; I, 302–3 *et passim*).

Even more revealing of an affinity with Wittgenstein's mature concept of philosophy and thus more directly relevant to our main theme here, however, is the analysis of how philosophical problems arise as we become dazzled by the efficacy of our own mental constructs (164; 352–3). The idea that knowledge is facilitated by building models of what we take to be reality implies that our analogies (i.e., models) are merely of *local* significance. Philosophical problems arise precisely when we try to generalize the significance of our constructs and pronounce upon reality as a totality. The habits that we have acquired according to which we are able to cope with the world on the basis of subsuming the particular phenomenon under the more general tempt us to produce a unitary picture of the world itself. Thus »residual dissatisfaction« (137; 319) at our inability to define concepts like number tempts us to overshoot the mark by producing metaphysical explanations to fill the gap. However, when we do that reason »overshoots the mark« (*die Anpassung schießt das Ziel hinaus*, *loc. cit.*). The result is that reason plummets itself into contradictions of the sort that Kant described under the rubric »antinomies« (i.e., a situation in which both of a pair of contradictory propositions can be proved) when it seeks total explanations for reality.

The philosopher, as opposed to the scientist, seeks explanations of the given, which explanations are of a different logical type from the empirically given explanandum. Thus arises the »need« to explain our experience in terms of a sort of being, i.e., God, whose nature is of a wholly different order than what we experience. Furthermore, this tendency stand in awe of the fact that anything exists at all seems to be so deeply rooted in the nature of the human mind that it is inextinguishable as Kant insisted. Philosophers' obsession with questions of »existence« of a sort that is wholly foreign to scientists was virtually perverse in Boltzmann's eyes, a matter to be handled by a philosophical pathologist. What we really need is a description of particular phenomena, which, as we have seen, should reduce problematic complexes into simple components of the same logical type. In philosophy we look for something more »profound« and in so-doing, on Boltzmann's view we loose sight of the simplest things, which turn out to be the most inexplicable, the most trivial, the most puzzling, (165ff; 353ff) as a result. In order to remedy this »... we must ... work against the irresistible urge to apply the laws of thought even where they overshoot the mark, so that in the end this urge gradually disappears altogether« (*so daß er allmählich ganz verschwindet*, 197; 401). For Boltzmann the »laws of thought« too are the results of evolutionary development. Thus Boltzmann will at once allow that they have an a-priori function with respect to thinking but at the same time deny that they are absolutely certain. Philosophers must be disabused of confusing the two. This would involve disabusing »idealists«, in the sense of philosophers obsessed by »ideal cases« (cf. *PI*, I 81 et passim) of their tendency to view the world from a »one-sided standpoint« (135; 315). This one-sided standpoint consists chiefly of posing questions of such vast scope that they cannot be answered. In stark contrast to metaphysics »natural science appears completely to loose from sight the large and general question; but all the more splendid is the success when, groping in the thicket of special questions, we suddenly find a small opening that allows a hitherto undreamt of outlook in the whole« (14; 26).

1. LUDWIG BOLTZMANN ...

Galileo's inclined plane, which »showed« bodies of differing weights falling at the same speed, is an example of a case where a »big« metaphysical problem was resolved scientifically on the basis of a seemingly small technical innovation. Thus science handles unanswerable »big« problems by reducing them to small manageable questions. Indeed, Boltzmann viewed the main objective in philosophy as that of giving »a clear account of the inappropriateness of overshooting the mark«, a recurrent metaphor in Boltzmann (167; 356). It should at once eliminate the »tangles« (*Verwicklungen*)[11] that lead to contradictions in thought and create a system such that »it stood out clearly when a question is not justified so that the drive towards asking it would gradually die away« (167; 356). This is surely the origin of Wittgenstein's notion that the aim of philosophy should be to »show the fly the way out of the fly-bottle« (*PI*, I, 309), i.e., put the philosophical mind to rest by eliminating the temptation of raise »tormenting«, because unanswerable, questions (*PI*, I, 133). Fully in the spirit of Boltzmann Wittgenstein insists that he must find or invent a series of intermediate case to wean philosophers away from their one-sided diet of examples. (*PI*, I, 122) Such a philosophy and it alone, Boltzmann insists, would be worthy of the name of the queen of the sciences. Thus, at least implicitly, on Boltzmann's view, in contrast to, say, Mach and Russell, it is clearly an error to identify philosophy and natural science. In his *Popular Writings* philosophy is above or below the sciences, i.e., as clarification of the methods of the sciences or as epistemological or cosmological speculation, but never on an equal footing with them as Wittgenstein would reiterate in the *Tractatus*.

In the matter of the demarcation between scientific truth and existential truth Boltzmann is absolutely unambiguous: the problems of life are the »higher« (although he does not use the term). He insists with Goethe, anticipating both the conclusion of the *Tractatus* and what Wittgenstein will say about religion in *Culture and Value*, namely, that »theory is gray compared with life« (36; 80, where the English translation makes explicit Boltzmann's elliptical allusion to *Faust*, I in the original German text).[12] Moreover, like the Wittgenstein of *On Certainty* (and Blaise Pascal[13]) Boltzmann will insist that religion and science belong to different »orders« of experience.[14] The two relate to one another as the inside and the outside of our experience, which have to be pictured or imagined in *completely* different ways (as, say, Schopenhauer would insist). »Nothing is more perverse than linking religious concepts which rest on a quite different and immeasurably firmer basis with the vacillating subjective picture that we form of external things« (142, 324–5), insists Boltzmann in a passage that clearly prefigures the relation between logic and mysticism in the *Tractatus*.

Here we have reached the point where we should begin to reconsider the implications of Boltzmann's influence upon Wittgenstein for the latter's development. As we have stated, the impact of Wittgenstein on Boltzmann will help us to understand 1) Wittgenstein's »originality« and 2) the curious fact that Fann and others have remarked upon that the later philosophy is, *in nuce* at least, earlier than the early philosophy. We shall proceed from the later to the former point. In order to do so we should begin by reconsidering how Boltzmann laid the foundation for Wittgenstein's subsequent development. However, that involves reconsidering what Wittgenstein got from the figures he mentioned as it bears upon his legacy from Boltzmann. This will permit us a certain sketch of his development that we can later fill out more fully. Our question, then, is none other than how it was that Boltzmann at once led him to the point of view that informs the *Tractatus* and at the same time gave him the impetus to transcend its limits. We have already seen something of how Boltzmann »influenced«[15] the concept of philosophy in the *Tractatus*. Let us now sketch his role in Wittgenstein's philosophical development generally.

In all of Boltzmann's philosophizing it is clear that his hero and authority is Heinrich Hertz. Boltzmann continuously emphasized how the Hertzian view that it was the mathematical structure of our models of nature that conferred their usefulness upon them was the key to understanding how science explores nature. However, as we have seen, Boltzmann failed, as Wittgenstein did not, to understand why Hertz was so adamant about insisting upon the mathematical permissibility and the empirical correctness of models or theories. For Boltzmann that was simply given with the notion of theory/model itself. In all of that he failed completely to recognize, as Wittgenstein did not, that there was for Hertz also a third absolutely crucial dimension, a rhetorical dimension, to our models, which was not merely of superficial significance as Mach believed but which helped us to understand how generalizing our models could confuse us. This suggested to Hertz that if the metaphysical problems of, say, physics (with, say, a notion like »force«) arise in the language of physics they must be solved, not by prohibiting the use of certain misleading metaphysical expressions in that language, but by articulating the subject matter in question in an alternative language/model such that the problem that has »tormented« us disappears in the very alternative representation.[16] Thus in the spirit of Boltzmann on the basis of Hertzian views of the clarificatory powers of alternative representations Wittgenstein's *Tractatus* would show on the basis of truth-tables that there was absolutely no need for axioms in logic. It was Hertz above all who gave Wittgenstein the crucial clue about the importance of »showing« in philosophy.

Jumping over Schopenhauer (to whom it will be necessary to return later), whose dualist view of the relation between the self and the world, i.e., as knowing and feeling subject, would reinforce the view that there are indeed radically different »orders« of human experience and lead Wittgenstein's thought in other directions (and ultimately to Otto Weininger[17]), for a moment, let us consider what the adolescent Wittgenstein might have learned from Gottlob Frege that is continuous with what he had learned from Boltzmann in these matters. Two points seem to be particularly important with respect to how Frege could be seen as relating to the philosophical claims of Boltzmann: the idea that the number could indeed be rigorously defined and the notion that mathematics is in fact a part of formal logic (the thesis of »logicism«) both of which were deeply rooted in his thinking from the *Begriffsschrift* onwards and central to the program that he developed for analytic philosophy. If logic, which here means the notion of a logical »function«, can be employed to define »number«, we have the solution to one problem that Boltzmann had in fact written off. Moreover, if logic was the heart of mathematics, then the secret of modeling was to be found there. So we can see on the face of it what might have led the juvenile Wittgenstein from Boltzmann to Hertz to Frege: a deepening of our understanding of depicting the exterior of experience (just as Schopenhauer and Weininger would aid him a bit later in depicting its interior).

Thus he could enlist enthusiastically as a volunteer in Bertrand Russell's campaign to finish the job of eliminating arbitrariness from logic that Frege had left to him. Russell's service to logic had been to show on the basis of an analytic technique, his so-called »Theory of Descriptions«, that the apparent logical form of a proposition is not its real one (*T L-P*, 4.0031). In doing so Russell demonstrated how the truth of propositions required that they stand in an isomorphic relation to the situations they represent and thus are not mere analogies as Boltzmann had insisted. Here Boltzmann's notion of models as analogies was abandoned for the view that they represent reality with an absolute exactitude. The basis of this view is the notion of the bivalence of the proposition: a proposition, to be a proposition, must be true or false. The early Wittgenstein was convinced that our propositions could not »reach out« to reality (*T L-P*, 2.1511) as they do, if that were not the case. Even if Hertz would give Wittgenstein the crucial clue to undermining the notion of a »philosophical logic« or logical theory of the sort that Frege and Russell had striven for in the truth table, which would definitively show all of the possibilities for distinguishing genuine propositions from pseudo-propositions, isomorphism would remain absolutely central to the early Wittgenstein. Thus his early view of knowledge would depart in central ways from that of his first mentor, while, nevertheless, building upon it.

These »influences« – an unfortunate expression but Wittgenstein's own – are clearly echoed in all of Wittgenstein's discussion of philosophy starting from what we find in the middle of the *Tractatus*, where Wittgenstein insists that it is not to be confounded with science (4.11–4.116). These remarks belong to Wittgenstein's early, »pre-mystical« draft of 1916 that Brian McGuinness has referred to as the proto-*Prototractatus*.[18] Although there are most definite traces of the ideas of Frege (anti-psychologism, 4.1121), Russell (philosophy as logical clarification, 4.112) and maybe even Karl Kraus (philosophy as an elucidatory activity, as opposed to theory, 4.112), the voices of Boltzmann and Hertz can clearly be detected in the background to these first formulations of its conclusion: Hertz in Wittgenstein's preoccupation with limits (4.113–4.115); Boltzmann positively for the demarcation from science (4.111), negatively as Wittgenstein distances himself from Boltzmann's highly esteemed Darwin (4.1122) and the notion »entanglement« in psychology (4.1121, a turn of phrase that will turn up again in the *Investigations* as well as in writings like *Culture and Value*. Above all, the idea that it is impossible to make assertions about the world as a whole, whose importance is stressed by Bertrand Russell in his introduction, is an idea that ultimately originates in Wittgenstein's early encounter with Boltzmann (however much it may otherwise owe to Schopenhauer and Frege).

Later, he came to have second thoughts about logical atomism. He criticized his own view in the *Tractatus* that atomic propositions are wholly independent of one another. His own reflections on the ways in which the whole system of colors is presupposed in any specific sensory discrimination whatsoever provided one set of grounds for that. To »see« that an object is blue is at one and the same time to »judge« that it is neither green nor violet.[19] Another was Piero Sraffa's objections to the idea that whatever is meaningful in human experience must have a logical form (the famous Neapolitan gesture of contempt[20]), which led him to reject the notion that meaning is essentially linked to propositions that have an isomorphic relationship to the world. Thus the door to the *Philosophical Investigations* was opened. In that work suddenly Boltzmann's notion of the primacy of analogies and examples in epistemology would come once again to the fore as Wittgenstein would insist upon the epistemological primacy the notion of following rules where there are no explicit rules but only examples to follow. In short the way beyond Frege and Russell was, at least to some extent, a way back to Boltzmann. For example, it would involve returning to the idea that human thought is rooted in evolution but would distinguish, as Boltzmann had not, between evolution as a description of our natural history and evolution as an explanatory theory.[21]

How does Wittgenstein conceive the task of philosophy after

his return to philosophy in 1929? The clearest statement, as we have said, is to be found between sections 89 and 133 of Part One of the *Philosophical Investigations* the only really authoritative »later« text from his own hand. We have already seen a number of points of similarity to Boltzmann that we should reiterate here for the sake of clarity. For example, Boltzmann's notion that we cannot define certain crucial concepts, i.e., a certain vagueness attaches to some of our concepts, finds echo at *PI*, I, 76–77. There we find at the close of his discussion of the questionable character of the notion of sharply defining all concepts the Boltzmann-like question »how did you learn the use of the word good? The notion that philosophical problems arise from a »one-sided« way of approaching questions is similarly echoed at *PI*, I, 593: »A main cause of philosophical illness – one-sided diet«, he then goes on equally in the spirit of Boltzmann to add, »we nourish our thinking with only one kind of example«. Similarly, a crucial part of the so-called private language argument invites us to imagine more or less the situation that Boltzmann described in his thought experiment involving the construction of an »ideally perfect« *Weltbild*. Thus Wittgenstein writes,

> Imagine this case. I want to keep a diary about the recurrence of a certain sensation. To this end I associate it with the sign 's' and write in a calendar for every day on which I have the sensation. – I will remark first of all that a definition of the sign cannot be formulated – ... But I speak or write the sign down, and at the same time concentrate my attention on the sensation ... and so as it were point to it inwardly. – But what is this ceremony for? For that is all it seems to be! A definition surely serves to establish the meaning of the sign. – Well this is done precisely by the concentrating of my attention; for in this way I impress upon

myself the connection between the sign and the sensation. But 'I impress it upon myself' can only mean: this process brings it about that I remember the connection *right* in the future. But in the present case I have no criterion of correctness. One would like to say: whatever is going to seem right to me is right. And that only means that here we can't talk about 'right' (*PI*, I, 258; cf. I, 199).

Here it is less that the positions or even the situations are identical but merely that they are sufficiently similar to suggest that Wittgenstein was in a sense returning to terrain familiar to him from his early reading of Boltzmann.

Let us consider a number of further points at which the later Wittgenstein and Boltzmann employ similar philosophical strategies or metaphors.

We can start with a particularly striking use of the city metaphor that is hardly accidental in Wittgenstein given what Boltzmann had written earlier. Boltzmann describes the advancement of science in the pre-modern era »just as an old town constantly grows through new buildings put up by industrious and enterprising citizens«. This contrasts with the development of science in recent times, which »resembles rather that of a modern American town which in a few decades grows from a village into a city of millions«. (77; 198) Wittgenstein asks what is lost in that development: »Our language can be see as an ancient city: a maze of little streets and squares, of old and new houses, and of houses with additions from various periods; and this surrounded by a multitude of new boroughs with straight regular streets and uniform houses.« (*PI*, I, 18).

Wittgenstein insists that the most important »facts« with respect to illuminating philosophical problems are concealed from the philosopher because they are too simple and familiar, always before us and therefore never problematic (*PI*, I, 129). Boltzmann in a similar vein describes a situation in which, »many problems are like the question once put to a painter, what picture he was hiding behind the curtain, to which he replied »the curtain is the picture«. For when requested to deceive experts by his art, he had painted a picture representing a curtain.« He goes on to ask, »is not perhaps the veil that conceals the nature of things from us just like that painted curtain« (15; 23).

In describing the fundamental problem of essentialism Wittgenstein writes (in a passage reminiscent of Nietzsche in some of his moods [cf. *Der Wille zur Macht*, III, 513),

> when philosophers use a word – 'knowledge', 'being', 'object', 'I,' 'proposition', 'name' – and try to grasp the *essence* of the thing, one must always ask oneself: is the word ever actually used this way in the language game which is its actual home? – What *we* do is bring words back from their metaphysical home to their everyday use.
> (*PI*, I, 116)

For Boltzmann's part,

> Progress in thinking must much rather be sought by eliminating ... concepts, which, experience tells us, do not advance but mislead and even entangle us in contradictions. These forms of inference and concepts always arise when originally appropriate modes of thought are transferred to cases where they do not fit. (67; 176).

Like Wittgenstein, Boltzmann would continually ask the metaphysicians how they learn to use a particular word in the first place.

Consonant with his view of how our concepts go astray when we loose an overview of their origins, Boltzmann defines what is to understand pragmatically. »What, then, is meant by having perfectly correct understanding of a mechanism? Everybody knows that the practical criterion for this consists in being able to handle it correctly.« (150; 335-6). Moreover, knowing what to do when the mechanism breaks down is an essential part of this, which, Boltzmann insists, cannot be defined. However, that is not problematic as long as our understanding of them always leads to the correct action. Thus Wittgenstein will insist that understanding is not at all a mental process but a matter of being able to continue a series, knowing what to *do* next. (*PI*, I, 154). Understanding shows itself, we might say, in the act of application. In a similar vein Wittgenstein reminds us in what is on the surface a most unlikely place, namely, his *Lectures on Aesthetics* that »physics is connected with engineering. The bridge must not fall down« (*L+C*, 25)[22]; whereas Boltzmann asserts, »it is precisely the practical technician who as a rule treats the complicated formulae of electric theory with a surer hand than many a prospective physicist« (34; 79). Indeed, the point of Boltzmann's insistence that, unlike the scientist, the engineer had literally to pay for his mistakes would hardly have been lost on the industrialist's son, who would later insist that one should do philosophy in a business-like way.[23]

Be that as it may the discussion of philosophy in Part One of the *Philosophical Investigations* (§§ 89-133) is introduced very much in the spirit of Boltzmann. The problems that traditional philosophers like Bertrand Russell pose arise because we are mislead by certain analogies between forms of expression into seeking a comprehensive account of the essence of language. Thus a simple thing in everyday life, a proposition, comes to have all sorts of queer properties. Their importance in life

1. LUDWIG BOLTZMANN ...

suggests to philosophers that they must have extraordinary characteristics. However, when philosophers succeed in giving an account of those remarkable properties, »purifying« or (in a most curious usage) »subliming« logic, they end up by making the familiar world of everyday experience wholly foreign and bizarre (as does, say, strong AI or Cognitive Psychology and much of what counts as philosophy of mind these days).

Of course, there is a major difference between them inasmuch as Boltzmann argues against the imperialistic incursions of metaphysical philosophy into science; whereas Wittgenstein would free philosophy from the tendency to imitate science and in doing so let in dubious metaphysical assumptions in the name of science through the back door. However, that in itself would be a theme for another discussion.

In conclusion, it is possible, of course, that such similarities are merely coincidental but, given Wittgenstein's way of mulling over texts and images that impressed him his whole life long, it is not likely. It is more likely that he had internalized good chunks of Boltzmann (as he did, say Frege or Schubert), if he did not actually go back to him later as he did, say, to Hertz. Boltzmann's wit and snappy style were much appreciated in the Vienna of his youth, so it is fair to say that any »Viennese« account of Wittgenstein must begin with him. It is clear that Boltzmann's writings led him to Hertz and probably to Schopenhauer, to whom Boltzmann seems to have had a somewhat schizophrenic relationship (as he did to other philosophers such as Kant and Hegel, whom he *both* criticized and built upon). Here are even parallels to the witty Frege of the *Foundations of Arithmetic*, whose deployment of examples to break down big unanswerable questions into smaller more manageable ones bears a certain resemblance to Wittgenstein. Moreover, Wittgenstein's belief that the metaphysicians of old were not to be ridiculed but that their perspective had been transcended by the development of knowledge certainly originates with Boltzmann, in whose writings the theme continually recurs (but who does reap scorn upon them for all that) Their respective philosophical concerns as well their strategies are surely significantly similar at a number of crucial points. Like Wittgenstein, Boltzmann sought to develop ways of putting the philosopher's tormented, but fundamentally perverse, questioning of the commonplace to rest. When Boltzmann said that philosophy got on his nerves he meant it literally; for he was what was then called a neurasthenic, which had been termed melancholic in the Renaissance and is today called manic-depressive. Philosophy disturbed him literally and he sought to put his mind to rest by dissolving abstruse philosophical problems into manageable scientific ones. Is it entirely accidental that Wittgenstein would later come to see the philosopher's questioning of what is clear to normal people as a kind of madness that could only be cured by somebody capable of thinking yet crazier than traditional philosophers?[24] Is it entirely accidental that he would strive to show how their intellectual torments were neither silly nor superfluous? Hardly.

To be sure, we cannot by a long way illuminate all of the questions surrounding Wittgenstein's concept of philosophy and its originality on the basis of Boltzmann or indeed exclusively on the basis of historical arguments alone; for many of the issues turn upon what sort of estimate we make of his later philosophical position. Nor is the point of the exercise to show that Wittgenstein was simply Boltzmann redivivus. That would be absurd. However, a close account of the genesis of his mature concept of philosophy can bring us a long way towards appreciating that there is much less arbitrariness than meets the eye in his efforts to show the fly the way out of the fly bottle.

1. LUDWIG BOLTZMANN ...

Wittgenstein was not an Athena cropping out of the head of Zeus adult and fully armed. He always insisted that he got his main ideas early in life. We do well to take him seriously in the matter. When we do so we find much that is mysterious and problematic about his view of philosophy is to be understood in terms of the work of important but neglected philosophers like Ludwig Boltzmann. Wittgenstein too could well have said with Newton that he stood on the shoulders of giants. In fact he did so. The peculiarities of his philosophical development have tended to blind us to the fact. To explore his intellectual origins in the history of philosophy in no way involves compromising his place in the history of 20th century philosophy but can only help to insure it by showing skeptics[25] how little is arbitrary in the strikingly »original« concept of philosophy that he developed with the help of Boltzmann, Hertz, Schopenhauer, Frege, Russell, Kraus, Loos, Weininger, Spengler and Sraffa.

CHAPTER 2

Heinrich Hertz: Alternative Representations

WITTGENSTEIN'S PATH FROM BOLTZMANN to Hertz, like so many other aspects of his development, cannot be documented precisely. However, it hardly seems difficult to reconstruct, for it is but a short step from Boltzmann's concern with models and his praise of »theory« to Hertz's concern with »Bilder«, their nature, their use and their misuse. Much of what Hertz had to say about these matters, for example, about the characteristics of models struck Boltzmann as too obvious to require articulation. However, it was precisely here that Wittgenstein would find considerably more than Boltzmann could in Hertz's philosophy of science – indeed, more than Hertz himself appears to have seen there – which is exactly the claim that Wittgenstein made about himself. Moreover, these intense reflections on Hertz go a long way to explaining the origins of the oft perceived but little understood hermeneutic moment in his philosophizing.

Hermeneuticists have long been fascinated but puzzled by Wittgenstein. They feel instinctively certain sympathy for his idea of »seeing the world rightly« in the *Tractatus* as well as with his views about, say, what it is to understand persons in the *Philosophical Investigations*. Yet, there remains something strange, even foreign to the hermeneutic tradition from Dilthey to Gadamer in Wittgenstein's philosophical writings. Like the hermeneuticists, Wittgenstein insists, for example that description must replace explanation in philosophy but what he understood by description has precious little to do with either the historically-oriented contextualism of Dilthey or the phenomenology of the early Heidegger. Wittgenstein's descriptions take the form of thought experiments, examples, aphorisms, analogies, metaphors and questions – the most interesting single fact about the *Investigations* is that it contains 784 questions of which only 110 are answered of which in turn 70 are answered falsely on purpose[26]. This is a very curious way to do hermeneutics indeed. Nevertheless, Wittgenstein, despite his insistence that philosophy was a kind of analysis (*PI*, I, 91), always distanced himself from the tradition of Logical Positivism by emphasizing that it was fundamentally about meaning rather than truth. Indeed, the later Wittgenstein's lack of concern for issues relating to truth in philosophy has been perceived by many, not least Bertrand Russell, as scandalous. His ways of »reminding« us of the multiple modes of interweaving words and gestures into meanings are, nevertheless, highly reminiscent of hermeneutic techniques. Yet, Wittgenstein's rejection of Positivism was never for a moment connected with a temptation to develop an anti-positivistic philosophy like those of Dilthey, Heidegger and Gadamer. The question is why? The answer is to be found in his background in philosophy of science – the last place that either a Positivist *or* a hermeneuticist would look.

Wittgenstein's mature concept of philosophy is in fact heavily indebted to the concept of philosophy of science developed by Heinrich Hertz in the long introduction to his *Principles of Mechanics Presented in a New Form* of 1894.[27] The fact that this is the case has long been recognized by Wittgenstein scholarship; its implications, however, have hardly been explored. In his efforts to show graphically that alternative modes of presentation of the principles of mechanics could eliminate the difficulties surrounding such problematic notions as »force« in mechanics that tormented scientists and philosophers alike, Hertz delivered Wittgenstein with a highly original hermeneutic technique, which would influence all his thinking and in fact become the cornerstone of his mature philosophical method. Most of the main features of Wittgenstein's mature conception of philosophy in fact emerge from his early encounters with the philosophy of science of Ludwig Boltzmann and Heinrich Hertz only to be complimented and embellished, but in no sense fundamentally altered, by his later encounters with thinkers of different moulds.

We forget at our peril that Wittgenstein was not only a lifelong reader of Hertz, who gave Hertz's Introduction to the *Principles* to his students as the paradigm for doing good philosophy,[28] but also actually contemplated taking his motto for the *Philosophical Investigations* from its pages[29] »when these painful contradictions are removed, the question about the essence [of force] is not answered, but the mind is no longer tormented and ceases to pose illegitimate questions«. (*PM*, 9) Moreover, it was his mature method for dealing with philosophical problems, i.e., his techniques for »discovering or inventing intermediate cases« (*PI*, I, 122) for drawing our attention away from the »one-sided diet« of examples (*PI*, I, 593) in terms of which traditional philosophers posed their problems, that Wittgenstein took to be his major contribution to philosophy. Hertz's technique of presenting alternative representations of mechanics to clarify its conceptual difficulties thus played a crucial role in the development of Wittgenstein's mature method for »dissolving« philosophical problems.

The crucial point about the concept of philosophy that the

physicist, Hertz, developed for handling metaphysical problems in science and bequeathed to Wittgenstein is the insistence on the *immanent* character of the philosophical enterprise: if philosophical problems arise *in* physics, then they must be handled in physics itself rather than in some theory *about* physics to paraphrase Wittgenstein. Physics must take care of itself as it were. In effect, what Wittgenstein saw here was the solution to a problem immanent in the then nascent logical positivist movement concerning the status of philosophy – and one that it would never adequately solve. What is philosophy if it is not science? Mach and Boltzmann polemicized against all forms of foundationalism, be they ontological or epistemological, in the name of science but those polemics themselves were not part of science but more an ideology. Hertz showed Wittgenstein a way around that problem, which would stamp all of Wittgenstein's thinking. How did he do that? What, then, did Hertz maintain to be the proper mode of procedure in philosophy of physics?

Hertz's new strategy for dealing with metaphysical problems in science was first and foremost a contribution to the resolution of debates about the role of concepts, in particular the concept of force, in Newton's physics. In order to understand the importance of Hertz's contribution to the philosophy of science we must begin by taking a look at the problems that bothered Ernst Mach, the founder of the (then) new discipline of philosophy of science.[30] Therefore it is necessary to begin our story with a brief recapitulation of the problems that led Mach to formulate his Principle of Economy with respect to scientific modeling and Hertz to want to emend the Machian view thereof. It should be emphasized from the outset that the aspects of Hertz's philosophy of science that most interest us are the points at which he departs from Mach.

For all its admiration for Newton's theoretical breakthroughs in physics, the critical spirit of nineteenth century positivism increasingly came to question the *form* of Newton's presentation of his physical theory. Scientists with an empiricist philosophical bent like Ernst Mach became increasingly discontented with conceptual framework upon which Newton's Platonic mathematical synthesis rested. Why, for example, should Newton base his system upon notions of »absolute space, time and motion« which could neither be perceived nor measured? In this context Newton's notion of »force« came under particular scrutiny. Like the »absolutes«, »force« is unobservable (but, of course, measurable); however, it is absolutely essential to Newton's development of dynamics. Thus scientists and philosophers were permanently tempted to ask the question what sort of *thing* is this unobservable cause of motion, the »force of gravity«? From Mach's positivist perspective[31] the confusion arising from the continual temptation to reify the concept of force was disastrous. Such confusing, i.e., metaphysical, elements in science offend against its essential characteristic, its »economy«: »It is the object of science to replace, or save, experiences, by the reproduction and anticipation of facts in thought«[32]. Mach considered scientific theories, even those that had to be considered among the greatest achievements of mankind, to be, nevertheless, embedded – and limited by – the culture of their epoch. Therefore, the language in which scientists expressed themselves was in continual need of purification from contingent cultural accretions. Since Newton's age was an age whose typical cultural idiom or mode of expression was theological speculation, his central concepts are not entirely free of the rhetoric of theology. His employment of a word such as force highly suggestive of a causal agency to express what is in fact a mathematical relationship between mass and acceleration reflects this sociological fact and is thus an indication of our need for a critique of scientific language. By inviting us to ask what the force is that works upon the mass in question the word force only obscures that exact mathematical description of physical reality which is the goal of physics. Therefore it must be eliminated from the vocabulary of science in a more enlightened era. Henceforth the goal of science should be the representation of observable phenomena in terms of the simplest mathematical relationships (functions) between observations. Observations were to be represented as points on a graph and the most adequate mathematical model of the situation would be the function which corresponded to the shortest line connecting the points. That in essence is Mach's Principle of Economy.

Hertz's question to Mach is as bafflingly straight-forward as it is unexpected: what is simplicity? »Here it is not certain what is simple and permissible and what is not,« Hertz writes (*PM*, xxv). In fact Hertz's query about the nature of simplicity turns out to be a series of questions about the role of what Kant termed »regulative ideas« with respect to scientific theory: what sorts of considerations have guided us as we shaped our models of physical reality in the past? what sorts of considerations should guide us as we shape our representation now? what sorts of considerations with respect to shaping our models of physical reality help us to understand how we confuse ourselves in the interpretation of models? To be sure Hertz's questions about the nature of simplicity are inspired by Mach's reflections and hardly hostile to them, (*PM*, xxviii) but it in fact reveal a very different perspective on the question of how to eliminate metaphysical problems from science (even if it should sometimes *seem* that there is little or no difference between their positions). Like Mach, Hertz believes that the aim of physical theory is the simplest representation of observed phenomena. However, Hertz, rather in the Pragmatist manner of C. S. Peirce[33] than the positivist

2. HEINRICH HERTZ ...

manner of Mach, poses a question that Mach had not at all mentioned: simple – for whom? Mach had drawn attention to the importance of the rhetoric of science, but he had not considered all of its implications. For Mach the rhetorical element of science is always distorting and never useful. For Hertz, who is well-aware of the distorting possibilities of scientific rhetoric, it is nevertheless something useful and necessary in the development of physical theory. For Mach the question »for whom« does not arise because he simply presupposes that the our representations are always made for the same audience of scientific experts, and *one* of these will always be the simplest mathematically for them. Indeed, here Hertz, the first great German physicist of Jewish origins, seems to have been paradigmatic of Wittgenstein's Jewish mind that sees more in the work of others than they do themselves (here the parallel to Hertz's insights into the meaning of Maxwell's equations as well as Helmholtz's interpretation of Maxwell is also worthy of mention[34]).

Be that as it may, Hertz proceeds from the view that even within science it is necessary to construct different representations of the same data depending upon whom you want to talk to. He offers us the analogy with presentations of grammar: pupils learning to master their mother tongue require an altogether different presentation of the rules of grammar than philologists do. (*PM*, 47) The more we consider the analogy, as Hertz does not, but as Wittgenstein assuredly did, the more complex it becomes; for it will soon become clear that students in the course of mastering their mother tongue will require a very different grammar from those foreigners who struggle with the same language, whereas different groups of foreigners will find different presentations of grammar more or less helpful depending upon the characteristic modes of expression in their own language, etc. For these different purposes we need different »pictures« or models of the rules of grammar. The same is true in physics: a representation that is suitable for theorists is hardly suitable, say, for engineers or for chemists working with the same subject, let alone introductory students. Thus Hertz differs from Mach at the very outset by emphasizing how it is that the normal development of science requires a plurality of representations.

For Mach, as for the early Wittgenstein, the underlying similarities between different presentations of the same theory, i.e., the common mathematical structure in its simplest expression, provided the key to understanding the nature of scientific concepts. Hertz in no way denies this. In fact he insists just as much as they do that it is only by means of a consideration of the mathematical structure of physical theories that we come to grasp their actual structures and actual ontological commitments. However, unlike them, he does not stop there. He goes on to stresses how close reflection upon the *differences* between these presentations would provide the key to eliminating philosophical perplexities concerning the nature of scientific concepts inasmuch as the rhetorical reasons why they arose in the first place would become crystal clear. In Mach's account of physical theory there are two questions which must be handled, in Hertz's there are three. For Mach our representation must be physically correct and logically coherent; for Hertz they must be rhetorically apposite as well, i.e., they must be constructed with a view to the communication situation in which the scientist finds himself. In other words the physicist's models must be fittingly constructed so as to be in a position to convey the sort of information that the audience wants to learn about in a form it can assimilate. The most rigorous and elegant presentation of a theory will be of no help to students who are just beginning to deal with the subject.

Thus Hertz will speak of three characteristics of our models of nature. They must be logically *permissible*, i.e., internally consistent, empirically *correct*, and communicatively *appropriate* or effective. (*PM*, 2) The third criterion for the acceptability of a model is its usefulness in a given situation. Without referring to Mach, Hertz actually criticizes him for failing to see (as Boltzmann would later) that representations have to be constructed with a view to the questions that are being posed to us. As well as accuracy and rigor *sensitivity* belongs to our models of physical reality. Put differently rhetorical adequacy is as important as architecture in the development of our models of physical reality.

Although Mach was hardly opposed to the idea that models are constructs, his concentration upon empirical accuracy and architectural simplicity led him to overlook the positive significance of the teleological element in modeling. Although Hertz is as sensitive as Mach to the demands of empirical accuracy and logical coherence (indeed, one problem with his introduction is that it on a superficial reading seems to be the case that he is merely restating Mach's view with a somewhat different emphasis), he is adamant in insisting that the crucial feature about models of physical reality is that *we construct them* »our requirement of simplicity does not apply to nature, but to the models we fashion of it.« (*PM*, 28). If we sometimes paint ourselves into a corner by so constructing our models as to confuse ourselves about the objects to which they refer as in the case of Newton's concept of force, we must eliminate the problem in precisely the way that we have created it, namely, by creating alternative models, which dispense with the unessential characteristics – Hertz refers to them somewhat confusingly as »contradictions« (*PM*, 9 *et passim*) – that we have built into those models which have come to puzzle us (we should not forget that Hertz's own contribution to physics, which led to the unit of frequency being named for him, was his clarification of the meaning of the mass of mutually inconsistent equations which Maxwell developed for interpreting the results of Faraday's experiments with electricity).

Thus Hertz's way of handling the metaphysical problems which arise in the course of developing physical theory entails literally a (mathematical) re-presentation of our theories such that we are able sharply to distinguish those elements in the model (*Bild*) which arise from logical necessity, and those that are matters of empirical evidence, from those that we have arbitrarily interjected into them with a view to rhetorical effectiveness. To be sure Hertz's emphasis upon purging our models of inconsistencies has a lot to do with logical analysis (i.e., the mathematical component in modeling). However, it is all too easy to be misled by his very real concern with logical clarification into thinking that it was the main element in his program; whereas he in fact wants to place the main stress on our capacity to achieve conceptual clarification in physical theory on the basis of alternative presentations of our theories. In short, Hertz wants to solve the sort of problems that bothered Mach in physical theory by working *within physics*, rather than developing a theory about the nature of physical theory as Mach did. Thus, his contribution to the conceptual clarification of foundational problems within physics came in the form of the axiomatic system that he presents in the body of his text (which, if successful, would amount fulfilling the Cartesian program for mechanics[35]). Again, the notion that his contribution to physical theory should take the form of an axiomatic system has tended to create the erroneous impression that his principal concern was with the formalization of mechanics pure and simple, rather than with demonstrating the value of that formalization for clarifying conceptual problems within scientific theory on the basis of an illuminating alternative representation of the same body of mechanical knowledge.

However, we forget at our peril that this axiomatization of mechanics, which would surely be a *tour de force* by any scientific standards,[36] is not an end in itself (as axiomatization would tend to become in Logical Positivism especially in the hands of Carnap) but part of a philosophical program for articulating the conceptual foundations of physical theory, whose sense is to be found in the ways in which that axiom system differs from the traditional Newtonian presentation and the alternative presentation developed at the turn of the century known as Energetics. Thus the task of his philosophical »Introduction« to the *Principles* is to present the two currently available systems of mechanics as an introduction to his own, which in turn is part of a way of doing what we would today call philosophy of science. The first of the representations the classical mechanics, which begins with an account of *statics*, i.e., the study of space and force without respect to motion, proceeding to *kinematics*, i.e., the purely descriptive study of motion without reference to mass or force, and culminating in *dynamics*, i.e., the study of bodies under the action of forces which produce changes in their motion. The basic concepts upon which Newton's development of mechanics rests are space, time, force and mass. Here Hertz is in full agreement with Mach concerning the conundrums that the Newtonian notion of force brings with it. (*PM*, 13–6) The very word tempts us to ask the wrong sorts of questions and thus into metaphysical speculations about the »nature« of forces, which only confuse us with respect to our empirical expectations.

The program of Energetics (developed by Wilhelm Ostwald, father of physical chemistry and later Nobel Prize winner) was a reaction to those conundrums strongly influenced by the development of thermodynamics in the nineteenth century. On the energeticist view the problems that the notion of force presents for classical physics can be avoided if all observable changes are treated as transformations of energy. (*PM*, 19) This entails basing mechanics upon the concepts of space and time as mathematical quantities and mass and energy as physical quantities. For energetics the properties of force are derived from fundamental laws and definitions, which function as ways of simplifying notation such that is becomes clear that they are matters of the appropriateness of the theory. In Energetics there are no intangibles; there are no »arbitrary and ineffectual« hypotheses. (*PM*, 22). However, the idea of a complex fundamental principle offends against our demand for simplicity with respect to principles in an analogous way to Newton's »force«, i.e., epistemologically rather than ontologically.

Hertz himself offers us a third possibility in the form of an axiom system which purports to deal with both of these problems in terms of what Helmholtz called »concealed masses and motions«. (*PM*, 31) In this third presentation of the principles of mechanics all mechanical phenomena are explained in terms of masses and movements, although the masses and movements that enter into explanations are not always perceived by us. Nevertheless, they are in principle identical with the sorts of masses and movements that we perceive and in no way »occult« qualities. In short, Hertz offers a way of going beyond our actual experiences without going outside of experience, i.e., by modeling possible experiences mathematically. Thus to speak with Kant all of mechanics is represented within the limits (*Grenzen*) of the empirical, but not within the bounds (*Schranken*) of the empirically given.[37] Whether Hertz succeeds or fails in his efforts to axiomatize classical mechanics is a question that need not concern us here, for it is his strategy as a philosopher of science that is so important for Wittgenstein.

Let us turn to Wittgenstein's mature conception of philosophy as presented in sections 89 to 133 of the first part of

2. HEINRICH HERTZ ...

the *Philosophical Investigations*. Coming from the Introduction of Hertz's *Principles* to Wittgenstein's text we ought to be struck at once by a number of similarities both in philosophical strategy and mode of expression—similarities that are hardly coincidental given the fact that Wittgenstein seriously considered giving the *Philosophical Investigations* a motto from the Introduction to Hertz's *Principles*. That is, of course, no secret, but its significance has been all too little recognized.

Like Hertz, who could marvel at »how easy it is to attach to fundamental laws considerations which are quite in accordance with the usual modes of expression in mechanics, and yet which are an undoubted hindrance to clear thinking« (*PM*, 6), Wittgenstein is concerned with the problem that our usual ways of speaking, like Newton's, conceal as much as they reveal of reality rather like spectacles that allow us to read but are not themselves »seen« (*PI*, I, 103). We are held captive by a picture (*PI*, I, 115) both in a general sense and in a specific sense. Generally philosophers have a picture of language as exclusively a matter of representing the world, that at once 1) leads them to consider the logical basis of representation as constituting an ideal language, and 2) systematically prevents them from seeing the most obvious fact about it, namely that there are a myriad speech acts which are both non-representational and irreducibly different from one another. Wittgenstein's discussion of the nature of philosophy thus begins with a consideration of how we tend to become fixated upon an ideal language when we do philosophy. Specifically, we are all like philosophers inasmuch as we are so tied to specific, one-sided ways, of seeing things that we forget that it is legitimately possible to understand words in startlingly different ways than we normally do. So we associate the word »cube« with the drawing of a cube, but there is also a very real sense in which it describes a triangular prism as well. (*PI*, I, 139) Although the latter is always there we need to be reminded of that fact occasionally. What we need in this situation is »eine übersichtliche Darstellung« or a synoptic view (*PI*, I, 122), which shows us what other possibilities there are. We need a »depth grammar« or logical grammar (*PI*, I, 664) that diverts our focus from the seductions of surface grammar and permits us to liberate ourselves from our »grammatical illusions« (*PI*, I, 110) and focus our attention upon a number of simple, commonplace truths, whose very obviousness prevents us from grasping them. In the preface to the *Investigations* Wittgenstein had already compared his task to that of a draughtsman (in ways reminiscent of Cezanne painting his various pictures of Mont Sainte-Victoire from different points of view) making sketches of a landscape from different directions in order to get a comprehensive overview of something that was most definitely visible but which could not be taken in with a single glance. It is precisely in aid of obtaining said »overview« that Wittgenstein speaks of the needs to discover or invent intermediate cases (i.e., language games other than that of representation) to help lead the philosopher away from the confusing exceptional cases and back to the rule, i.e., away from the tendency to want to speculate about the nature of thought and reality and back to the things we actually do with words. Just as in Hertz an alternative to time-honored ways of thinking in physics shows us how those ways of thinking go astray, so Wittgenstein wants to »teach us differences« to paraphrase Kent in *King Lear*, which was another of the mottos he considered for the *Investigations*.[38] Similarly the metaphor of being entangled in our own rules is no less suggestive of Hertz. Further, Wittgenstein likens the confusions of philosophers to people inexperienced with machinery who confuse an idling engine with one that is running (*PI*, I, 132); whereas Hertz will describe the role of »forces« in physics as »idling side-wheels« that have nothing to do with the machine's functioning (the standard translation obscures the similarity between Hertz and Wittgenstein here by rendering *leergehende Neberräder* as »sleeping« – Americans would say silent – »partners« in a business, *PM*, 14). Thus on Wittgenstein's view the traditional philosopher is »whipped« (*gepeitscht*) by questions that seem logical but in fact are not answerable (*PI*, I, 133), because they are not questions at all; whereas in the very passage that Wittgenstein contemplated as motto for the *Investigations* Hertz speaks of the mind of the physicist ceasing to be »tormented« (*gequält*) by the contradictions in a concept like force or electricity (*PM*, 9). What the philosopher needs to discover is the spectacles on his nose to put his vain questioning to rest.

The influence of Hertz would seem at this point to merge curiously with that of Freud; for philosophy thus becomes a therapeutic art (*PI*, I, 133) that seeks to assemble techniques for attaining the goal of disabusing the philosopher of his obsession with seeing the relationship between language and world *exclusively* as a matter of representation[39]: He has to be put into a position where his difficulties cease to be difficulties and he finally attains peace of mind. Lest this expression seem an overly religious description of Wittgenstein's concept of philosophy it is important to note that in the very same text he asserts that to so eliminate the source of our questioning in philosophy is to find the »redeeming word«. an expression that he first used in his struggle with fear of death as he manned a searchlight in World War I. (*GT*, 21.XI.14) Already in 1914 in his daily encounters with death as the ideal target for enemy fire Wittgenstein was insisting that in philosophy as well as in existential matters the solutions to our most distressing problems must be immanent ones: the problem of life must be solved in the living of it and the problem of representation must be solved in the act of representing and not in some theory about it: »the hard problems have to dissolve of themselves before us« (*GT*, 26. XI, 14; cf. *C+V*, 31); whereby it is clear that he refers to both his personal problems and the problems he was having understanding the nature of mathematics (*GT*, 6–7. VII. 16; cf. *N*, 39, 54, where the English translation misleadingly renders the phrase as »the key word«).

If the above is correct there ought to be other earmarks of Hertz both in Wittgenstein's other mature works as well as in his development generally. What might these be? In fact the closer we look, the more similarities we find in the form of 1) shared claims, 2) deep concern for appropriateness of presentation as a means to attaining clarity, or 3) for showing us how alternative modes of presentation and representation can dissolve philosophical problems, 4) inter-textual similarities, and, finally, 5) striking similarities of tone.

One surprising place where we encounter a clearly Hertzian notion is in Wittgenstein's last work, *On Certainty*, where Wittgenstein denies that there is a fixed distinction between the propositions which function normatively, i.e., as criteria, in our inquiries and those which have merely empirical status. For Wittgenstein it is a matter of choice (although by no means arbitrary) which propositions are, in Wittgenstein's words, »hardened« into the systematic framework of scientific inquiry and which remain »fluid« as empirical facts (*OC*, 96). Here we find a direct parallel both in substance and tone to Hertz's idea that »the concept of a mechanical principle has not been sharply fixed« (*PM*, 4). In the course of articulating his position that the principles of mechanics ought to be developed in various ways with a view to showing how fundamental difficulties are in fact more a matter of our modes of representation than they are of ontology. Hertz came to see clearly that what in one presentation functioned as a principle could be a corollary or a mere proposition to be demonstrated in another. (*PM*, 4) Thus Hertz anticipated Pierre Duhem, Otto

2. HEINRICH HERTZ ...

Neurath, and W. V. O. Quine as well as Wittgenstein himself in rejecting the analytic/synthetic distinction. It is noteworthy that Wittgenstein's way of alluding to the propositions which have been »hardened« into the framework for raising empirical questions is strikingly similar to that of Hertz. Thus Hertz writes at the very beginning of the Author's Foreword to the *Principles* about what we know with certainty as that which »stands fast« (*steht fest*, [*PM*. xxv]); whereas Wittgenstein will assert, »I do not explicitly learn the propositions that stand fast for me« (*die Sätze, die für mich feststehen, lerne ich nicht ausdrücklich* [*OC*,. 151]) and »what I hold fast to is not *one* proposition but a nest of propositions« (*Das, woran ich festhalte, ist nicht ein Satz, sondern ein Nest von Sätzen* (*OC*, 225, cf. *OC*, 125, 144, 235, 343). The point is that for both Wittgenstein and Hertz there is no such thing as a principle as such only propositions whose functions change in differing representations of physical systems (cf. *OC*, 318–21).

This takes us right to the heart of the matter with respect to the continuity in Wittgenstein's thought; for it is too seldom recognized how closely the view that there is no qualitative distinction between what belongs to the conceptual framework and what is an empirical matter in our scientific inquiries in *On Certainty* is related to the Tractarian view that there are no logical propositions that are by their nature axioms. Let us ask ourselves how this idea enters into the *Tractatus*.

If one simply reads the seven propositions that constitute the mains ideas of the *Tractatus* consecutively one quickly comes to the realization that the book's center is in fact propositions 5 and 6. Proposition 5 tells us that all meaningful sentences are truth functions; whereas 6 tells us that double negation is the general form of all truth functions. The force of this assertion is that all of the propositions of logic are of equal logical significance. The philosophical significance of the truth table method of representing propositions (as opposed to its significance as a logical decision procedure) is literally to show that nothing that is a proposition can be anything other than a tautology, a contradiction or an empirical proposition (*T*, 5.101). If this is true, not only is the Kantian notion that the propositions of philosophy are synthetic a-priori truths shown to be logically nonsensical, the Fregean notion in the *Begriffsschrift* that logic is based upon privileged propositions designated as axioms turns out to be equally nonsensical.[40] Thus Wittgenstein's central concept, paradoxically a development of a notion of Frege's, which in fact rules out there being a theory of logic, in the *Tractatus* directly parallels the Hertzian view that there are no principles as such in science. The best that one can do is get straight about what makes a proposition a logical truth, on the one hand, and what we do when we apply representations to the world, on the other. No theory can help us with the latter because logical form cannot be represented logically. Once we realize this we arrive at the limits of logic and, like good Hertzians, cease to be bothered by unanswerable questions.

It is evident from Wittgenstein's correspondence with none other than Gottlob Frege that the latter found such a Hertzian conception of clarity incomprehensible. It seems that his views on clarity and Wittgenstein's were profoundly different. »I cannot pass a judgment on your treatise, not because I am in disagreement with its content, but because its content insufficiently clear to me,« wrote Frege (*Fr*, 20). Yet, for Wittgenstein the whole of the *Tractatus* was nothing but an exercise in clarity. If what he had written was not clear, then it was worthless. Thus enormous frustration emerged on both sides. For Frege, who saw the whole task of philosophy as that of producing a razor-sharp distinction between the intelligibility (sense) and the object (reference) of an assertion, clarity is a matter of strict formal consistency[41] (Hertz's idea of obtaining clarity on the basis of axiomatization would thus hold great appeal for him).

Wittgenstein accepted this account of clarity in his early work inasmuch as it bore upon scientific statements. However, even in his early phase philosophical clarity was more than that. For better or worse philosophical clarity in the *Tractatus* is something that is neither an empirical nor a formal matter, but first and foremost a matter of obtaining the right perspective on the relation between the empirical and the formal, i.e., something that neither empirical nor logical propositions can say, but is in fact a matter of the application of propositions (*T*, 5.557).[42] In short, Wittgenstein understood clarity as something essentially attached to showing the limits of language *appropriately*. Thus the point of his *Tractatus* essentially related to the way Wittgenstein presented his thoughts. The ever perspicacious Frege only dimly recognized this; but he rejected Wittgenstein's »showing« gesture as being more artistic than scholarly (*Fr*, 19), which seems to have been convincing to Wittgenstein, who would later describe the book as »strictly philosophical and at the same time literary« to Ludwig von Ficker (*F*, 23). That is why the extremely curious very first sentence of the preface, which asserts that only those persons who have already had the thoughts contained in it will understand the book, was »disturbing« (*befremdlich*) to Frege (*F*, 19). To his credit the skeptical Frege recognized, as nearly all commentators since then have not, that the importance of the *Tractatus* to its author lay in its *form* and was thus principally a matter of aesthetics to him, which in turn is probably why Wittgenstein was to turn to a literary publisher, Ludwig von Ficker, when it became clear that Frege would not agree to publishing the book in any form but that of a logical treatise. (*F*, 22).The importance of the book's form is again stressed towards the end of the preface Wittgenstein insists that the achievement that he sees in his book bears upon the way it expresses the thoughts it contains. Wittgenstein makes no claims to novelty (something that always seemed absurd to his readers, since there is considerable, even astonishing, novelty in the book), rather he insists that what is really important about the book is the form in which it presents the results of his wrestling with the nature of logical symbolism. Rather like the author of an ancient tragedy Wittgenstein claimed only to tell a well-known story in a more powerfully nuanced language than it had yet been related. Seen from seen from the point of view of Russell and Frege's (Machist) project for the purification of language this had to be a virtually incomprehensible thing to do; however, from the point of view of Hertz Wittgenstein was doing exactly what a good philosopher of science should do: presenting a strictly immanent account (F, 22), as he wrote to Ficker, of the limits of the domain of language (viewed as a representational system) as opposed to Russell's profoundly disturbing but continual efforts to solve problems in logic by means of dubious stratagems such as the Axiom of Infinity or a Theory of Types, which arbitrarily stipulated how things *had* to be in logic from without.[43] It is not my intention to examine all of the various ways in which Hertz had an impact upon the *Tractatus* here; that would go far beyond the scope of this essay, rather, I want to identify yet another echo of Hertzian thinking with respect to the problem of the aims and goals of philosophizing that illuminates what is normally taken to be a very curious text.

Wittgenstein's encounters with Schlick and the Vienna Circle proved to be no less frustrating to his interlocutors than that with Frege. There is much to be said for the fact that what made Wittgenstein's views, say, of contradiction so puzzling was the Hertzian perspective he had upon the matter. In

2. HEINRICH HERTZ ...

those discussions Wittgenstein returns repeatedly to Hilbert's attempt to introduce technique for proving that a calculus does not contain a contradiction. (*WWK*, 119) Wittgenstein was totally convinced that this was an entirely false approach to mathematics. He insists that it is not a proof that is required here, but an analysis that substitutes a clear expression for a vague one, because the contradiction does not arise in the mathematics but in our mode of projecting mathematical problems. (*WWK*, 120) If I am confused in formulating my mathematical problems, no proof will help me. If I am clear about how I pose them, the question of contradiction does not arise. In no case does clarity bear upon proof, rather it has to do with what has to be done before proof is possible. Thus Wittgenstein insists that we need to get clear about our frame of reference, our mode of posing problems (cf. *BBB*, 169), in order to eliminate our problems with respect to contradictions, which do not arise from our doing mathematics, but from the sorts of questions we pose mathematically. This view connects the frequently expressed Tractarian idea that there are no surprises in logic and a-fortiori mathematics (*T*, 6.1251, 6,1261; cf. 5.473, *N*., 42, 2) with the view expressed in the *Investigations* that philosophy does not resolve contradictions in mathematics but seeks to get clear about the situation in mathematics that led us into contradiction (*PI*, I, 125). From the Hertzian perspective of a non-dogmatic empiricism contradiction merely indicated that it is necessary to form another representation of the situation at hand to extricate ourselves from this entanglement in our rules. It is in no way a catastrophe, rather a challenge to our ingenuity to reformulate our way of representing matters such that the tension that our model has introduced disappears. If there is nothing to fear in a tautology, then there is also nothing to fear in its logical equivalent, contradiction. (*WWK*, 131) The challenge is to find out how our normal procedures for projecting problems have gone astray. The matter is as »clear« as that.⁴⁴

There would seem to be yet other echoes of the Hertz in Wittgenstein that are perhaps not entirely obvious or documentable, but which also should not simply go ignored. I refer to the role that alternative modes of presentation plays in Wittgenstein's way of writing philosophy, which he compared with writing fiction: *Philosophie dürfte man eigentlich nur dichten* (*C+V*, 28). We have seen that »discovering and inventing« intermediate cases to correct the philosopher's bad diet of examples is fundamental to the sort of therapy that Wittgenstein wants to employ for the sake of extinguishing our urge to raise philosophical questions of the traditional sort. Wittgenstein's »dissolution« (*GT*, 26. XI. 14) of philosophical problems is accomplished by showing us aspects of reality that were invisible because they were always before our eyes. To make us astonished at the »splendor of the simple« to employ a phase of Heidegger's⁴⁵ Wittgenstein became increasingly convinced that he had to invent concepts, even natural histories, whose peculiar, striking character could shock us out of our intellectual fixations on the representational character of knowledge. By giving us examples of how things could be, but in fact are not, Wittgenstein shows us how many different ways there are of »weaving language and actions« (*PI*, I, 7) together. This is, of course, something quite different from what Hertz did in his *Principles* but it could well be seen as continuous with Hertz's philosophical strategy, a kind of variation on a theme as it were – a consequence of understanding Hertz better than he did himself.

Alois Pichler has argued insightfully on the basis of a thorough analysis of materials from Wittgenstein's *Nachlass* that Wittgenstein's almost absurdly painstaking mode of formulating and reformulating questions, assertions, observations and the like involved collecting alternatives such as »we could say

...«, »we might say ...«, »one is tempted to say ...«; »could one say ...«; »or – could one say ...«, »we are tempted to say ...« and literally hundreds of variations are essentially related to his philosophical goal of obtaining clarity about how philosophical problems arise through our tendency to misunderstand the logic of our language.[46] Wittgenstein seems to have seen variation in mode of expression as a mode of battling against our tendency to let ourselves be bewitched by language. This too would seem to be part of his Hertzian heritage.

Even Wittgenstein's *Wörterbuch für Volksschulen* bears traces of this Hertzian concern with the ways in which alternative ordering of material can either confuse us or prevent confusion. This example is particularly interesting because it has nothing directly to do with philosophy and because the speller is merely made up of a list of words that pupils have had problems with, i.e., it contains no text; it is simply a list that has to speak for itself. Here Wittgenstein is primarily concerned with preventing confusion. So he must consider the relative merits of alphabetical presentation in relation to that of presenting groups of etymologically related words with the derivatives following the base word, which would clash with the alphabetical principle. (*WV*, xxviii) How should he organize the series *alt* [old], *Altar* [altar], *Alter* [old age], *Altertum* [antiquity], *altertümlich*, [antique], etc? (*WV*, xxix) The usual modes of presentation for adults are sure to be either confusing to children or to make too sophisticated demands upon them. Appropriateness thus dictated to Wittgenstein that he opt for an unorthodox, but practical, solution:

ALT, das Alter
der Altar
D[d]as ALTERUM, altertümlich
etc.

Thus the central list in emphatic print contains the alphabetic order; whereas the derivative follow the base but are printed normally. In every instance Wittgenstein follows Hertz by asking systematically what is the appropriately simple, the »natural« order (cf. *PI*, Preface) of presentation – a question that would preoccupy him till the end of his life with respect to the ordering of his philosophical thoughts in the *Investigations*. Here too we have an exercise in Hertzian hermeneutics.

What is remarkable in all this, however, is that the scientific origins of the kind of analytic hermeneutics[47] that Wittgenstein practiced should have remained so long obscure. We are accustomed to associating hermeneutics with a philosophical tradition that has tended to be suspicious of, when not overtly hostile to, science, as well as to analytical philosophy.[48] Failure to take Hertz seriously as a precursor to Wittgenstein's philosophical method has gone hand in hand with locating his mature thought in the Machist tradition and then in an incapacity to understand how it could possibly be that anyone could at once belong to that tradition and want to undermine its central tenets about the nature of philosophy. Or it has led to a superficial identification of Wittgenstein's views with the much better-known hermeneutics of Dilthey and Gadamer. Such hermeneuticists who have found something congenial in Wittgenstein's mature philosophy have nevertheless been deeply puzzled at the absence of any reference to typically hermeneutical themes such as historical narrative or the relationship between texts and contexts in the *Investigations*. Such puzzlement now becomes understandable in terms of the little known and less understood Hertzian hermeneutic program for the elimination of metaphysics within mechanics. A good part of the reason why the scientific origins of Wittgenstein's linguistic hermeneutics certainly rests generally with Hertz's obscurity as a philosopher of science, but more specifically with failure

2. HEINRICH HERTZ ...

to grasp the importance of his notion of »appropriateness« and alternative modes of presentation as the basis for a kind philosophical thinking which is at once analytical and hermeneutic. It also helps us to understand why Wittgenstein never moved in a more conventionally hermeneutic direction. There was simply no reason to do so.

However, another part of the reason why the scientific origins of Wittgenstein's mature thought have remained obscure bears upon the fact that we have been accustomed to dividing his development into an early, more or less positivistic phase and a later assault upon positivism. This is something that Wittgenstein himself wanted to avoid, for example, in insisting that the *Tractatus* be published along with his later work. Maurice Drury has pointed out that even Sraffa's devastating critique of his views of the dependence of meaning upon »logical form«, which left him like a tree bereft of its branches, did nothing to disturb the »roots« of his thinking.[49] These, Wittgenstein insisted came to him early in life. Indeed, K.T. Fann insisted long ago that perhaps the »later« philosophy was in fact earlier that the »earlier« philosophy in its origins.[50] This sketch of the Hertzian origins of Wittgenstein's concept of philosophy should help us to understand more clearly what that claim means. Till we have a complete picture of Wittgenstein's texts all discussions of his development will be to some extent speculative; however, that is not to say that such speculations must be idle. There is any amount of evidence from the extant notebooks that Wittgenstein kept during World War I that themes such as the distinction between wishing and willing (*N*, 88), the emphasis upon use and application (*N*, 82), the idea of the importance of »etc.« (*N*, 89-90), and even the more existential idea that in the course of fighting he sometimes became like an animal that he discussed there (*GT*, 29.VII.16) clearly anticipate central ideas in the so-called »later philosophy«.

Indeed, it seems to be the case that Wittgenstein's return to philosophy was a matter of taking out the notes he kept and studying them carefully by continually revising them and producing alternatives of them as was his wont: he seems to have done this after returning to philosophy around 1930 and once more at the very end of his life in the manuscripts that have come to be known as *On Certainly* and *On Color*. There is at least some inter-textual evidence for this hypothesis. If this is true, there is no less reason to believe that he returned to Hertz as well with equal enthusiasm.

Further, Hertz himself distinguishes the a-priori procedures of a »mature« science from the more expedient modes of concept formation in practical scientific work in a way that clearly anticipates Wittgenstein's perspectives on *Bilder* both in the *Tractatus* and in the *Philosophical Investigations*: »in mature knowledge logical purity has to be taken into consideration above all. Only logically pure models [*Bilder*] are to be tested for correctness, only [empirically] correct models are to be compared for appropriateness. Pressing need frequently prompts us to proceed in the reverse manner: models are invented that are suitable for specific purposes, then tested for their correctness, and finally cleansed of inner contradictions« (*PM*, 12). There is much to be said for the thesis that Wittgenstein wrote the *Tractatus* with the first half of this text in mind, the *Investigations* with the second.

Finally, approaching Wittgenstein's later philosophy after reading the Introduction to Hertz's *Principles* it is clear why a scientifically-oriented thinker would maintain that there were no theses to advance in philosophy, no explanations to offer only a description of how our concepts systematically confuse into thinking that we need theories to explain the nature of concepts when we really only need to get straight about their functioning. After Hertz it becomes clear how philosophy can

2. HEINRICH HERTZ ...

dissolve problems by leaving everything as it is, i.e., by giving us a new perspective upon what has till now puzzled us such that we no longer are impelled to raise questions, without lapsing into a know-nothing anti-scientific irrationalism. Finally, after taking Hertz seriously as an influence as profound as it was early in Wittgenstein's career, we can understand more easily how »unscientific« thinkers as different as Kierkegaard and Weininger, Tolstoy and Lichtenberg, Spengler and Kraus could have impressed him to the point of taking on profound philosophical significance for him, i.e., by presenting radically striking alternatives to the clichéd »absolute presuppositions« informing both everyday thinking and philosophy. In short, in Wittgenstein's eyes they were capable of offering just the sort of freshly liberating points of comparison that could bring philosophy to rest. They were allies in the battle to gain clarity, not about some specific object before us, but about the ways in which *our preconceptions* about said object often systematically confuse us by leading us to ask inappropriate and impossible questions. If this is true, then Wittgenstein's turn to religion during World War I was preceded by his encounter with Hertz, which explains why the scientific and religious elements in his thought, which all of his contemporaries, both Positivists and Hermeneuticists, took to be absolutely incompatible, could nest comfortably in his thinking.

Of course, the paradox is that Hertz never saw himself as a hermeneuticist nor would he have seen a connection between his main achievements in the philosophy of science and religious thought as Wittgenstein did. Little wonder that Wittgenstein would claim to understand him better that he did himself. In any case, it is the heritage Hertzian hermeneutics that paved Wittgenstein's way to a refined highly unusual philosophy of showing, rather than saying, that would form the prelude to his reception of both Gottlob Frege and Karl Kraus.

CHAPTER 3

Arthur Schopenhauer: The Opaque Self

DESPITE WITTGENSTEIN'S REMARK TO Maurice Drury about Schopenhauer's shallowness[51], there is plenty of evidence that Schopenhauer exerted a profound influence upon Wittgenstein. Both his own statements about his philosophical development and intertextual evidence from his crucial notebooks from World War I as well as other texts provide us with ample documentation of that. Indeed, to the extent that one may speak of a »Continental«, as opposed to an »analytic«, side of his thought, it is ultimately (but not exclusively) traceable to Schopenhauer. (For the historian of philosophy these polemical categories »Continental« and »analytic« philosophy are a completely misleading, sloppy, unscholarly way of characterizing the differences between twentieth century philosophers.) In any case, however much the influence of Oswald Spengler on Wittgenstein explains about the similarities between him and thinkers like Nietzsche, Heidegger and Foucault, it is the influence of Schopenhauer that ultimately explains these similarities. Thus he would say to Miss Anscombe that his first philosophy at age 16 (1905) was a Schopenhauerian idealism, which he was disabused of by his encounter with Frege and Russell.[52] However, here too, the considerations that made the *Tractatus Logico-Philosophicus* seem »disturbing« (befremdlich) to Frege (Fr,19) and left Russell with a certain »intellectual discomfort«[53] are assuredly those which are rooted in his Schopenhauerianism (even when they are not attributable to Schopenhauer alone). Moreover, we have the infamous text in *Culture and Value* where Wittgenstein insists that his philosophical work of clarification was influenced by Schopenhauer among others. Just as this list is chronological, it seems that the figures earlier on the list paved the way to those who come later. So, just as Wittgenstein found his way from Boltzmann first to Hertz and then to Schopenhauer, Schopenhauer paved his way to Kraus, Loos, Weininger and Spengler.

Since the Wittgenstein-Boltzmann relationship is especially important as background to Wittgenstein's Schopenhauer reception, we shall do well to consider certain aspects of it as they form the prelude to Wittgenstein's encounter with the great pessimist. Briefly, Boltzmann's witty polemic, parodying Schopenhauer's own style and turning it against him in the lecture »On a Thesis of Schopenhauer's« which Boltzmann was restrained from naming »Proof that Schopenhauer is fundamentally and irrevocably a mindless, ignorant, nonsense scribbling, philosophaster, who unhinges minds on the basis of his unsurpassed phrase mongering« (*ein geistloser unwissender, Unsinn schmierender, die Köpfe durch beispiellos hohlen Wortkram von Grund aus und auf immer desorganisierender Philosophaster*) is probably the source of Wittgenstein familiarity with Schopenhauer. The irony is that Schopenhauer used precisely that phrase to describe his archenemy G.W.F. Hegel[54]. Boltzmann's wit and sense of style assuredly left a strong impression on the teenage Wittgenstein (c. 1903 or 1904). Moreover, Boltzmann's own concern with what he termed the confusion (*Verwirrung*) of solipsism probably did a great deal to orient Wittgenstein's early reading of Schopenhauer. However, Boltzmann's view of metaphysics as the result of succumbing to our inclination to over generalize our theories and his view of how techniques can help us solve intellectual puzzles, as well as other aspects of Boltzmann's view of philosophy, also left their mark upon Wittgenstein as he approached Schopenhauer.

Thus the concerns that brought Wittgenstein to Schopenhauer were basically different from the intellectual concerns that drew him to Boltzmann and Hertz; they were as personal as they were philosophical. He was doubtless drawn to Schopenhauer because the framed the philosophical quest in terms of *the problem of the world*, which is at once a problem about knowledge *and* a problem about myself, which are *inextricably and mysteriously, almost distressingly, linked, but yet distinct.* In short, Schopenhauer presented Wittgenstein with a perplexity that we need to get clear about. Thus he would write in his wartime *Notebooks*, »There are two godheads: the world and my independent I« (*N*, 8.7.16) In any case, Schopenhauer's influence upon Wittgenstein seems to have been a complex matter bearing upon both his existential and his intellectual concerns and running through all phases of his thought from first to last. It is present most prominently in the dramatic swing to concerns about God and the meaning of life that came in his notebooks at the beginning of July 1916 not to mention the dramatic reflections upon suicide with which those notebooks close. Briefly, in posing the series of questions beginning with »what do I know about God and the purpose of life?« a wholly new element enters his philosophizing. Moreover, it was precisely that element that was so puzzling to Frege and Russell but was so deeply rooted in his personal psychic constitution, as we can clearly see from the private or »secret notebooks« (i.e., as opposed to the philosophical, public ones, which he kept simultaneously). There is no doubt whatsoever that these new philosophical questions were prompted by

Schopenhauer, above all by his concept of the self in its twofold character as knowing and as willing subject:

> First of all it [knowledge] is bound to the form of representation; it is perception and decomposes as such into subject and object. For not even in self-consciousness is the ego absolutely simple; rather it consists in a knowing element and a known element: intellect and will respectively. The former is not known and the latter is not knowing, even if both flow together into the consciousness of an ego. However, for that very reason this ego is not entirely familiar, as it were transparent; rather, it is opaque and thus remains a riddle to itself. (*Werke*, II, 254)[55]

In sharp contrast to, say, Descartes, for Schopenhauer it is of the essence of knowing that mind (the self, the ego, the will [to know]) can understand itself only with the greatest of difficulties. We only know the will's act but never the will itself. In an extended analogy that certainly would have pleased Wittgenstein Schopenhauer compares the relation between the two to that between the branches and the roots of a tree (*Werke*, II, 261f.). So there will always be something extremely mysterious about the ego as Schopenhauer emphatically reiterates in numerous passages throughout his works. For Schopenhauer mind is in the very middle of nature, not outside of it. The power to represent things, intellect, is an instrument that unconscious nature in us employs to prevail in the biological struggle for survival (cf. »Von den wesentlichen Unvollkommenheiten des Intellekts,« *Werke*, II, 176-190). Briefly, humans are thinking animals but animals none the less: »The human intellect is only a higher gradation of the animal's ...« (*Werke*, II, 188) – a theme that returns in Weininger and Spengler albeit in very different ways. As such the mind is only darkly aware of itself. The ego (self/will) is never the object of scientific knowledge. It is something we know in the sense that we feel something within us such as our own pulse. This is what it means to claim that the self is opaque: it is absolutely incapable of a God's eye view of things, not to mention itself, but must, nevertheless, struggle to get a sense of itself in its relation to the world. This opacity never ceased to fascinate Wittgenstein.

Reflections based upon Schopenhauer's notion of the complex relationship, at once of complementarity and opposition to one another, between mind and nature, which is prior to mind, dominate Wittgenstein's philosophical notebooks after July 1916. The mystical dimension to the *Tractatus* – a feeling of the world as a totality with logical limits – was Wittgenstein's response to Schopenhauer's challenge to get clear about the relationship of the self to the world. When these thoughts, which were previously at best, a private, personal matter entered his philosophizing, Wittgenstein ceased to be preoccupied exclusively with Bertrand Russell's problems, i.e., rewriting the first eleven chapters of the *Principia Mathematica*,[56] and his own distinctive philosophy with its peculiar aesthetic form began to take shape. Thus trains of thought originating in his encounter with Schopenhauer would run through the *Tractatus* into the *Philosophical Investigations* right down to *On Certainty*. What follows is a sketch of that path.

In the so-called *Secret Notebooks* Wittgenstein writes that he went to war to subject his character to trial by ordeal (*GT*, 10. VIII. 14). On his own account, from the very start of the war Wittgenstein needed philosophy in the everyday sense to survive. In that vein he would ponder a bit later what sort of philosophy his pianist brother Paul would need to overcome the loss of his arm and therefore his profession. Fear for his life nightly as a search light operator and perfect target of enemy fire, the banality of his comrades in arms and even his own sensuality as they contrasted with doing his duty and being decent (*anständig*) generally haunted him. His thoughts regularly turned to suicide. In the *Secret Notebooks* he set down his most intimate thoughts of these torments, including his occasional incapacity to behave as anything other than an animal thoughtlessly seeking satisfaction (*GT*, 29.7.16). Discovering Tolstoy's *The Gospel in Brief* with its doctrine that we are powerless in the flesh but free through the spirit was an immense help to him in finding the personal philosophy that would pull him through. For it was true, only his work on logic gave him a sense of satisfaction. Did Schopenhauer play a role here? His name does not turn up here but there are nevertheless distinct traces of his influence in the *Secret Notebooks*. What are they?

We know that he was later in life fond of quoting from Schopenhauer's *Aphorisms for Living Wisely*. At least four Schopenhauerian themes in the secret diaries seem to indicate that he knew the work already during the war: the need to live in the present, the need to be decent, the liberating nature of work and, surprisingly, the necessity of fighting a duel with a certain Cadet Adam to defend his honor, which discussed extensively by Schopenhauer turn up there (Schopenhauer, *Werke*, V, 430–466; Wittgenstein, *GT*, 11.2.15). All of these elements are present in Schopenhauer's Baroque reflections on how to be happy. However, the very conception of a eudaimonology itself seems to run through Wittgenstein's whole text appearing explicitly only here and there. At a crucial point in July 1916 Wittgenstein wrote in his private notebooks a scant few days after having written the dramatic entry in his philosophical notebooks about God and the purpose of life, which have already been mentioned in connection with Hertz and to which we shall have occasion to return in connection with Weininger, which clearly illuminate how he saw his life and his work:

> Colossal strain in the last month. Have reflected much about everything but curiously incapable of producing the connection with my mathematical lines of thought. However, the connection will be produced! What cannot be said cannot be said! (*GT*, 6–7. VII. 16).

The implicit point of this text would bear out Schopenhauer's notion that happiness consists in self-sufficiency. How is that so?

To answer that question we must look more closely at the text cited. The first point is that Wittgenstein is seeking a connection between the solution to his mathematical, i.e., logical problems, and his existential ones. I take this to mean that he was seeking a technique comparable to the truth table method of representation, which he had developed along lines suggested by Frege in the *Begriffsschrift*, a pellucid, foolproof, strictly mechanical method for determining the logical status of a proposition. In effect, the logical status of a given proposition simply showed itself on the basis of representation in a truth table. So the problem of whether it was a tautology, a contradiction or a substantive proposition simply disappeared. Wittgenstein thus appears to be seeking a similar solution to the problem of the meaning of life. The solution is that the problem should simply disappear in the living of life itself. However, at a closer look we find him insisting that he must *produce*, as opposed to discover, the link between logic and life. How can we make the problems of life disappear? His answer is that it has to be a matter of living in such a way that those existential problems do not arise in the first place. At this stage Wittgenstein's notion of happiness is clearly a matter of what Schopenhauer would term the denial of the will, i.e., a matter made complicated by the elusive, opaque nature of the self. However, we cannot discount the impact of Frege's antipsychologism on him even here, for he is sure from the start that this is not merely a matter of wishing for something but of actively willing it. In any case, Schopenhauer's central ideas about the opaque self increasingly found their way into his philosophical notebooks, in which the question of how to live happily is absolutely central.

Two days after the remark about his colossal strain (8.7.16), for example, he would write the parenthetical remark »I do not yet know what my will is.« What follows is an extended reflection upon the relationship between the self, i.e., the will and the world that is too well-known to have to be summarized here. What is easily overlooked is that this is all part of a project to rid himself of fear and thus live happily. It is worth considering some of the things Wittgenstein says about the self in this context. First, it is one of two godheads, the other being the world. Second, it is something deeply mysterious. Third, the ego is a philosophical problem inasmuch as the world is my world. Thus history has nothing to do with me, i.e., I have only a contingent relationship to temporal developments around me. Here it is certainly significant that Wittgenstein speaks of a problem here; whereas Schopenhauer speaks of a riddle. He seems to have been campaigning to eliminate riddles from his own thought and philosophy generally. At this stage Wittgenstein was, nevertheless, content to express himself entirely in Schopenhauerian terms: »Just as the world is my representation, my will is the world will.«

However, Wittgenstein seems to think that Schopenhauer needs to be qualified by Frege here if we are to get straight about the will/self – which is, of course, consonant with the idea that Frege led him away from his early Schopenhauerian idealism. Thus Wittgenstein insists in Frege's spirit on eliminating all traces of psychologism and subjectivity from the Schopenhauerian picture. He will distinguish sharply between the knowing subject for whom the world is object (the »metaphysical« or transcendental subject) and the psychological subject, which, he insists is of no interest to philosophy. Similarly, in specifying what he means by will, he will sharply distinguish between wishing and willing. The latter is action and not a mere psychological state. Neither is the will an object in the world nor an object of knowledge in any sense. Enter the mystical: something entirely foreign to the original project of rewriting the first 11 chapters of the *Principia Mathematica*. The difference was the impact of Schopenhauer and the new set of problems he brought with him to Wittgenstein – problems whose solution would lead him to Weininger's notion that seeing the world rightly entails acknowledging that the world and the self have limits.[57] This was a matter of problematizing the world as such in a Schopenhauerian way:

> Philosophy is essentially wisdom with respect to the world. Its problem is the world and the world alone. It lets the Gods in peace and expects in return that they will leave it in peace as well. (*Werke*, II, 243)

This idea is surely related to Wittgenstein's project in the *Tractatus*, and reflected in to the provocative first and last sentences, which in fact came to frame his reflections upon logic.

Wittgenstein's world is a far cry from the logical atomist's inasmuch as it consists of both objective facts and a subjective mood that is at once inseparable from them and, nevertheless, completely independent of them. In fact this Schopenhauerian notion of the world is more reminiscent of St. Augustine, Pascal or even Husserl than it is of Russell and the Positivists.

In any case, Wittgenstein agrees with Schopenhauer that we have to get straight about the nature of the world without ever being in a position where we can be said to know anything in the strict sense about the totality except that it is our representation. At the same time, unlike other animals, we are aware of our own mortality. Knowledge of the fact that we must die presses us to make sense of the whole of our experience at the cost of transgressing the transcendental limits of the knowable. Wittgenstein's *Logisch-philosophische Abhandlung* in the form that we have it was the result of those deliberations. Thus Wittgenstein could remark in early August 1916, »my work has extended from the foundations of logic to the nature of the world,« which seems to signify that his Schopenhauerian project had come to compliment, indeed, swallow, as it were, his original Russellian task. What further Schopenhauerian elements enter into that work?

At least five points can be mentioned apart from the mystical element that we have already encountered in the *Notebooks 1914–1916*: the impossibility of their being a hierarchy of languages, the problem of solipsism, denunciation of the belief in causality as superstition, the identification of the world and life and the concomitant notion that ordinary language is in order as it stands.

Many philosophers right down to today take the grounds for Wittgenstein's denial that there could be a hierarchy of languages to be a matter of empirical fact: since nobody had succeeded in producing one at the time he wrote the *Tractatus*, he did not think it was possible to do so at all. Those figures, with Rudolf Carnap being the principal agent, believe that the mystical conclusions of the *Tractatus* could be avoided by a metalanguage. However, this misses Wittgenstein's point massively. In fact Wittgenstein's point is a transcendental one that he owes to Schopenhauer (and through him ultimately to

Kant). The latter writes in his dissertation on the principle of sufficient reason, »thus there is no knowledge of knowledge, because that would require that the subject separated itself from the act of knowing and now knew knowing as an object, which is impossible«, *Werke*, III, 169). In terms of the *Tractatus* the idea that the subject of a science of knowledge would have to be logically prior to himself means that a metalanguage would be every bit as much a construct of the subject as the object language, only that fact would be all the less obvious. The crucial assertion is that we can foresee only what we construct. A metalanguage is every bit as dependent upon the subject as an object language, so it cannot solve any problems in philosophy. To be sure this is in a much more pragmatist vein than Schopenhauer's view but it does not differ from it with respect to the transcendental standpoint that both share. The impossibility of a hierarchy of elementary propositions is entailed by their dependence upon the subject, not by developments in logic but by the application of logic as the mind constitutes the world.

Since Wittgenstein's transcendental standpoint is not well understood we shall do well to spell out its central features here. The chief characteristics of this transcendental perspective are that it 1) conceives the mind as active, i.e., as constructing knowledge rather than discovering it 2) takes philosophical problems to be immanent in the very language which employ as we construct knowledge and 3) only soluble in the sense that they are »dissolved« into insights into how we have constructed our representation of reality 4) won on the basis constructing alternatives to our usual modes or expression, 5) which alternatives thus show us the limits of specific modes of representation in the sense of how they can mislead us.[58]

Wittgenstein's solipsism is a difficult but crucial theme within the *Tractatus*, which David Pears has insisted must be traced back to Schopenhauer's influence upon him (although, as we have seen, its philosophical roots go back to his beginnings in Boltzmann – and doubtless to profound existential concerns about whose exact nature we can only conjecture). Indeed, Pears goes as far as to assert that Wittgenstein seems to be playing Russell off against Schopenhauer in the matter of solipsism.[59] Beginning from his encounter with Russell's views about solipsism in 1913, where Russell observes that my experience of a given object is somehow more than that object, Wittgenstein became increasingly fascinated by the way in which the self is a correlative of the world. However, in the course of the War there was a radical transformation in Wittgenstein's attitude to this problem. Indeed, Russell's way of conceiving the problem of the relation between the self and the world could hardly inspire the sort of »obsession with limits«[60] that we find in his *Notebooks*, which would characterize all of his future philosophizing. Pears ascribes that transformation to the influence Schopenhauer who transformed Wittgenstein's thinking about the matter as well as the intensity with which he pursued the issue. In any case, the idea that the world is my world is absolutely central to the author of the *Tractatus*. There is an uncanny relationship between the self and the world that can best be expressed by saying that seeing the world rightly is to feel it as a limited totality as I feel my pulse. I sense, literally, that I am the microcosm but I cannot really say anything about what I feel, except perhaps that I do so grasp the world. However strange this might strike a Bertrand Russell, it could well be a commentary upon the closing passages of the *World as Will and Representation*:

> If, however, it should be absolutely insisted upon that somehow a positive knowledge is to be acquired of what philosophy can express only negatively as denial of the will, nothing

would be left but to refer to that state which is experienced by all who have attained to the complete denial of the will, and which is denoted by the names ecstasy, rapture, illumination, union with God, and so on. But such a state cannot really be called knowledge, since it no longer has the form of subject for an object; moreover, it is accessible only to one's own experience that cannot be communicated.
(*WWR*, IV, § 71, 410 [tr. Payne], *Werke*, I, 556-7).

The early notebooks as whole leave no doubt that Wittgenstein was striving for just such a denial of the will. It seems that he had had precisely that mystical experience that Schopenhauer describes here. The odd thing, however, appears to be that he was convinced that anybody who was prepared to ponder the objective, logical, as opposed to a mere psychological, construction of the world, as he did, would be forced to the same conclusion. However, that solipsistic illumination paradoxically entails letting the self shrink to an extensionless – and therefore indescribable – point. Thus solipsism coincides with Fregean realism.

In any case, it is absolutely clear from this text how much hangs upon the Schopenhauerian point of departure, the absolute opposition of knowing subject and object of knowledge and what consequences it had for the early Wittgenstein. Here is we come to a suitable point for taking up Wittgenstein's reception of the Schopenhauerian notion of causality upon which Wittgenstein's transcendental standpoint ultimately rests. Like Wittgenstein's mystical thoughts, the anti-Russellian notion that belief in the causal nexus is superstition seems to come out of thin air. However, when one sees Wittgenstein's early philosophy of philosophy as it were as emerging from a Schopenhauerian as well as a Russellian *Fragestellung*, this is comprehensible. The result of Schopenhauer's critique of Kant's theory of knowledge is that the system of categories is superfluous. Only one category is really necessary, causality. On Schopenhauer's view causality is given with the very mental representation itself. Representation becomes experience because causality is the exclusive a-priori condition for representation. Put differently, for Schopenhauer we can only understand what we perceive in terms of causes, i.e., we understand perception on the basis of causal connection, which physicists designate as laws. Thus Wittgenstein would assert, following Schopenhauer, that the law of causality (i.e., the basis of pre-Kantian metaphysics) is not a law but the form of law. For this reason the law of causality cannot be extended to the whole of experience, i.e., the whole of experience as such cannot be represented; its form can only be shown. Thus the law of causality cannot be extended to explain experience as such as he points out in the chapter explicitly dedicated to the misuse of the law of causality in his dissertation on the fourfold root of the principle of sufficient reason (*Werke*, III, 116). This is precisely what Russell had done in the *The Problems of Philosophy* with respect to explaining sense data. In an argument that Russell himself admitted was weak, he asserted that the simplest assumption that coheres with our experience is that physical objects cause them. This is precisely what Wittgenstein wants to deny. Science cannot by its nature give an answer to traditional metaphysical questions, for they have an entirely different status than scientific questions do. It is the point of Schopenhauer's essay on human beings' need for metaphysics that creatures aware of their finitude must pose such questions even though they cannot be answered. In short, Schopenhauer's philosophy contains at its core an explanation of how human reason is limited and why human beings have an innate tendency to run up against the limits of reason – a favorite theme of Boltzmann's. All of Wittgenstein's philosophizing shows that he took up these concerns with a passion, not least in his conversations with Moritz Schlick, to whom he said:

> Human Beings have an instinct to run up against the limits of language. Consider, for example, amazement at the question why things exist at all. It cannot be expressed as a question and there is no answer for it. Everything that we can say about it can only be nonsense a-priori. Nevertheless we run up against the limits of language. (*WWK*, 68)

This is part of his Schopenhauerian heritage.

However, Wittgenstein's concerns came to turn increasingly upon the ways in which these questions are embedded in language itself. With that we come to two closely related points at which we can perceive Schopenhauer's influence in the *Tractatus*: the idea that the world and life are one and the notion that everyday language is in order as it stands. In fact these are points at which the author of the *Tractatus* anticipates the author of the *Philosophical Investigations*. Thus discussing these theses leads us to the implications of Schopenhauer's thought for the later Wittgenstein.

The idea that life and the world are one is, once more, hardly a notion that we find in Bertrand Russell; it is, however, a completely Schopenhauerian thought. Unfortunately we have no way of knowing why Wittgenstein included it in the *Tractatus*. It, like most of the thoughts that he took over from Schopenhauer, is an excellent example of a proposition that should in fact be a chapter heading. There is no question that it is continuous with Wittgenstein's later thoughts about dissolving philosophical problems on the basis of understanding human natural history. In any case, it is precisely that thought that moved Schopenhauer to assert that philosophy is in the end wisdom with respect to the world. For Wittgenstein the notion that the world is life seems to emphasize that the world is more than the totality of facts, even though there is nothing beyond them that we can describe.

No less striking is the thought, also completely undeveloped, that ordinary language is completely in order as it stands. For positivists, who took the task of philosophy to be the clarification of thought on the basis of logical analysis it is hardly comprehensible but for a Schopenhauerian less surprising than one might think. Let us take a look at the relationship between logic and language in Schopenhauer with a view to grasping the continuities between Wittgenstein and Schopenhauer as well as within Wittgenstein's own thought here.

It is hardly a secret that Wittgenstein's concern with demolishing the notion that there could be such a thing as a private language is absolutely central to the *Philosophical Investigations*. Professor Pears has argued convincingly that Wittgenstein's position with respect to the incoherence of the idea of a private language is a continuation of his concerns about the nature of solipsism and *a fortiori* of his confrontation with Schopenhauer's opaque self. In the later philosophy the extensionless point that correlates with the world in the *Tractatus* expands into the collective, social subject that determines use.

However there are a several other aspects of Wittgenstein's mature thought that ultimately derive from his encounter with Schopenhauer. These bear upon the fact that practical logic is implicit in language, which has the corollary that the learning of language is tantamount to learning to think, i.e. to learning practical logic. This a subject upon which Schopenhauer waxes eloquent:

> Thus learning this [language] brings the whole mechanism of reason, so the essentials of logic, to consciousness. Clearly

3. ARTHUR SCHOPENHAUER ...

> this cannot come about without great intellectual work and intense attentiveness, i.e., without the power which confers upon children their desire for learning as evidenced when they see something really useful and necessary before them but appears weak if the child thinks that we are trying to force something inappropriate upon him. (*Werke*, III, 123)

Schopenhauer goes on to insist that the genuinely concrete logic, not a matter of formal rules but a matter of their application. He goes on to make just the sort of analogy that Wittgenstein was fond of, asserting that the child's relation to logic here resembles the way a musical person who has taught himself to play the piano has come to master the rules of harmony and general bass.

Further Schopenhauerian thoughts can be found in *Zettel* and In *On Certainty*. Let us round off our survey of the points at which a Schopenhauerian influence is clearly observable by a brief consideration of those traces.

It is often overlooked that Wittgenstein believed that, »in philosophy it is significant that such-and-such a sentence is makes no sense; but also that is sounds funny«, where funny is the English rendering for »komisch«, i.e., odd strange, curious or perhaps best peculiar. *Zettel* contains a number of humorous philosophical anecdotes:

> Imagine someone saying: 'Man hopes'. How should this general phenomenon of natural history be described? – One might observe a child and wait until one day he manifests hope and then one could say 'Today he hoped for the first time'. But surely that sounds queer! Although it would be quite natural to say 'Today he said "I hope" for the first time' (Z, 468).

or

> So he is having real pain and it is the possession of this by somebody else that he feels doubt of. –But how does he do this?–It is as if I were told: 'Here is a chair. Can you see it clearly?—Good,– now translate it into French!' (*Z*, 547).

or

> If someone were now to tell us that he eats involuntarily— what evidence would make one believe this? (*Z*, 578)

Some further examples from other works:

> Why can't a dog simulate pain? Is he too honest?;
> (*PI*, I, 250)

and,

> 'A rose has no teeth.' This ... is obviously true! It is even surer than that a goose has none. – And yet it is not so clear. For where should a rose's teeth have been? (*PI*, II, xi, 221)

These questions are less to be answered than to be thought through by Wittgenstein's reader. That these questions seem to verge on the absurd is intentional:

> We speak of red hot or white hot but we do not speak of brown hot or gray hot? (*OCL*, I, 34)

or

> (Why do we speak of brown rather than reddish green? (*OCL*, 11).

All of these points are conceptual and all of them tend to makes us laugh. Schopenhauer gives us an explanation of why: such ludicrousness arises from the misuse of reason. Using the language of the old logic he tells us that we have subsumed a representation under the wrong concept (»Zur Theorie des Lächerlichen,« *Werke*, II, 122), something that since Ryle's

3. ARTHUR SCHOPENHAUER ...

The Concept of Mind has been known as a category mistake. For Wittgenstein such howlers are typical of metaphysicians. From the point of view of everyday usage metaphysicians' mistakes are grounds for questioning their sanity (*OC*, § 467). The point is entirely Schopenhauerian and probably the explanation for why he came to take Karl Kraus so seriously – it is significant that he lost his interest in Kraus in the course of the 1920s when he ceased to find Kraus funny.[61] In any case, Wittgenstein's lifelong concern with nonsense, which went as far as to be the basis for a collection of texts in his *Nachlass*[62], most like goes back to his encounter with Schopenhauer. It is no less relevant to his relation to Frege, as we shall see.

Be that as it may, one of the most radical ideas in all of Wittgenstein occurs in *On Certainty* where he asserts,

> I want to regard humans here as animals; as a primitive being to which we grant instinct but not reasoning. As a creature in a primitive state. Any logic good enough for a primitive means of communication suffices, we do not need to be ashamed of it. Language did not emerge from a reasoning process. (§ 475 – where Wittgenstein employs the, for him unusual, Schopenhauerian expression for abstract reasoning, *Raisonnement*).

This is not the kind of thing that one expects from a Logical Positivist or even a conventional analytic philosopher but it is hardly strange in a Schopenhauerian, with his notions of mind's rootedness in nature and the concomitant need to get straight about the relationship between the human and the animal. Moreover, the animal nature of thought explains why Wittgenstein did not cringe at the suggestion that, in the end, the logic of human thought was not describable. The point is that right up to the very end we find Schopenhauerian themes, not least that of the opaque self from which I have taken my point of departure, echoed at crucial junctures in Wittgenstein's thinking. It is clear from his own remarks about his development that this is anything but accidental. Here it is important to reiterate that it is less Schopenhauer's solutions but his transcendental perspective on knowing and the questions it suggested to Wittgenstein that are important for his philosophical development. Moreover, Schopenhauer seems to have shown him the way to Weininger (limits of the self, animality), Kraus (wit and irony) and Spengler (language, tacit knowing).

However, if all that I have said to this point is correct I end up with a problem: why should Wittgenstein have complained of Schopenhauer's superficiality to Maurice Drury? There is a clue in *Culture and Value* where he writes:

> Schopenhauer, you might say, is a completely gross [roh] mind, i.e., he is refined but his refinement suddenly stops at a certain depth and he is as gross as the grossest. We could say about Schopenhauer: his depth stops where real depth begins. One could say he never examines his conscience. (*C+V*, 41)

Drury's own conjecture about how to construe Wittgenstein's contrast between shallowness and depth is an important hint here. He writes, »a shallow thinker may be able to say something clearly but ... a deep thinker makes us see that there is something that cannot be said«.[63] This suits Schopenhauer when viewed from a Wittgensteinian perspective.

Perhaps we can best appreciate what Wittgenstein is getting at if we contrast Schopenhauer's attitude to his own philosophizing with Wittgenstein's mature perspective on his subject. Both as a human being an as a philosopher Wittgenstein was his whole life long intensely self-critical. He continually subjects his own beliefs to scathing criticism. For Wittgenstein criticism most decidedly begins at home; it is most decidedly a form of examination of conscience. Moreover, the other side of that coin is that self-criticism requires taking almost infinite patience with the erroneous thoughts of others. Thus in what is perhaps the most widely discussed aspect of his mature philosophy, his reflections upon private language, Wittgenstein wrestles for some 75 paragraphs to establish the conceptual incoherence of a view whose problematic character he had already underscored in posing the question whether following a rule is something that a single person could do only once in his life (*PI*, I, 199). This is what we for the most part find wanting in Schopenhauer.

The critical spirit in Schopenhauer, to be sure, frequently manifests itself as subtle critique of the views of other philosophers: his critique of Kant is a case in point. However, as often as not Schopenhauer's criticisms of other philosophers degenerates into polemic and outright name-calling. Thus his works are strewn with invective that occasionally verges upon the common. Here we should note that it was precisely this aspect of Schopenhauer's thought that Boltzmann parodied in his lecture on Schopenhauer, which, as we have seen, he originally entitled »Proof that Schopenhauer is fundamentally and irrevocably a mindless, ignorant, nonsense scribbling, philosophaster, who unhinges minds on the basis of his unsurpassed phrase mongering« precisely to emphasize that he was treating Schopenhauer just as Schopenhauer had treated Hegel.

If the sources of the temptation to metaphysics that lie at the roots of philosophy are really »deep disquietudes« innocently concealed in the outer forms of grammar such *ad personam* arguments get us nowhere – except perhaps counterproductively inasmuch as they confirm the criticized person his or her errors. In short, Schopenhauer's polemics overlook frequently his own insights into the ways that philosophical problems are puzzles, not least that of the opaque self, that confuse and torment philosophers, not superstitions that they have naively adopted. In fact Schopenhauer's ubiquitous polemics are the very opposite of the kind of therapy which should put the philosophical mind to rest. It would be Gottlob Frege who would teach the young Wittgenstein to distrust subjectivity in all its forms.

Note

What had Wittgenstein read of Schopenhauer? It is not easy to give a precise answer to that question. He seems to have known *The World as Will and Representation*, as well as Schopenhauer's commentaries upon the main text in his essays, well. Brian McGuinness suggests that the *Aphorisms for Living Wisely* were particularly important to him. Matters discussed in the secret diaries as different as his concern for establishing the nature of happiness and his curious reflections on the necessity of fighting a duel with a problematic comrade at the front seem to confirm this. It is virtually impossible that he did not know the essays on death and, in particular, the one on man's need for metaphysics. Professor McGuinness questions G. H. von Wright's view that Schopenhauer's dissertation *On the Fourfold Root of the Principle of Sufficient Reason* played much of a role in his thinking. There is simply too much history of philosophy that was completely foreign to him in it. He could hardly have understood it. Yet that are thoughts expressed in it such as Schopenhauer's methodological notion that in any investigation we must at once strive to produce a balance between generalization and specificity appropriate to the subject of investigation that clearly anticipate one of Wittgenstein's central ideas. Even more impressive in this respect is the notion that acquiring language is nothing less than mastering the whole mechanism of reason (*Vernunft*) including what is essential to logic. The similarities here are hardly accidental. Moreover, direct references to problems like Kant's problem with the left and right hand glove in Wittgenstein's *Notebooks of 1914–1916* are difficult to explain without reference to that work.

CHAPTER 4

Gottlob Frege: The Quest for Objectivity

»Heiliger Frege!«
Wittgenstein, marginalia commenting upon
David Hilbert's refusal to be driven from Cantor's paradise.[64]

IT IS ANYTHING BUT a secret that Gottlob Frege exerted an enormous influence on Wittgenstein in all phases of his philosophical development. For example, during his confinement in the Italian prisoner of war camp at Cassino after World War I he urgently requested on 24.5.1919 that Paul Engelmann send him a copy of Frege's *The Basic Laws of Arithmetic* (*E*, 19). Similarly, he would request with no less urgency a year and a half later on 31.10.1920 that Engelmann send him his own copy of the same work via Anna Knaur. (*E*, 37) In the Preface to the *Tractatus* he would claim inspiration from the »great works of Frege« (*T*, p. 3). Indeed, the very heart of that lapidary work is the elaboration of an idea of Frege's, which led him to the construction of truth tables, which with the help of the Scheffer function, simultaneous negation, a single operation that at once affirms and denies, which allows the derivation of all of the propositions of logic from, which in turn enables Wittgenstein clearly to *show* what Frege himself others had vainly tried to say about the status of logical propositions[65] and thus to pass over what had hitherto been considered the philosophical problems in logic in silence.[66]

Still later he would remark on at least two occasions upon how deeply he was impressed with Frege's style (*C+V*, 99; *Z*, 712) and upon the profound, if from the reader's viewpoint, imperceptible, influence it had exerted upon his way of writing: »the style of my sentences is extraordinarily strongly influenced by Frege. And if I wanted to I could really pinpoint this influence, where *prima vista* nobody would see it« (*Z*, 712). In the fragments that would later become *Culture and Value* he originally began the list of figures that had influenced his philosophical work of clarification with Frege.[67] Indeed, the impact of Frege upon Wittgenstein was so enormous that it has in recent years evoked an approach to his work, the so-called »New Wittgenstein«, which is almost exclusively based upon his relationship to the Jena philosopher.[68] However one-sided that slant may turn out to be, it is impossible to ignore Frege when considering any aspect of Wittgenstein's development. At the same time it is no simple matter to give an account of Frege's impact upon his thinking about philosophy (as opposed to logic). It certainly is not much help to anyone interested in reconstructing the genesis of his mature philosophical method as we are here.

Our concern, then, is a very specific one, namely, with trying to establish just what impact Frege had upon Wittgenstein's *mature concept of philosophical method*. It is to establish how Frege fits into Wittgenstein's infamous list of »influences« upon him in *Culture and Value*. Our endeavors thus bear upon an aspect of his reception of Frege, which has for the most part neglected in the huge literature that has grown up around them. So our investigation must begin by looking at the residual Fregean elements in the *Philosophical Investigations* reconstructing the continuities between central themes and argumentative strategies in Frege's work and the mature Wittgenstein. Then, if we are to follow Wittgenstein's list in *Culture and Value*, we must trace the way from Boltzmann to Frege in the *Tractatus*

4. GOTTLOB FREGE ...

as well as account for how a certain impetus in Wittgenstein's thinking would push Frege into the background without by any means eliminating him in the *Investigations* – I take it that Frege's originally coming first on the list means nothing less than that, despite prior interests in philosophy, it was Frege, who turned Wittgenstein into a philosopher.

To reiterate: the goal of our search, then, is to see what Frege contributed to the genesis of Wittgenstein's mature strategy for doing philosophy. That search has less to do with the profound impact that Frege had upon the *Tractatus* (which is not say that said influence is entirely irrelevant to our story) than it does with what Wittgenstein inhaled in intense readings of the man who reinvented logic after 2,000 years. How did he exhale Frege again in his philosophical strategy in the *Philosophical Investigations*? to borrow a metaphor from Goethe. The intensely musical Wittgenstein often had tunes in his head, as music lovers frequently do, but, like so many poetry fanciers, he also had texts in his head as well. Not the least of these were texts of Frege, such as the Introduction to *The Basic Laws of Arithmetic*, many of which he had learned by heart as a young man.[69] So we can be certain that Frege's *central ideas* were indelibly impressed upon him sometime between 1905, when he came under the influence of Schopenhauer, who precedes Frege on the list, and 1911, when he met Russell, who comes after him. These would inspire much of the *Tractatus* directly; however, even after he abandoned the idea that representation is the exclusive function of language they would continue to *resonate* within his thoughts over the years at the roots of his thinking rather than determining their substance. That makes the task of reconstruction all the more difficult.

We can safely start our investigation by considering the three principles that Frege emphasizes as encapsulating his central points of departure in the philosophy of mathematics with a view to finding echoes of them in the *Philosophical Investigations*. It is simply impossible that Wittgenstein would not have been acquainted with them.

1) It is necessary to distinguish sharply between the psychological and the logical, the subjective from the objective.
2) We must inquire into the meaning (reference) of words in the context of propositions and not in isolation.
3) We must not lose sight of the distinction between concept and object.[70]

How do these notions or notions clearly derivable from them enter into Wittgenstein's mature philosophy?

Really to be in a position to answer that question we need to grasp what Frege understands by *objectivity* – a theme that is not noncontroversial within Frege scholarship.[71] In the *Foundations of Arithmetic* he writes that objective means: what conforms to law, the conceptual, what can be judged, what can be expressed in words *(was sich ausdrücken läßt)*. Frege opposes what is objective to the »reality« given in pure sensory intuition *(das reine Anschauliche)*,[72] which cannot, he believes, be communicated. Frege insists that what is objective is not real in the sense of being the object of perception. Objectivity seems bound to the logical (transcendental?) conditions that make thinking what is true possible in the first place. So the earth's axis and the equator, for example, are objective for him without being real. Such objective unrealities form the basis of the system of presuppositions upon which scientific knowledge rests. For all their unreality, they are anything but fictional, distinctly not fictions as, say, Frege's contemporary Hans Vaihinger would claim, but objective in an unusual sense that bears significant comparison with, but is not entirely identical with, that of

Plato or even Immanuel Kant. The point is that Frege's realism is considerably less medieval than, say, that of Bernhard Bolzano (at least in the version we find in *The Foundations of Arithmetic*).[73] Without necessarily agreeing with the substance of Frege's thought on the matter, Wittgenstein shared in principle his preoccupation with the idea that objectivity is essentially bound to the conditions of the possibility of something's being intelligible (i.e., not in the Kantian sense that conditions of possibility are synthetic a-priori propositions). This notion profoundly influenced his concept of philosophical method (and probably the course of his life as well).

In fact, Frege's injunction to objectivity, i.e., distinguishing sharply between the psychological and the logical can also be found *inter alia* in a vehement form in the Preface to *The Basic Laws of Arithmetic*,[74] a text that Wittgenstein had largely committed to memory. It is hardly accidental that a variation on that theme turns up, albeit transformed, at a central, if not the central, juncture in the *Philosophical Investigations* I, at § 202 where Wittgenstein denies the possibility of there being such a thing as a private language – as, indeed, it does in one form or another at every crucial stage in Wittgenstein's development.[75] He writes:

> ... following a rule is a practice. And to believe that one is following a rule is not following the rule. For that reason you cannot follow a rule privately, because otherwise believing that you follow the rule would be the same as following the rule.

The distinction between following the rule and imagining that I am doing so (which is also the core of *On Certainty*) is the mature Wittgenstein's way of distinguishing the objective from the subjective. He has in fact transformed Frege's variation on traditional ontological realism, i.e., realism based upon the reference of names occurring in propositions, into what, following a clue from Rudolf Haller, we might term a »praxiological«[76] realism if we need a label for it: in Wittgenstein's mature thought practice rather than formal logic introduces an order that is not arbitrary, and therefore objective, into thinking. In any case, no element in Wittgenstein's mature philosophy is more central than his rejection of the notion of a private language, which is based upon the profound difference there is between subjectively believing – or even »being certain« – of something and its actually being the case. That is clearly continuous with Frege's rejection of subjectivist pyschologism. It is precisely this sort of continuity that is crucial to appreciating Frege's impact upon the *Philosophical Investigations*. Indeed, Wittgenstein's least Fregean work with respect to its substance, *On Certainty*, which is in fact continuous with the so-called private language argument in the *Investigations*, is, paradoxically, also inspired by Frege's anti-psychologism despite its anti-Fregean position, say, with respect to the mythological character of the logic involved in human reasoning.[77] It is assuredly no less accidental, given Frege's emphasis upon the central role of judgment in human thought, that the epistemological center of *On Certainty* is the notion of judgment, admittedly construed in a different way from Frege.[78] Briefly, it is impossible to over-estimate the importance of Frege's concept of objectivity for Wittgenstein at all stages of his development after 1910. Indeed, it is even plausible to see his struggle to cope with fear in the face of death in World War I as indebted to Frege; for the solution that he sought to his existential problems should be parallel to the solution to his »mathematical« problems that he found in Frege. However difficult that influence may be to reconstruct the Fregean injunction to objectivity was always at the forefront of Wittgenstein's thinking in all matters of philosophy.

Indeed, Susan Sterrett's recent exploration of the parallels between Wittgenstein's early investigations into the relationship between language and the world and the problems and strategies of the fledgling theory and practice of aeronautics, *Wittgenstein Flies a Kite*[79] emphasizes (with heavy but highly constructive reliance upon Brian McGuinness' *Young Ludwig*) how Wittgenstein was to make a choice for philosophy and against aeronautics and psychology in the course of his first year at Cambridge. Moreover, that decision would highlight Wittgenstein's commitment to Frege's principle of anti-psychologism in philosophy. Sterrett's account raises the significance the story of Wittgenstein asking Russell to tell him whether he was a complete idiot, in which case he would pursue a career as an aeronaut, or not, in which case he would become a philosopher from the realm of the merely anecdotal and at the same time allows us to identify the point when Frege exerted his decisive influence upon him a bit more closely. Thus we must revise the superficial notion already presented that Frege's influence upon Wittgenstein had to be before he met Russell – another reminder of the complexity of our undertaking here. In fact, it seems to have been Russell's positive evaluation of the written work that he had assigned Wittgenstein that was the point of his full-fledged breakthrough into philosophy and the point at which Frege made him into a philosopher as it were.

However, to return to the point, the role of Frege's other two admonitions in Wittgenstein's mature thought is easier to identify. Let us turn to Frege's second admonition not to inquire into the meanings of words in isolation. If Frege was adamant in the matter, the mature Wittgenstein was no less adamant that we cannot establish the meanings of terms apart from the contexts is which they are employed: don't ask for the meaning look at the use (*PI*, I, 43) is perhaps the best known slogan from his mature period. Like Frege, he will insist that meaning is related to the role that logic allots to an expression. However, the mature Wittgenstein had come to understand logic very differently from Frege. In fact, he construes logic as the behavioral *grammar*, i.e., the sense of the implicit order, which must be incorporated in the actions of an animal that speaks. That means on the basis of what it is to follow a rule in a situation where there are no formal rules but only *examples* that function as *standards to be imitated* to go on. In short, the way in which a word is woven into practice determines its meaning. Everything depends upon the language game that is being played. No less than Frege, Wittgenstein considers that words (signs, symbols etc,) taken in isolation have a way of dazzling us into thinking that we can specify their meaning, when that is actually only possible in terms of their context. Thus Wittgenstein asks us how we know which direction we are to follow when we encounter a sign post (*PI*, I 85). Only familiarity with the practice of following sign posts permits us to answer the question.

However, unlike Frege, who considers that formal logic provides the sole frame of reference in which meaning can be determined, Wittgenstein recognizes a plurality of possible contexts coterminous with the plurality of ways of interweaving words and actions that Wittgenstein understands under »language games« (*PI*, I, 24). However, this is a matter of showing and not saying in Wittgenstein. Moreover, it is no easy matter to do so. Indeed, a major strategic difference from Frege emerges here despite an undeniable continuity in their thinking.

For Wittgenstein, however, it is not enough to warn the erring philosopher, the philosophizing mind must be *lured* away from its tendency to psychologistic explanations back to understanding *how* philosophical problems dissolve into

4. GOTTLOB FREGE ...

practice when they are properly understood. How and why that should be so are part of the story that unfolds below. He believed that he had to eliminate the »deep disquietudes« that tempt us to philosophize entirely. It will not suffice simply to *admonish* either the psychologizing (or Platonizing) philosophers of mind on account of their beliefs. They must be *persuaded* to discard them. It is the point of all of the mature Wittgenstein's thought experiments, questions answered and unanswered, examples, analogies etc. to disabuse traditional epistemologists of their tendency to subjectivity as well as their quest for absolute certainty. They are not directly part of what Wittgenstein took over from Frege lock, stock and barrel but definitely *inspired* by his encounter with him as we shall see.

That brings us to Frege's third injunction: not to loose sight of the distinction between concept and object. Although there is little surface similarity between the two here, there is a crucial parallel to Frege in Wittgenstein's insistence that it is not the sign (word, proposition etc.) but the way that it is used that we have to grasp if we want to understand how language functions. It is central to Wittgenstein's pluralistic account of language that there are *radically different* ways in which words fit into our experience. It is not simply that the notion »meaning is use« implies that meaning is contextual but that there are fundamentally different sorts of contexts, ways of doing things with words that are essentially diverse. Frege's concern, like that of the young Wittgenstein, was with the logical presuppositions for producing true propositions. Language was thus identified exclusively with one of its functions. The mature Wittgenstein considered his effort to establish the essence of language on the basis of determining the general form of the proposition to be a major mistake in his early work. His later work emphasizes that commands, questions, promises, expressions of pain, aesthetic responses and a variety of other things are distinct ways of interweaving words and actions existing alongside of and are in no way reducible to the representational function of language. So the statement »I am in pain« is not a report upon something but a covert way of expressing pain (*PI*, I, 244). Rather than screaming, the »natural« reaction to pain, or crying out, the »childish« reaction to it, I utter a sentence that replaces the scream or the exclamation. That sentence does not represent my pain; it *is* my pain itself in a sense, rather than a remark about it. Similarly, aesthetic assertions are sophisticated aesthetic reactions (*L+C*, 13, §10), pleasure at seeing or hearing or smelling something delightful, revulsion at seeing or hearing or smelling something repulsive. They are not reports but joyful, disgusted, surprised, enchanted, bored responses to things. The vast differences between Frege and Wittgenstein with respect to their accounts of the relationship between concepts and objects should not blind us to the fact that the considerations which led Wittgenstein to take up such problems originally came from Frege's injunction to bear the distinction between them in mind in the first place (even if the substance of his message here originated with Spengler as we shall see later). That is true in two senses: first, certain central preoccupations came from Frege as should now be clear; second, the *intensity* with which he attacked his problems was equally inspired by Frege. Let us consider the latter point.

The most accessible work by Frege, *The Foundations of Arithmetic*, unlike *Concept Script* or *The Basic Laws of Arithmetic*, seems to have been written in the informal mode and with copious references to the works of other writers explicitly with a view to compensate for the idiosyncrasies of his earlier, neglected, *Concept Script* in which he first developed the notion of logic based upon the idea of truth »functions«. Here Frege goes out of his way to meet *any and all* opinions to the contrary of his own views. It is as if his principle to develop a completely

4. GOTTLOB FREGE ...

deductive exposition of mathematics with no logical gaps whatsoever (as he repeatedly emphasizes) was being applied in responding to his critics.[80] In fact, Frege leaves no stone unturned in his efforts to come to grips comprehensively with contrary views. Not only the views of Kant and Mill but those of contemporaries like Baumann, Schröder, Schlömilch and dozens of other writers on mathematics are analyzed in depth. One informed commentator describes his fourfold approach to the view he would criticize as follows,

> ... he takes remarks by his opponents absolutely literally; he draws consequences with absolute rigor; he brings large-scale claims down to earth with very concrete counter-examples; he searches out hidden inconsistencies.[81]

Frege's critique of, say, Benno Erdmann in the Preface to *The Basic Laws of Arithmetic*[82] is a perfect example of this strategy, which could just as easily be an account of Wittgenstein's strategy as a critic.

Wittgenstein's aim in his mature philosophy, as we have said, was to *dissolve* rather than resolve philosophical perplexities on the basis of questioning relentlessly the *presuppositions* which led people, including Frege, to propose theoretical answers to philosophical/conceptual questions. The techniques that he developed had to be as complex as the confused presuppositions that led unreflective philosophers to those theories in the first place i.e., notions such as the Cartesian view that ideas have to have clear and distinct boundaries or the notion of a private language. Indeed, we do well to consider that Wittgenstein found all of the twists and turns in the 70-odd paragraphs that make up the »argument« against the notion of a private language (*PI*, I, 243-317) necessary to restore the bemused philosophical mind to health. So Wittgenstein could write in the preface to the one mature work that he clearly considered completed with in his lifetime, *Philosophical Investigations,* part I, merely an album. In it he did not succeed in expressing his thoughts in a »natural and unbroken sequence« (*in einer natürlichen und lückenlosen Folge,* Preface) in manner of a conventional philosophical treatise. In short, he could not live up to Frege's ideal. However, at the same time he insists that only such a seeming potpourri of fragments could *fittingly* express his message, i.e., that he, nevertheless, endeavored to do so in the only manner that fit the nature of *his* subject: how language itself misleads us into posing metaphysical questions, which by their very nature cannot be answered. In other words, the very objectivity that Frege inspired in him demanded that he produce a set of highly ordered fragments, whose purpose it is to remind philosophers of what they knew as human beings, i.e., before they began to pose philosophical questions. Wittgenstein would be every bit as preoccupied as Frege with »Zwischenglieder« (intermediary cases)[83] but in a very different sense from his. Wittgenstein's strategy seems to owe its inspiration both to Frege's ideal of systematicity, which Frege insists means »Lückenlösigkeit«[84], and his practice of criticizing positions he disagreed with so thoroughly that the force of their arguments simply disappears. The natural and unbroken sequence of thought in the *Philosophical Investigations,* such as it is, emerges from the need to penetrate this veil of confusions parading as a paradigm of clarity. Thus he would write in *Culture and Value* that you had to think even crazier than the philosophers to solve their problems (*C+V,* 75). However, even this thought seems to originate in Frege, who accused contemporary psychologistic logicians holding to a relativistic view of the laws of thought as suffering from a new form of craziness (*Verrücktheit*).[85]

As we have seen, the mature Wittgenstein's thought centers around the notion of following a rule where there are no formal rules but only examples to be imitated. That center dictates that his philosophical method is (somewhat oversimplified) itself largely a particular way of employing examples where traditional philosophers have had recourse to formal arguments. It was crucial to Wittgenstein that these examples neither be obvious nor simple. They had to be sufficiently subtle and imaginative to put our thinking onto new tracks as it were. This strategic use of examples was part of the heritage he bore from Ludwig Boltzmann and Schopenhauer but it was certainly profoundly stamped by Frege as well. Consider only Frege's way of undermining the importance of the notion of »what you obtain by the continual augmentation by one« for understanding the concept of number:

> Our case might most easily be compared with the following. You have noticed that the temperature in a bore hole regularly increases with depth; you have previously hit upon highly differentiated layers of rock. It then is clear from the observations, which you have made at the bore hole that it is not possible to conclude anything about the constitution of the deeper layers and, whether the regularity of the temperature distribution would be further confirmed, cannot be determined. Under the concept 'what is being hit upon by continued boring' falls both the previously observed as well as what lies deeper but that is not very useful here.[86]

Both inductive reasoning and arithmetical augmentation never justify as explanations of what will come next. The analogy has that stringent, apposite character that we have become accustomed to in Wittgenstein's examples. Moreover, the tone, to use a favorite expression of Wittgenstein's (cf. *E*, 43; *F*, 12), is one we are familiar with from the latter's works. Such examples abound in Frege.

We have noted a certain continuity with respect to the use of examples in Boltzmann and Frege but what is as striking as it is unmentioned in the literature on Wittgenstein is the fact that Frege, like Boltzmann, was a writer of considerable *wit*. Frege's wit is nowhere more in evidence than in *The Foundations of Arithmetic*, which abounds in hilarious ripostes to his adversaries. Thus Frege will speak of the kinds of confusions that arise in philosophy as the sort of gaffs we would make were we to speak of a blue idea, a salty concept or a chewy judgment. This involves a philosophical error of the sort that Ryle called a *category mistake*. Boltzmann's witty lectures and Schopenhauer's disquisition on the philosophical sense of the ridiculous in the supplementary essays to *The World as Will and Representation* helped prepare him to appreciate the philosophical importance of Frege's humor, which, paradoxically, helped to pave his way to Karl Kraus – something that would radically alter his view of philosophy and, ultimately, evoke the desire to present both logic and ethics as transcendental conditions of there being a world at all in the *Tractatus*. In his mature thought, as in Frege and in Kraus, humor is essentially linked to taking one's opponent by his word and exposing the superficiality and latent inconsistencies his position by a rigorous analysis of his mode of expression. Be that as it may, Wittgenstein, too, would tend to see philosophical problems as arising when we give in to the temptation to ask an inappropriate question and he would find the result just as laughable as Frege (and Kraus as we shall see). Moreover, he would find the sort of questions that traditional philosophers pose »mad« in *On Certainty* (§ 467) and thus in a sense funny.

Another example of Frege's humor comes at the point where he is discussing Immanuel Kant's notion that we have an intuition corresponding to each number similar to the intuition we have of fingers or points when we use these numbers. This seems reasonable enough with respect to 1, 2 and 3 but, Frege asks, what is the intuition of 37,863 fingers like? If Kant's view of the role of intuition in arithmetic was correct we would have to have an intuition of 135,664, 37,863 and 173,527, when we added the first two numbers together to get the third. Moreover, the correctness of the third number as sum of the first and second would have to be immediately apparent, which it obviously is not.[87]

In rejecting Baumann's view that the concept »one« rests upon a mental intuition of undividedness and demarcation Frege writes:

> If this were correct, we would have to expect that animals as well could have a certain idea of unity. Whether a dog looking at the moon has even a definite idea of what we designate by the word 'one'? Hardly?[88]

Similarly Frege would remark, with respect to the notion that we should term a proposition empirical, as opposed to a-priori, if we need to have made observations to be conscious of its content that the stories of Baron Münchausen would also be empirical in that sense because their author would have had to make a considerable number of such observations to invent them.[89] Indeed, there can be little doubt that Frege was a master in the deployment of the philosophical witticism: There are no cheap laughs here but penetrating wit. It is a pity that Frege's wit would degenerate in his frustrated late polemics, which are excessive by any standards.

As we shall see later in connection with Karl Kraus, Wittgenstein was capable of appreciating the place of such humor in philosophy: »in philosophy it is significant that such-and-such a sentence makes no sense; but also that it sounds funny«, (where »funny« *komisch* should be understood as peculiar, *Z*, 328).

So we have something to go on when we look for the continuity in style between Wittgenstein and Frege. However, there are specific passages in Wittgenstein that are clearly influenced by Frege in a way that a simple intertextual comparison will immediately reveal. It is probably not accidental that these passages should be in the prefaces to both his major works, each of which clearly echoes passages from Frege's *The Basic Laws of Arithmetic*, which Wittgenstein knew by heart. In general, the almost melancholic tone of Wittgenstein's prefaces, with their skepticism at finding an adequate reader, seems clearly related to the virtual despair of Frege, completely isolated in the German community of mathematicians and philosophers, at finding a reader at all. Just as Wittgenstein seems not particularly sanguine with respect to fulfilling his goal of giving pleasure to a reader capable of understanding him, Frege seems to doubt that he can find a reader with patience enough to follow him step by painstaking step. Nevertheless he writes: »May I be fortunate enough to find such a reader and judge« (»Möge es mir glücken, einen solchen Leser und Beurteiler zu finden«).[90] Similarly the preface to *The Basic Laws* closes with ... may this book, if belatedly, contribute to a renewal of logic« (»... möge dieses Buch, wenn auch spat, zu einer Erneuerung der Logik beitragen«).[91] Wittgenstein, on the other hand, remarks after insisting that his aims was to express himself in the most appropriate manner but he knows that he has not really fulfilled it: »May others come and do a better job of it. (»Mögen andere kommen und es besser machen,« *T*, 4). Frege, for his part hoped that he had always found the shortest proof for a given lemma asks »those who have something to complain about in this respect to do it better« (»Wer in dieser

4. GOTTLOB FREGE ...

Hinsicht etwas zu tadeln hat, der mache es besser«).[92] With respect to the *Philosophical Investigations*, we find Wittgenstein despairingly asserting that, although it was not impossible that his book could enlighten somebody about the nature of philosophical problems it was not likely that it would in such darkly troubled times.

One final intertextual point of reference should not go unnoticed here. It is the common use of the word »Wink«, »hint«, »gesturing by waving the hand« that Frege employs to assist readers dedicated sufficiently to the subject to put up with his demands. This is what he does when he needs to show something that he cannot say. The same goes for Wittgenstein both in his early and his later works. Thus in his crucial discussion of »Menschenkenntnis« (*PI*, II, 575), i.e., that kind of knowledge that people who understand expressions of human feelings have, and what it is to teach it to somebody, it turns out to be a matter of giving someone learning the right »Wink« at the right moment. This too would seem to be a residual part of his heritage from Frege. It also is reflected in the notion we find in *Zettel* that Wittgenstein explains gestures by words and words by gestures. (*Z*, § 227)

At this point it is necessary to shift to pursue a different line of questioning. How did Wittgenstein find his way to Frege? The answer to that question is not altogether clear either.[93] However, when we consider Frege's place on the list of influences with respect to his philosophical work of clarification one thing is especially striking: one of Frege's main contentions in the philosophy of mathematics was that he could rigorously define number as a logical object.[94] This would certainly be a brilliant breakthrough on any account, an achievement of the first magnitude. Indeed, to have defined number would have been so to accomplish something so difficult that Wittgenstein's first philosophical hero, Boltzmann, considered it to be impossible. For Boltzmann number was one of those concepts like species that science must make use of without being in a position to define. Indeed, Frege's achievement was so far beyond anything that his first mentor could have imagined that it had to have shaken Wittgenstein to the core. Little wonder that Frege could woo him away from the Schopenhauerian idealism to which he was attached as a teenager. At the same time Frege would also woo young Ludwig away from Boltzmann as well (albeit not permanently).

Let us consider Wittgenstein's earliest statements about philosophy in the *Tractatus*, which form a commentary upon 4.11: »The totality of true propositions is the totality of the natural sciences«. The sentiment is one that Boltzmann could thoroughly endorse but, in fact, Wittgenstein's commentary is inspired by Frege and runs against Boltzmann. Summarizing:

- Philosophy is not a natural science but something above or below it.
- The purpose of philosophy is the logical clarification of thought.
- Philosophy is not a body of doctrine but an activity.
  It does not yield propositions but clarity about vague and ambiguous thoughts.
- Psychology is no closer to philosophy that any other science.
- Wittgenstein's philosophy of logic is a study of the process of thought.
- Darwin's theory has no more to do with philosophy than any other scientific theory.
- Philosophy sets a limit to natural science by distinguishing strictly between the thinkable and the unthinkable.
- It intimates what cannot be said by clearly representing the sayable.

4. GOTTLOB FREGE ...

- Everything that can be thought can be thought clearly.
- Everything that can be expressed can be expressed clearly.

Indeed, taken together they might well be considered to be a Fregean critique of Boltzmann. Although the basic ideas about the relationship between philosophy and science could well be taken as having been inspired by him, the rejection of Darwinism and the identification of his »Zeichensprache« as the basis of our thought processes, not to mention the emphasis upon clarity as the result of logical analysis, clearly smart of a critique of Boltzmann based upon Frege. All of that is obvious enough. What is more important for us is what happens to Frege later when Boltzmann becomes reinstated. We are seeking here to understand the mature Wittgenstein. However, we cannot hope to do so until we have seen what brought Wittgenstein to Frege – and then away from him. In any case, the propositions 4.11ff. are Wittgenstein's early Fregean statement of what philosophy should be. Before he finishes writing his *Abhandlung* he will graft significant themes from Schopenhauer and Weininger onto it to form the *Tractatus* as we know it.

How, then, can we recapitulate Wittgenstein's philosophical development up to this point (i.e., c. 1910)? From our genetic point of view his first notion of philosophy had the following shape. Briefly, Boltzmann had taught him that the search for substantive laws of thought was vain. This notion would figure in his confrontation with Frege in helping him get clear about the idea that the only necessity is logical necessity (an idea that remained central in his thinking in all phases). Moreover, Boltzmann, like Frege, had insisted that the task of philosophy of science was to lay bare the presuppositions of theorizing. After Frege there seemed to be good reasons for identifying them as its purely formal presuppositions. That would change later as Wittgenstein ceased to identify language exclusively with its representational function, which entailed something of a return to Boltzmann's view about the nature of models and the danger of overshooting the mark by generalizing fallaciously from our models.

Hertz gave him the view that thoughts are pictures in the sense of being conscious constructs (*Darstellungen*), not merely mental images which reproduce perceptions (*Vorstellungen*). This idea could nest easily with Frege's objectivist rejection of »Vorstellungen« as the vehicles of thought. What made Hertzian »Bilder«, i.e., models, permissible in physics in the first place was their logical structure, which guaranteed that they could be employed to understand the empirically given. Hertz further taught him that philosophical problems could not be solved on the basis of theories, rather their dissolution had to be shown on the basis of alternative representations of the problematic subject matter. Frege would similarly insist that the objectivity of logic rested upon the complete representation of it as a system. This was something that had to display itself: »mathematica sunt, non leguntur«[95]. He himself could at best make hints or gestures (»Winke«) that would help us to understand the achievement in presenting logic as a complete system. Its fundamental »truth« had to show itself; it could not be said.

In any case, Hertz would help Wittgenstein to understand propositions as »Bilder«, with a clearly limited capacity to depict reality. Frege's notion of the bivalence of the proposition as such would make it possible to represent all possible truth functions in terms of matrices, which, in turn, would be mechanical decision procedures for determining the validity of arguments.[96] That idea inspired Wittgenstein (independently of Post) to devise the truth table, which so represents the relationship between the propositions of logic (tautologies), empirical propositions and pseudo-propositions (contradictions) such that the idea of necessarily true, propositions of substance, i.e., metaphysics, was literally shown to be nonsense. It was a mechanical technique that could eliminate theory from logic as well as all forms of metaphysics at one go. The truth table technique was crucial for Wittgenstein's project of turning philosophy from a theory of reality into a craft for dissolving philosophical conundrums. In the vast transformation that took place in his thinking between the *Tractatus* and the *Philosophical Investigations* he did not loose sight of the project of dissolving philosophical puzzle on the basis of a technique but came to realize that the infinite complexity of our actual language, which continually gives rise to tormenting philosophical questions cannot be tackled on the basis of a single tactic. Thus the mature Wittgenstein would require a whole repertoire of techniques for dissolving the illusions that give rise to philosophical problems (*PI*, I, 133).

Despite the fact that Frege demolished Wittgenstein's youthful Schopenhauerian subjective idealism: the world of the *Tractatus* is not my idea but all that is the case as Brian McGuinness has put it,[97] the ideas of the founder of mathematical logic and the great pessimist nest uncomfortably in the *Tractatus* and, in fact, Schopenhauer's view that our representations of the world are rooted in nature rather than »mind« would ultimately lead him away from the substance of Frege's thought. The project of the *Tractatus* as Wittgenstein published it was profoundly influenced by Schopenhauer's view that it is an essential task of philosophy to get straight about the nature of the world (see Chapter 3 »The Opaque Self«, above). This meant getting straight about its twofold nature: as the object of thought and as life pulsating within me. After Frege's demolition of psychologism there could be no more talk of the world as my subjective idea (*Vorstellung*). However, this posed a problem to the young Wittgenstein: what is the relationship of my subjective torments, my anxiety in the face of death, to my objective situation? Indeed, even in the *Notebooks of 1914–16* we find Wittgenstein insisting in a Fregean vein seeing the world rightly is a matter of objective willing rather than subjective wishing, i.e., a matter of how one lived rather than what one believed. It is for that reason that the person who lives happily considers the comforts of the world »only so many graces of fate« (*N*, 13.8.16).

In any case, our representations of the world presuppose logical form, as Schopenhauer in one of his more Kantian moments insisted, and are, therefore, objective. However, Schopenhauer did not understand what logic is. Yet, explaining the objectivity of a world made possible by logic correctly did not exhaust the Schopenhauerian task; for objectivity is only one aspect of the world as I find it. There are a whole series of questions about the *meaning* of what is objective itself that remain distressingly open. Wittgenstein poses them in his notebooks, clearly inspired by Schopenhauer (although his answers to them would ultimately come from Weininger, see below, Chapter 8). Our applications of logic to the world – because they are *our* representations – are not capable of representing the world as I find it as a totality: the representing subject can never be captured in the act of representing nor can the absolutely uncanny fact that the world is objective reality and at the same time *my* world. In short, human experience as a *totality and in its depths* becomes all the more puzzling the more deeply we reflect upon it. These thoughts would ultimately lead Wittgenstein to his Weiningerian reflections upon the limits of the self and the world and to the mysticism of the *Tractatus*. Yet, even they would build upon Frege's distinction between what we could define and what one could merely wave at[98], which presages

4. GOTTLOB FREGE ...

Wittgenstein's distinction between saying and showing upon which his infamous reflections on the mystical are, for better or worse, grafted.[99] Paradoxically, Frege (and Russell) would lead him to Kraus (see Chapter 6 below), who would both compliment Frege's influence upon him and at the same time broaden the scope of his philosophical investigations.

However, residues of Schopenhauer would remain puzzlingly and uncomfortably sitting in the middle of the *Tractatus*, which would ultimately lead Wittgenstein, with Spengler's help, to a view of language and philosophy that was very different from Frege's even thought it would still bear his stamp indirectly. Two of these ideas are the notion that all of the propositions in everyday language are in order as they stand (*T*, 5.5563) and the notion that everyday language with its subtle tacit conventions is a part of the human organism and no less complicated than it is (*T*, 4.002). The Wittgenstein that returned to philosophy in 1929 – and soon fell under the sway of Oswald Spengler – was a decided critic of Logical Positivism, who would come to emphasize how language is rooted in the natural history of a particular kind of animal. Yet, the spell of Frege would remain crucial in the background to his philosophizing against Cambridge philosophy.

But let us return to the mature Wittgenstein. In the so-called philosophy chapter of the *Philosophical Investigations* (I, 89-133) it is clear that target of his philosophizing is Russell and Frege himself (not to mention the author of the *Tractatus Logico-Philosophicus*). At least all of the ideas against which he polemicizes are traceable back to him: the notion that logic is sublime, the idea that the proposition is something remarkable, the idea that thinking is unique, the view that the essence of language is connected with some kind of a super order, which is concealed from us, the idea that vagueness and sense are incompatible with one another, the idea that philosophy stands in an intimate relationship with mathematics, the notion that philosophy should essentially involve a reform of merely concentrate upon Wittgenstein's target, we miss something very important, namely, the notion that these preoccupations are not mere prejudices rooted in ignorance or bigotry. Rather, they are »deep disquietudes« as Miss Anscombe has rendered it, whose roots are as deep as the forms of our language and whose importance is no less than that of language itself, which for Wittgenstein is tantamount to human nature itself. Thus Wittgenstein's intense confrontation with Frege left him convinced that the kinds of questions that Frege posed were louring in the very forms of language themselves waiting as it were, for the unwary, would-be philosopher. Only an effort of the will could withstand the temptations to pose the sort of questions Frege did. His mature philosophy was an effort to build up a set of techniques to wean us away from those tendencies. In Wittgenstein's eyes putting us into a position to stop doing philosophy had to be a monumental and in many respects thankless undertaking. Nevertheless, it was his way of remaining true to Frege's commitment to a philosophy of objectivity.

How, then, die Frege influence the mature Wittgenstein's concept of philosophy? In three ways, all of which are indirect but no less continuous with Frege's thinking for all that: first, as a *target*, i.e., by providing him with clear evidence of how the philosophizing mind, however, brilliant, is continually under the temptation to misunderstand the logic of language; second, in the form of *themes*, with which he must preoccupy himself: objectivity, contextualism, the relationship between words and things and third, in *spirit*, i.e., in the very *intensity*, *thoroughness* and *wit* with which he pursued his *Philosophical Investigations* and without which they would not have been possible. Little wonder that, for all their differences, Frege would, as Russell would not, remain always a revered figure in Wittgenstein's eyes.

CHAPTER 5

Bertrand Russell: Loaded Questions

The power of language to make everything look the same, which is most glaringly evident in the *dictionary* and which makes the personification of *time* possible: something no less remarkable than would have been making divinities of the logical constants.
C+V, 22

UNLIKE ALL THE OTHER figures on Wittgenstein's list of figures, who had exerted an influence upon his »philosophical work of clarification«, we know *exactly* what Wittgenstein incorporated into his mature approach to philosophy from Bertrand Russell (which is not, it must be emphasized, identical with Russell's overall influence upon his philosophical development, which, like Frege's overall influence upon him, is a far wider subject than ours). Thus Wittgenstein wrote at *Tractatus* 4.0031:

> All philosophy is a »critique of language« (though not in Mauthner's sense). It was Russell who performed the service of showing that the apparent logical form of a proposition need not be its real one.

The reference is clearly to Russell's so-called theory of descriptions, which Wittgenstein is known to have admired.[100] It was central to the concept of what a proposition is in the *Tractatus* and the insight it contains about the ways that language itself misleads the questioning mind would be permanently illuminating to Wittgenstein with respect how even the most brilliant thinkers are tempted into metaphysical speculations. Here we shall be covering well-travelled philosophical terrain familiar to all students of 20th century philosophy.

Like Frege before him, Russell was increasingly aware after the turn of the century that the grammatical structure of a sentence can be fundamentally misleading with respect to the reference of the terms it contains. Thus the concept »man« in the sentence »all men are mortal« means something very different from the individual I refer to when I say »I saw a man«. Reflections about such differences led Russell to the awareness that there is a very significant difference between proper names and definite descriptions that is by no means obvious at first glance. Moreover, even the astute Frege had failed to recognize that difference. Here was a gap, which clarity demanded be filled. On the face of it »James Joyce« and »the author of Ulysses« seem to be interchangeable – and indeed they are. Whatever is true of the one is true of the other. The problem is that not all definite descriptions stand to individuals in this way. Thus Russell, writing in the Edwardian age could distinguish between the seemingly equivalent propositions »The King of England is bald« and »The King of France is bald«. The former is true – or was at the time of writing (the first of the three versions of the relevant essay, »On Denoting« was published in *Mind* in 1905[101]) – whereas the latter is not. However, this proposition's not being true does not entail its falsity, as it should, for its opposite, »The King of France is not bald«, is no less false, for there is – or was – no such person.

Logic demands that we be in a position to say »yes« or »no« to any given proposition, which is another way of saying that a proposition, in order to be a proposition, must be either true or false. However, the fact that there is no such individual as the current King of France makes it impossible for us to affirm or deny the proposition without landing in the difficulty that we have posited the existence of a non-existent King. Moreover, this was the kind of paradox that Russell came to be increasingly preoccupied with once he had, under Moore's aegis, finally parted ways with idealism, which had sought to resolve such contradictions »at a higher level«. Russell now found them potentially threatening to the effort to produce an ideal language and, therefore, had to solve them on the basis of immanent analysis.[102]

Russell's achievement consisted, first, in recognizing the pitfalls that awaited the unwary in dealing with propositions whose subjects were definite descriptions and, second, in providing a technique for representing such proposition in a way that would cease to confuse us. He argued that what seemed to be one proposition was in fact implicitly three: two existential statements and a predicative assertion. Thus he analyzed »The King of France is bald« into the following:

1) There is at least one current King of France.
2) There is at most one current King of France.
3) That person is bald.

Represented in this way the confusion disappears. The proposition, as Wittgenstein says, is only apparently well-formed. Its sentence structure is perfectly in order as it is; the sentence does not all appear to be problematic in character. It is only upon logical, as opposed to grammatical, analysis that is becomes clear that the proposition in fact contains three assertions and not one. Such analysis would become paradigmatic for the nascent form of philosophy that we now term (logically enough) »analytic philosophy«. Its Russellian center is the thesis that the meaning of a proposition can only really be firmly established when we have analyzed it into its logical constituents. Thus originated the doctrine of »logical atomism«, i.e., the view that the logical constituents of propositions enter into combination with each other without loosing their own proper identities (in contrast to the idealist doctrine of »internal relations« which maintains that the relations that things enter into in fact determine their essence[103]). Such logical atoms are the basic constituents of facts. Russell developed these views to some extent out of his discussions with Wittgenstein before World War I. They would certainly figure prominently in the *Tractatus*, as the huge literature on the subject indicates.

Our concern here is principally with Russell's impact upon Wittgenstein's mature view of philosophical method, especially in the *Philosophical Investigations*. Here the matter also seems relatively clear cut. Although Wittgenstein had long put any notion of logical atomism behind him, he was more than ever concerned about how it is that the grammatical forms of language, what he terms »surface grammar« confuses us to the point of tempting us to pose metaphysical questions about the structure of the mind, intentions, certainty etc. Thus he would distinguish between the surface grammar and, what he refers to variously as »depth grammar« or »logical grammar« (*PI*, I. 664).

These expressions are not entirely fortunate ones, especially after Noam Chomsky appropriated the phrase »depth grammar« to cover precisely the kind of formal depth structure that the mature Wittgenstein rejects entirely in his account of meaning and understanding.[104] However, Wittgenstein's own use of the family of words »grammar«, »grammatical«

etc., which in fact come to play the role that »logic«, »logical« etc. do in his early thought, is seldom easy to follow. It is not obvious why he should employ the word »grammar« in his mature account of meaning. On the face of it, it seems to trivialize what it ought to deepen. In any case, it will do well to consider what Wittgenstein means by such terms and why he wants to employ them.

Depth grammar is opposed to surface grammar, which is the sort of grammar pupils in school have to master, i.e., the rules of correct syntax. Depth grammar by analogy pertains to the rules of correct or appropriate usage. It is a matter of pragmatics, rather than semantics to employ the terms of C. S. Peirce. It is what establishes the categorical differences between concepts like »thinking« and »believing« (*PI*, I, 574) – it is hardly accidental that this central example harks back to Frege's attack on psychologism. Concepts like »time« (*PI*, I 90) or »composite« (*PI*, I, 47) are highly complex and used in a plethora of situations. Thus Wittgenstein reminds us of how many different kinds of things we say about duration, past, present and future or about the essential difference between talking about the physical constituents of a tree, i.e., its cells and the logical constituents of the concept tree, i.e., wood, plant, perennial, roots, trunk, branches, leaves etc. Similarly, the question, »what is the world made of?« can have a variety of answers depending on whom you ask. In fact, there are several questions confusingly rolled into one here. Competent physicists, chemists, biologists and ecologists will give us different answers all of which will be »true« without being reducible to one another. Demanding a simple straightforward answer to such complex questions is what gives rise to metaphysics, as Wittgenstein had long learned from Boltzmann.

Logical grammar calls our attention to the variety of questions that lurk behind that seemingly simple one. Grammatical distinctions in Wittgenstein's sense of logical grammar are thus reminders about the different ways in which a single word can be used in radically different contexts (»language games«) with a view to redressing the confusions that arise when we fail to take the multiplicity of referents that word can have into consideration. The point of Wittgensteinian grammar is to get clear about how linguistic usage can be ruled-governed and at the same time open-textured, i.e., without constituting a system that can be clearly represented. Grammar describes how the problems we have with a word like »thinking«, which tempt us to try to produce a theory of thinking, arise when we try to reduce this most important element in human existence to a precisely specifiable unity. When we do this the very effort of seeking a definition for thinking focuses our attention away from the innumerable ways in which we normally and legitimately refer to thinking. Thus the search for definitions of words like »thinking« or »knowledge« systematically obscures precisely what it would illuminate. This is in fact the origin of metaphysics on the mature Wittgenstein's view. Once we manage to describe the multiplicity of the things that we *do* when we think, i.e., when we employ words, the urge/need to explain them disappears.

Thus the very core of Wittgenstein's strategy in the *Philosophical Investigations* is determined by a certain understanding of how the surface grammar of a term entices us to misunderstand what it represents in more or less the same way that the apparent logical form of a proposition, see the case of definite descriptions, entices us to misunderstand what a proposition represents. Philosophical problems arise because we confuse empirical and conceptual matters in a single question in just the way that Russell described. Thus Wittgenstein asserts in the *Philosophical Investigations* that »the results of philosophy are the uncovering of one or another piece of plain nonsense

5. BERTRAND RUSSELL ...

...« (*PI*, I, 119) The implication is that traditional philosophers deal in covert nonsense without being aware of it. This is not because they are stupid or narrow-minded but because, as in the case of definite descriptions, language tempts us into confusion. So, he will go on to say, »... and of bumps that the understanding has got by running its head up against the limits of language. These bumps make us see the value of the discovery«. However, for Wittgenstein it will turn out to be of the utmost significance that normal people in ordinary circumstances (admittedly something devilishly difficult to determine) do not make this kind of mistake. They are more typical of the theorizing mind like Russell's himself. Thus it should not turn out to be surprising that much of Wittgenstein's philosophizing, early and late, is directed against Russell. We must now turn to that theme, since it is highly relevant to the development of Wittgenstein's mature conception of philosophy.

Wittgenstein's encounter with Russell started with a bang. No sooner had they been introduced they began to argue vehemently. The story has often been reprinted about how Russell reported with fascination that he could not convince Wittgenstein that there was no rhinoceros in the room as they talked. Later he would report to Lady Ottoline Morrell that »his German« as he liked to call him did not believe that anything was empirical.[105] This is usually cited as an entertaining story and nothing more (except by Brian McGuinness[106]). However, when seen in the context of the broader story we are telling here, it has much wider implications. Wittgenstein was more than a fearless Siegfried breaking Wotan's spear; he was a young philosopher with an established philosophical point of view that was radically different from Russell's empiricism right from the start. Russell, whose deepest philosophical interests remained epistemological, rather than logical, as is the case with Wittgenstein and Frege, never seems to have really comprehended the gap that separated him from Wittgenstein here: the former's philosophizing was dominated by epistemological considerations; whereas logic was at the core of Wittgenstein's thinking first last and always.[107] Thus, for all their friendship and for all the profound influence that Russell would exert upon the young Wittgenstein, fundamental philosophical differences would always mark their relationship. So, in the end, it should not surprise us that in the 40s Russell would accuse Wittgenstein of having become lazy and Wittgenstein Russell of having lost his sense for problems and become shallow.[108]

Although we do not have a full account of what transpired when they first met, it is possible to reconstruct Wittgenstein's strategy on the basis of what we know about his development up to 1911. There is no doubt that by the time met Russell, Wittgenstein had already digested both Hertz and Frege. Together they had already turned him into a kind of super-Quinean critic of dogmatic empiricism *avant la lettre*. McGuinness' view that the thrust of Wittgenstein's argument here turns upon the idea that no complex of objects can be supposed to exist in virtue of there being no rhinoceros in the room[109] does not contradict this view. The views of Hertz and Frege would have armed Wittgenstein to do battle with a confirmed empiricist. From Hertz he had learned that it was always possible to readjust the balance between observation and assumptions such that a recalcitrant observation – or a missing one – could be accounted for by changing our set of presuppositions. Just as Hertz had endeavored to eliminate the metaphysical elements in Newton by literally re-presenting mechanics in an alternative form, Wittgenstein could employ such a strategy to defeat Russell's continual appeal to sense data. Later Wittgenstein would insist that it is always possible to reject a question with the riposte, »it all depends upon what you mean by ...« (cf. *PI*, I, 47) Is it not plausible that he did so here? He was assuredly in a position to do so. Indeed, his exposure to Frege's anti-empiricism would have given him all the more grounds to challenge Russell, who never seemed to grasp that he and Frege were at odds about the relation between logic and empirical knowledge as the grounds of objectivity.

By the time that Wittgenstein got to Cambridge he had fixed opinions about philosophy, which is not to say that he had a closed mind or that he would not further develop, but that there were certain ideas and techniques to which he was completely attached that determined the spirit in which he would take up Russell's project. This anecdote is clear evidence of that, for all the intensity of his collaboration with Russell in the years before World War I he was his own man as it were from the start. In the course of the War their differences became even more pronounced in ways that Russell only vaguely seems to have realized. The latter was more inclined to attribute Wittgenstein's dissenting views to psychological idiosyncrasies or simple obstinacy, rather than an alternative concept of just what the philosophical task at hand was. Here we must turn to examine the tension that exists within the *Tractatus* and the significance of that tension for the development of Wittgenstein's concept of philosophy. The former point has been explored by Professor McGuinness, who serves as our point of departure here.

The *Tractatus* originated as an effort to re-write the first eleven chapters of the *Principia Mathematica*. This project was in some sense completed already in 1917. Brian McGuinness has called attention to page 71 of the *Prototractatus* where Wittgenstein has conspicuously drawn a line under proposition 7.110 He conjectures plausibly that there is in fact a caesura there, for the line is drawn after propositions 6.4 »All propositions are of equal value« and 7 »Whereof one cannot speak, thereof one must remain silent«. He has termed this part of the manuscript the *proto-Prototractatus*«. He suggests that what comes before that line are the substance of Wittgenstein's original reflections on the problems he had taken over from Russell and Frege before the war as he had developed them *before* his encounter with Paul Engelmann in Olomouc (Olmütz) in 1916 (in which Wittgenstein really does pass over matters beyond the scope of the nature of the proposition in silence). What comes after them, including his remarks on value and the »mystical« are basically a foreign accretion stemming from intense personal reflections fundamentally without philosophical significance in the strict sense in the summer of 1916 and strongly reinforced by his discussions with Engelmann and the Engelmann Circle in Moravia concerning poetry and religion in the fall of that year. He goes on to suggest that the mystical was an illegitimate extension of Wittgenstein's previous train of thought, which resulted in a lack of coherence in the resulting book, which has come down to us as the *Tractatus Logico-Philosophicus.*

The advantage of reading the *Tractatus* this way, as Russell in fact did in his introduction to the bilingual edition of 1922 (which Wittgenstein found »impossible«. *E*, 31), is that it clearly demarcates two aspects of Wittgenstein's completed project that nest together uncomfortably. We might refer to them as Russell's *Tractatus* and Wittgenstein's *Tractatus* respectively. The former, roughly propositions 1–4 of the printed version, i.e. all that bears upon the world, facts, states of affairs, pictures, thoughts and sense, in short, the Leibnizian »ontology«, might be so termed because it is a continuation of the project, which began with Russell's work on Leibniz in 1900 and continued with the *Principles of Mathematics* and the *Principia* itself. It is certainly not accidental that numerous readers right down to today have taken this part of the *Tractatus*

5. BERTRAND RUSSELL ...

to be its center, regardless of what Wittgenstein might have said and regardless of how the final version of Wittgenstein's text looks. These are the readers who have, for the most part, proven impatient with Wittgenstein's style of writing, wanting frequently to rewrite or even formalize its content. It is an important aspect of what Brian McGuinness has called attention to here that the demand for such reformulation, which was totally abhorrent to Wittgenstein himself is not entirely unreasonable. After all, the most concentrated elements of the text, certainly its most familiar elements, seem to be in the first half of the book; whereas the properly Wittgensteinian elements, entering massively into the text from proposition 5 onwards – especially in the so-called mystical parts of the work from proposition 6.4 onwards – are decidedly more oracular and, on the face of it, cryptic than the first four propositions. Little wonder that Wittgenstein's *Tractatus* left Russell with »a certain sense of intellectual discomfort« (*T*, xxi).

McGuinness goes so far as to suggest, on the basis of a close study of the text-genesis of the *Tractatus*, that there is but a dubious link between the »mystical« part of the *Tractatus* and the »logical« part that precedes it. Thus he concludes his paper on the topic with the following reflections:

> It will be seen that I think the propositions about value and the mystical in the completed *Tractatus* were indeed extracted from Wittgenstein somewhat against his original intention. This can be interpreted in two ways – that they were a questionable extension of his insights (this was the view of one wing of the Vienna Circle) or that they are all the more trustworthy because, metaphysical as they seem, they forced themselves upon him. Whether the choice between these two alternatives is a matter of logic or sympathy I find hard to decide.[111]

However, we should note with respect to Prof. McGuinness' presentation of these alternatives is that they are anything but dichotomous: it is certainly possible that the mystical is both a questionable extension of Wittgenstein's thoughts on logic and that it forced itself *psychologically* upon him. Indeed, Professor McGuinness seems to want to reconcile positivist qualms about the coherence of the *Tractatus* with Wittgenstein's own convictions about the mystical in this way. However, the possibility that the mystical is a *legitimate* »logical« extension of what has come before it, i.e., because it forced itself upon Wittgenstein *philosophically,* seems to be rejected *a-priori* without any reasons for doing so. It is this possibility that will be explored here. The ensuing digression should serve to clarify the issue of the coherence of the *Tractatus* and to frame the relationship between Wittgenstein and Russell philosophically at the time of the book's publication as well as provide an important hint about the continuity in Wittgenstein's thought with respect to the notion of »use«.

As we have already seen, Frege was convinced that it was possible to gesture at aspects of a formal development of logic that the resultant system showed: Moreover, he was convinced that a hint in the form of a verbal gesture, a *Wink*, was the appropriate way of making a point that otherwise would have involved appealing to metamathematical discourse. This is one of the origins of Wittgenstein's notion, so central to the *Tractatus*, that logic shows things that it cannot say (Hertz's mechanics is the other). On the basis of what he had already written about logic, for example, we know that propositions show that a logical constant corresponds to nothing empirical (*T,* 4.0621), Wittgenstein's basic idea or »*Grundgedanke*« as he refers to it (*T,* 4.0312) and it is clearly the case that »what can be shown, cannot be said« (*T,* 4.1212). Here we are, for better or worse, at the very heart of the logical part of *Tractatus*. It turns out that Wittgenstein's notion of »showing« is crucial to any possible resolution of the question of the relationship between the logical and the mystical in his early work. If we are to take the opening remarks of the *Notebooks* seriously, Wittgenstein had already found the »unsayable« solution to his »mathematical lines of thought« in the notion that a sign must be able to »take care of itself« by signifying on its own by the fall of 1914 (*N*, 22.8.14).

Indeed, three closely interrelated points that we have already touched upon are of come into play here:

1) the notion that there are aspects of logic that cannot be said: a theory of signs is not possible; their use can only be shown,
2) the closely related notion that »logic must take care of itself«: a theory of logic is not necessary
and
3) the notion that the »hard problems must dissolve of themselves«: a theory of logic would be superfluous anyway.

All three are aspects of what is to »show«, rather than say, something. The first point involves the rejection of the idea of a »complete analysis«, of the sign. The reason for this rejection brings us to the very core of Wittgenstein's thinking. The *use* of the signs in question shows that »p« and »~p« can say the same thing and thus that the constant »~« corresponds to nothing empirical. At a later stage in the writing of the *Tractatus* Wittgenstein will reject the idea that we can employ a metalanguage to clarify the vagaries with respect to the way signs signify on the grounds that a hierarchy of elementary propositions is an impossibility: it is not the invention of forms but the conditions of their possibility, which is philosophically important. Letting logic »take care of itself« turns out to be a matter of understanding how we use signs and how certain of our »theoretical« problems surrounding signs »dissolve« in an understanding of their use. Similarly tautologies show that they are tautologies in what we can – or cannot – *do* with them. The same is true of signs that are »identical«. (*T*, 4.1212) Nothing could be more fundamental to Wittgenstein's philosophizing at any stage of his development than this idea. Indeed, in a sense certain crucial aspects of the »later« Wittgenstein's philosophizing seem to be implicit here. For the early Wittgenstein we cannot describe the use of a sign because it shows itself; whereas in the later philosophy we cannot describe in propositions, say, what expert judgment is with respect to genuineness of feelings or what it is to follow a rule.[112]

From the very start of writing the *Tractatus*, then, this immanent way of »showing« seems to have been Wittgenstein's fundamental principle in coping with philosophical problems; however, it also seems to have become a kind of intellectual discipline that he submitted himself to (presumably, astonishing as it might seem, in conformity with Frege's ideas about objectivity *and* Hertz's views about our ability to make problems disappear) and ultimately his guide to right living in his encounter with death during World War I as the *Notebooks* and *Secret Notebooks* respectively indicate. In the *Tractatus* Wittgenstein's distinctive contribution to logic is his truth tables. They are nothing less than an Hertzian alternative representation in the sense of a technique for showing what cannot be said about the nature of propositions. They constitute an alternative mode of presenting propositions, which displays with crystal clarity the difference between tautologies, contradictions and empirical propositions at the same time that they show that metaphysical propositions, i.e., necessary truths about the empirical world are not logically possible. They are a way of showing the limits of language. However, they too offer precious little with respect to what we find on the far side of the distinction between the sayable and the unsayable. To be sure they show us that the propositions of logic, tautologies, are »sinnlos« (senseless) but what is senseless is sharply distinguished from what is »unsinnig« (nonsense). Of course this in itself hardly brings us closer to demarcating the domain of God and values from ordinary discourse. Nevertheless, it should be clear that showing is the essential notion in »elucidating« philosophical problems about propositions on Wittgenstein's view in a twofold sense: first, propositions show what they say; second, philosophers must show what cannot be said by gesturing with words – the famous Fregean »Wink« (see above p. 113) As he would elsewhere say, you have to look, not think (»denk nicht, sondern, schau«, *PI*, I, 66) – and philosophy is a way of bringing people to look at what they do. We shall have to return to this point.

How, then, is showing the key to understanding questions of ethics and the meaning of life? In his wartime notebooks Wittgenstein emphasizes that the problems of life must be solved objectively in the living and not subjectively on the basis of convictions, i.e., a set of beliefs, about it or expectations from it (i.e., what philosophers conventionally term »ethics«). That is what turns out to be »mystical« about ethics in the *Tractatus*. The problems of life must disappear in the living. Happiness is a matter of learning that I can only master the world (the facts) by making myself independent of them (*N*, 11.11.16), Wittgenstein claims, in a Spinozistic turn, that independence is a matter of taking a position with respect to the world (»eine Stellungnahme zur Welt«, *N*, 4.11.16), i.e. to will. Echoing Frege's emphasis upon the distinction between psychology and logic, he insists that to will is not merely to wish but to act, to *live* without »wishing«, i.e., without fear and hope. Fear and hope, it should be noted, presuppose that I identify myself with what I possess or what I want to possess – in the most extreme case with life itself considered as something which I *have* as opposed to something which I *am*. Fear and hope presuppose loss and gain as well as a past and a future in which said loss or gain can transpire. When I abandon the idea that life is a possession to be hoarded the problem of life disappears. I have nothing more to fear. Thus it would seem that an evil life would be one in which I expected to be rewarded for my actions. In short, it is nothing other than a life so completely self-centered that the very idea of limits, even in the sphere of knowledge, is »intolerable« as Weininger put it in a passage that Wittgenstein certainly knew well.[113] On the other hand, the happy life, as Wittgenstein insists both in the *Notebooks* and in the *Tractatus*, is a life in which our actions are by their nature rewarding because they are »harmonious«. Thus Spinoza passes over into Aristotle (with the help of Frege) at this point as ethics and aesthetics become one in a profound sense. Such a happy life is one dedicated to work in the form of the pursuit of knowledge, i.e., exactly what those »Secret Diaries« show Wittgenstein striving for in the face of death. It is only possible to the extent that we are prepared to recognize that we are limited by the nature of the world itself.

This turns out to be where the question of moral values enters into the philosophy of logic, even though it does not find its way into the text of the *Tractatus* or the *Notebooks*. Russell was wont to cheat a bit in logic when it fit his purposes. When it suited him he could revert from the rigors of deduction and simply stipulate that there were an infinite number of »objects« for logical operations because it was convenient that there be. Moreover, he would cover his tracks by proclaiming the resultant swindle to be »The Axiom of Infinity«. Just the sort of arbitrary subjectivity that Frege wanted to banish from logic asserted itself here. In this sense moral values clearly play a role in logic but it is, in a sense, not a 'logical' role. It was this tendency to »immorality« in Russell, his desire to have the world as he liked it to be, rather than to accept it as it is, that Wittgenstein always found questionable in Russell. Is it absurd to suggest that such considerations played a role in leading to the mystical?

In a sense Russell could be seen as a kind of Peer Gynt of philosophy (central aspects of Wittgenstein's views about what is ethical ultimately can be traced back to Weininger's essay on Ibsen's *Peer Gynt*), whose claims often far outstripped his ability to back them up.[114] Consider his treatment of the nature of our knowledge of the ego. In 1912 he insisted that it was known only by acquaintance. A year later he insisted with equally adamantly that it could only be known by description. At the bottom of all this there was an irresponsible frivolousness that could only be circumvented by attaining philosophical bedrock. This is something Russell steadfastly refused to do in Wittgenstein's eyes. The former's attitude was summed up in his »shilling shocker«, *The Problems of Philosophy*, which concluded on the note, »philosophy is to be studied, not for the sake of any definite answers to questions, since no definite answers can, as a rule, be known to be true, but rather for the sake of the questions themselves ...«[115] This is a far cry from the unassailable and definitive solutions to the problems of philosophy that the author of the *Tractatus* sought precisely by showing how the realm of discourse is limited in the only rigorous way, i.e., from within (F, 23, undated, probably October 1919).

Like Frege, Wittgenstein wanted to become absolutely, clear about the relation between the sign and what is signifies. Absolute clarity involved that nothing be arbitrary in the relationship between signifier and signified. For Wittgenstein this meant refraining from saying anything about that relation and letting logic thus speak for itself. It is what is »mystical« about logic. However, a certain moral demand is made upon the logician who would see that point, one which Russell was not always prepared to meet. It is at this point that the two parts of the *Tractatus* overlap. In the end the question of what is shown is indeed a matter of a »feeling« of the world as it is limited by the logical conditions of its possibility to speak with Kant. The latter for Wittgenstein include the actions involved in using a sign. Those actions can only be gestured at. Russell seemed to lack that very feeling. Little wonder that the notion of the mystical with which the *Tractatus* closes would leave him with a touch of intellectual dyspepsia.

Let us return to the question with which we began this digression: is the *Tractatus* consistent? Obviously not in the strict sense or we would not have to wrestle with these problems as we do – but that is not to say that it is incoherent. Although it is not possible to establish the consistency of the *Tractatus* definitively in the sense of being able to show how the ethical follows from the logical (or vice versa), we can lay bare the path from logic to mysticism that it follows. The starting point is the notion (inspired by Hertz) that propositions show things that they cannot say. What is shown is shown in the application of logic, i.e., in the course of making logical models of situations. In this very process there is thus an »unsayable« element that can only be gestured at, which is present on Wittgenstein's view from the start. This unsayable aspect of propositions is what makes logic philosophically problematic; for the »scientific mind« is inclined to demand that everything essential to our representation of the world can itself be the object of representation. Since this is not true, philosophical conundrums about the nature of propositions press themselves upon us. However, these perplexities are not to be confused with scientific problems; for they entail questioning where the questions involved cannot be explicitly answered. Philosophy can only gesture in words at what is shown in the course of employing a sign, symbol or sentence. Philosophy's concern is thus with establishing the limits of the sayable in »elucidating« the distinction between the saying and showing (in comparison with his later philosophy, we have to say that Wittgenstein, on his own account, did not do a very good job here). Yet, establishing those limits offers us a glance at what is on the other side – as does the effort to transgress them. Philosophy, then shows on the basis of an analysis of the propositional microcosm, what the metaphysican tries vainly and nonsensically to say about the macrocosm.

This by no means assuages all of our intellectual discomforts with respect to the mystical but it does at least indicate a path along which one can travel to see how Wittgenstein might have considered that he had legitimately connected logic and what now in the *Tractatus* could indeed be called the realm of the religious. The central point, however, is that the path referred to begins with an acknowledgement that there is a dimension to knowledge that can only be »shown« but goes beyond Russell's epistemology as well as Frege's philosophy of logic. The result has to be disappointing to the traditional philosopher as Wittgenstein points out in his Foreword to the *Tractatus;* for it only shows how little is achieved when the problems are solved. The problems of philosophy (i.e., Schopenhauer's »world as representation«) turn out to be of a different order (in the Pascalian sense) from those of life (the »world as will«), although there is a common strategy for coping with them. There are no sets of strict implications between them but a certain kind of continuity that can clearly be perceived in his later »philosophical« investigations as well as in investigations of themes related to »culture and value« but which would never again be handled in a single text.

It remains to discuss the continuity between the *Tractatus* and the *Philosophical Investigations* with respect to the ways that words confuse us in philosophy. We can start from the Tractarian notion that what signs fail to express is shown in their application (*T*, 3.262). The step from this view of application to the notion that meaning is use is short indeed. Logic and its application, Wittgenstein insists, are, obviously enough, intimately related but they are not identical nor can they be (*T*, 5.557). This means that the application of logic, which is identical with thought (*T*, 5.5) and, in fact, decides what propositions are in a given case elementary (*T*, 5.557), can only be shown. In effect, Wittgenstein asserts already here that there can be no theory of practice. Use cannot be described, only shown. The plot thickens further when we consider that this is all part of ordinary language as it functions, for Wittgenstein insists that it is in order as it is (*T*, 5.5563). Not only that: everyday language is as complex as the human organism itself (*T*, 4.002). Already in the *Tractatus*, it follows that the tacit conventions of everyday language can only be shown. The sort of complexity that Wittgenstein refers to with respect to everyday language is connected to the idea that in everyday language it is frequently the case that the same word has different applications and thus different meanings (*T*, 3.323) or that two apparently different symbols are employed in the same way and are thus really one. Thus there is a need »to take a look« at how we use language already in the *Tractatus*. Indeed, Wittgenstein recommends investigating the actual usage of words and propositions already there (*T*, 6.211) Moreover, the sort of confusion that results when we fail to recognize such differences (»is« functioning as copula, a sign for identity or asserting existence) are typical of philosophy (*T*, 3.324). It was to avoid such pitfalls that

5. BERTRAND RUSSELL ...

Frege and Russell developed their concept script (*Begriffsschrift*), which is here explicitly described as a logical grammar (*T*, 3.325). This view clearly owes its inspiration to Russell's critique of language in »On Denoting« and it is what determines the search for the dissolution of philosophical problems on the basis of differences in linguistic usage as his mature critique of language. All of these notions would increase in importance to the extent that Wittgenstein abandoned the notion that representation was the essence of language. In short, they would turn out to be absolutely central to the *Philosophical Investigations*, where philosophers are continually reproached for failing to recognize how words have a multiplicity of scarcely related meanings. If the Wittgenstein of the *Philosophical Investigations* enthusiastically endorsed Kent's promise in *King Lear* »I'll teach you differences« in philosophy, it was Bertrand Russell who first showed him why that should be so important. The theory of descriptions showed him why it was so important to assemble reminders of how we actually weave words into actions.

CHAPTER 6

Karl Kraus:
Style as Strategy

> Wittgenstein always looked for the striking, even the syncopated, expression of an insight – it should become dazzlingly obvious; and for refutation he relied on a rephrasing of views he disagreed with that made them seem absurd.
>
> Brian McGuinness[116]

THE EXACT NATURE OF Karl Kraus' influence upon Wittgenstein's philosophical »work of clarification«, like that of several other figures on the list, is not easy to determine. We know from Brian McGuinness' magisterial biography of the young Wittgenstein *what* must have interested him personally in Kraus: »It is obvious enough what he liked about Kraus ... the style *and* the man. The satire, the exposure of shabby moral attitudes, the scorn were conveyed by a use and criticism of language which was more ethical than literary. Ludwig all his life had Kraus' habit of taking his opponent at his word and reading from a single ill-judged sentence a whole moral character«.[117] Moreover, the fact that Wittgenstein *ceased* to be interested in Kraus in the mid-twenties when, on the philosopher's view, the satirist's work ceased to be funny[118] gives us a further clue concerning what drew Wittgenstein to Kraus. However, that information is more about Wittgenstein the man than his philosophy. At best it provides us with clues to

145

the impact Kraus had on his philosophical »work of clarification«. The latter is the important issue. Lack of documentary evidence as well as the subtle, indirect character of Kraus' influence upon Wittgenstein, then, implies that our investigation of Kraus' influence upon Wittgenstein necessarily has a conjectural character. Yet, that by no means implies that it is in vain. The synergy that develops within the context of our analysis forms a background against which his appearance after Russell is considerably less mysterious than it seems at first glance.

According to Georg Henrik von Wright,[119] Wittgenstein's list of »influences« upon him is chronological. If this is so, the fact that Kraus comes after Russell but before Loos is a clue in establishing what Wittgenstein probably read at the decisive moment. We know that Wittgenstein first encountered Russell at Cambridge in 1911 and that he first met Loos in July of 1914. Given the intensity of Wittgenstein's Cambridge interactions with Bertrand Russell in 1911 and 1912, it seems safe to infer that Wittgenstein's profound encounter with Kraus most likely took place in Norway – and not Vienna or Cambridge – in 1913. Of this very special, extremely important and little documented period he would say 18 years later: »When I was in Norway in 1913–14 I had original thoughts, at least it looks that way to me now. I mean it seems to me as if had given birth to new movements of thought within me (maybe I am mistaken). Whereas I just seem to be applying old ones now«. (*C+V*, 17). However, we have no documentary evidence that he came under Kraus' influence then. What we do know is that Kraus became philosophically important for him after his encounter with Frege and Russell and that is all. This has to strike us today as very odd indeed. In fact, Frege's steadfast distinction between the subjective and the objective would condition his receptivity to Kraus' language-based critique of moral duplicity in Viennese life; whereas Russell's sensitivity to systematically misleading expressions would doubtless assist him to appreciate the Krausian techniques for unmasking moral nonsense. But that is to run ahead.

What, then, do we know about Wittgenstein's general interest in and knowledge of Kraus? Not much. We know that Wittgenstein had been reading the *Fackel* from his youth,[120] and had it forwarded to him religiously in Norway in 1913 as well as later during the war.[121] Concerning Wittgenstein's thinking in this period of seclusion, which he considered to be perhaps his most creative, we know nothing beyond what we find in his correspondence with Gottlob Frege and his Cambridge friends and colleagues. There are no references to Kraus in those letters. However, it is reasonable to assume that Kraus' development in that period is somehow connected with Wittgenstein's interest in him. In that period we know that Kraus' second volume of aphorisms, *Pro domo et mundo*, appeared in 1912 along with a reprint of essays from the *Fackel* collected originally in 1910 under the title *The Great Wall of China* (*Die chinesische Mauer*, whose title essay laments Viennese ethnocentrism). It is probably not entirely accidental that in 1914 Wittgenstein would refer to the Chinese language when he wanted to give an example of something that was so foreign as to be incomprehensible and thus scarcely compatible with the human: »If we hear a Chinese, we are inclined to take his speaking for an inarticulate gurgling. Someone who knows Chinese will recognize it as *language*. Thus frequently I cannot recognize the human in people« (*C+V*, 1; cf. *Z*, 219). That could, of course, be pure co-incidence but it is interesting that the *aperçu* is from August 1914. Be that as it may, Kraus, along with Weininger, was certainly later an intense topic of conversation with Paul Engelmann and his Olmützer Circle in the crucial discussion of 1916, during which his ideas about »the mystical« and »the limits of language« crystallized.[122]

Edward Timms has called our attention to a number transformations in Kraus' writing in the crucial period between 1911, when he began to write the *Fackel* alone, and September 1913, when he fell in love with Sidonie Nádhérny, that are important here. In this period bitter polemic in aid of social reform gave way to satire as the liberal social critic became disillusioned with the unreformable character of Austrian politics. Thus the social reformer came to be overshadowed by the literary artist and irony gave way to declamation, casuistry to monologue, as the objects of Kraus' attacks came increasingly to be described with hyperbole. At the same time Kraus' own literary ego assumed exaggerated, monumental proportions. In short, Kraus took on the role of the Old Testament prophet welcoming the destruction of a corrupt western civilization. »The challenging dynamism of the satiric monologue arises precisely because apocalyptic conclusions are drawn from such apparently commonplace material and trivial symptoms«,[123] writes Timms in a passage that directly reflects Brian McGuinness' estimate of what drew Wittgenstein to Kraus and is certainly highly relevant to Wittgenstein's interest in Kraus. Might it be that, then, the apocalyptic tone of the *Tractatus Logico-Philosophicus*, as we know it, is a reflection of Kraus' tone? Certainly. However, it is not clear how. What is clear is that tone was a direct reflection of an author's moral and aesthetic worth in Wittgenstein's eyes as in the cases of Trakl (F, 12) as well as Ibsen and Tagore (E, 43). Indeed, Kraus emphasized at this time that the society around him was nothing less than a world turned upside down, a world in which appearance and reality were inverted, a world in which everyone wore a mask.[124] What claims to be justice is wholly unjust; what claims to be morality is utterly immoral; what claims to be art is mere entertainment; what claims to be respectable is corrupt. »Justice is a whore«[125], wrote Kraus in defense of helpless prostitutes, made into criminals by unnatural, arbitrarily enforced laws. He thus found himself confronted with the task of setting things straight. The Krausian techniques of performing a moral »analysis« on perverse speech acts are, in a curious way, reminiscent of Frege in the *Foundations of Arithmetic*. Like Frege, Kraus takes his opponent »at his word« and demolishes his pretenses. Over time he developed this technique to the point of simply quoting his antagonist or juxtaposing, say, morally »uplifting« editorials from prominent liberal newspapers with dubious personals from the advertising pages to expose hypocrisy in its own words, rather than decry it.[126] Here was a distinction between »saying« and »showing« literally with a vengeance. The parallel to Wittgenstein's moral and aesthetic task in the *Tractatus* of helping us to see the world aright by showing us the limits of language suggests itself at once, although, on the face of it, their respective subjects could hardly be farther removed from each other. Moreover, the synoptic contrast that the technique of juxtaposition offered Kraus seems distantly related to the kinds of comparisons that should help us to dissolve philosophical problems in Wittgenstein's later works.

In any case, it is at this time that the crucial ethical notion of the *Ursprung*, with its heritage harking back to Herder and the Romantics, the origin or source of all true value, emerges in Kraus' work. *Ursprung* refers to »a world of idyllic naturalness and pure spirituality«[127] corresponding to Lichtenberg's utopian vision of a language in which grammatical as well as moral errors would not be possible. This notion would become the Archimedean point for Kraus' critique of cliché-ridden notions of Progress and Enlightenment characteristic of the fashionable positivism of the day after he had lost faith in politics. The poem »Two Runners« *(Zwei Läufer)* is a kind of Krausian parable of the *Ursprung*:

> Two runners down time's road have sped,
> one bold, the other full of dread:
> The one from nowhere who reaches his abode;
> the one from the source of life who dies on the road.
> The one from nowhere, after he's arrived,
> has to make way for the one who died.
> The latter, though his days are full of fear,
> knows that the source of life in always near.[128]

While this notion is foreign Wittgenstein's understanding of language and to his philosophizing generally, a reference to the poem does turn up in his self-commentary in the *Culture and Value* (doubtless under the influence of Paul Engelmann[129]): »In the race that is philosophy the one who runs slowest wins. Or: he, who reaches the goal last.« (*C+V*, 40). He seems to have deeply appreciated the Krausian transvaluation of values it implies.

In Kraus' development at this time the aphorism comes increasingly to take on importance for Kraus. From 1908 onwards Kraus began reprinting articles from the *Fackel* in books such as *Morality and Criminality (Sittlichkeit und Kriminalität)* and *The Great Wall of China (Die chinesische Mauer)*. These works were thus presented to the public at one remove from their polemic origin and thus took on a more purely literary meaning. From 1909 onwards Kraus further concentrated and »de-contextualised« his thoughts, as it were, by excerpting aphorisms from those writings (a certain similarity to Wittgenstein's mature method of writing philosophy suggests itself but the comparison is all too easy to strain). Wrenching them from first from their polemical and then from their satirical contexts at the same time involved further monumentalizing his literary ego. Thus, what began as social critique came increasingly to lay claim to literary merit and, ultimately, to being a kind of oracular wisdom, which, like, say, Lichtenberg, but unlike, say, La Rochefoucauld, is deeply rooted in a punning style.

The step from polemical social reform to aphoristic social satire was in fact a step from direct involvement in politics into the much-neglected tradition of practical philosophy at least as old as La Rochefoucauld, embracing Pascal and the French moralists as well as German writers such as Lichtenberg and Goethe, not to mention Schopenhauer and Nietzsche. We do well to remind ourselves of the functions of the literary form of the aphorism in that virtually forgotten tradition of practical philosophy. The aphorism, like the metaphor, condenses a judgment authoritatively into a phrase that has paradigmatic character by commanding our attention in a particular direction.[130] However, its mode of concentrating simultaneously releases energy in the part of the reader. When the aphorism works the imagination of the reader is set into motion. The aphorism thus functions to open the fantasy to possibilities hitherto concealed from it. Thus the sense of an aphorism, as J. P. Stern emphasized in his excellent study of Lichtenberg forty years ago[131] is to help us to take a second look at something of importance whose very familiarity permits us to take it for granted and thus to ignore it in everyday life. The successful aphorism's strange and surprisingly complex configuration of words hides an integrated antithesis. As the literary emblem of the paradox it is at once literary and philosophical in an antisystematic sense. The crucial point is that is forces us to take a fresh look at something we are prone to overlook.

Aphorisms induce precisely the sort of reflection on what we actually do, as opposed to what we think or say about what we do, that Wittgenstein always sought to occasion in his reader. In short, it is a highly appropriate vehicle for attaining a certain kind of Socratic self-knowledge. As such aphorisms, again, like metaphors, transcend truth, as Kraus wrote, the aphorism is either a half truth or a truth and a half.[132] To employ a phrase to which Wittgenstein attached much importance both in philosophy and in life a successful aphorism presents us with »das erlösende Wort«, the saving word, which »allows us to grasp what has burdened our consciousness in an increasingly intangible way«.[133] It is anything but continuous with »business as usual« and this is precisely what Wittgenstein needed to wake philosophers from their dogmatic slumbers. On Wittgenstein's view Socratic self-awareness requires that we have to be awakened from a dream-like state: »Human beings – and perhaps whole peoples – must awaken to wonder« (C+V, 7). It is not difficult to see a parallel to Kraus' desire to awaken us to the evils of the double standard and moral responsibility here. In the punning aphorism, for example, new aspects of the use of words dawn upon us. It is significant that Wittgenstein would compare the depth of philosophy with the depth of a grammatical joke: »Let us ask ourselves: why do we feel a grammatical joke to be *deep*? (And that is what the depth of philosophy is.)« (PU, I, 111). Kraus was, of course, the master of the grammatical joke, which, however, plays no role whatsoever in Wittgenstein's philosophizing.

In any case, style takes on a profound philosophical significance in Kraus' Socratic exercise in collective self-understanding. Punning aphorisms, such as Kraus', have a way of reversing meaning, of wrenching a word/concept of its conventional context and *showing* us something important about meaning, namely, that our conventional ways of speaking and thinking emphasize one aspect of meaning at the cost of concealing others. Here we will do well to remind ourselves of some of Kraus' typical gems in this genre. »Je größer der Stiefel, desto größer der Absatz« plays on the meanings of the words »Stiefel« (= boot; nonsense) and »Absatz« (= heel, paragraph, sale), such that the boot and its heel are at once images of commerce and journalism and at the same time morally dubious precisely in their reciprocity.[134] For Kraus the substance of the joke is important for showing us something about the relationship between capitalism, journalism and nonsense; for Wittgenstein the form of the joke shows us something about meaning itself. Here accident and necessity merge in an uncanny way. Yet, wordplay, as such, does not enter at all into Wittgenstein's philosophizing at all. Indeed, Wittgenstein would later go so far as to question the dazzling character of Kraus' aphorisms. However, for all Wittgenstein's mistrust, he does imply that Kraus' aphorisms and his own way of writing philosophy are connected (C+V, 76).

Let us consider a very different example of Krausian word play from *Sprüche und Widersprüche*: »Man lebt nicht einmal einmal« »You don't live once once« or »You don't even live once«.[135] In this example the negating force of the second »einmal« should not pass unnoticed. Indeed, Kraus' extraordinary use of negation and double negation in these aphorisms is noteworthy: »Nicht grüßen genügt nicht. Man grüßt auch Leute nicht, die man nicht kennt« (»Not greeting does not suffice. We also do not greet people, whom we do not know«)[136], »Man weiß nicht nur im Ausland nicht, was hier geschieht: man weiß es auch nicht hier (»It is not only that people abroad do not know what is happening here; people here do not know either«.[137] It could hardly have passed unnoticed by a logician who insisted that the general form of the proposition was simultaneous negation. On the basis of this operation one could construct truth tables, which showed in a foolproof way which propositions were tautologies, i.e., had logical status, and which were not. In this way he eliminated the need for axioms in logic. This procedure of simultaneous negation, on Wittgenstein's views, showed that not only that axioms could be dispensed with in logic, but that theory itself was superfluous: the very idea of calling his as yet unnamed book »Philosophical Logic« would strike Wittgenstein as absurd in 1922: »There is no such thing as philosophic logic« (*O*, 2). Indeed, the logical force of Wittgenstein's conception of showing in the *Tractatus* is bound to the notion that the application of logic should solve the problems for which Frege and Russell had introduced the notion of logical theory in the first place. In any case, at the very logical heart of the *Tractatus*, strange as it seems, there seems to be an echo of Kraus.

In any case, fascination with word play and its ability to focus our attention on neglected nuances of things around us is certainly nothing new in philosophy. We forget at out peril, for example, the fascination that word play exerted upon, say, ancient Pythagorean philosophers.[138] From the latter the fact that the word for body, *soma*, was virtually identical with the word for tomb, *sema*, was evidence that there was somehow a deeper sense in which the body was like a tomb or was in fact a tomb as it came to be seen in the Pythagorean-inspired Platonic tradition. This is certainly one way in which philosophers have been seduced by the outer forms of language into seeking some »inner« source of depth. However, there is nevertheless something to *wonder* at, something *puzzling*, a bit like a riddle, in which we can at once delight and challenge our understanding.[139] This is important.

As we have seen, philosophy in Wittgenstein's sense was a matter of waking us up (*C+V*, 7) to the richness, variety and complexity of the everyday and of the constitutive role that language plays in forming human experience. As such his philosophical mission bears a certain resemblance to Martin Heidegger's in *Sein und Zeit*. In both cases stylistic peculiarities are intimately linked to philosophical tactics. The difference is precisely in their respective methods of »describing«.[140] For the phenomenologist, Heidegger, at least in comparison with

6. KARL KRAUS ...

Wittgenstein, describing is a relatively straight-forward matter of directing our attention from theory to practice and thus of producing an alternative to the traditional philosophical way of describing what it is to know and act. Wittgenstein faces a similar problem made yet more complex by the realization that external grammatical forms disguise meaning and confuse the philosopher in his efforts to attain clarity. However, he insists that it is not mere stupidity or a certain *deformation professionelle* that prevents us from »seeing the world rightly« but »deep disquietudes« rooted in the external forms of language, its surface grammar. Surface grammar tempts us to see the world wrongly and thus make »the world as I find it« devilishly difficult to describe. It should not be surprising that we find Wittgenstein saying in this context that »philosophy is a battle against the bewitchment of our minds by means of language« (*PI*, I, 109). The source of the depth typical of the philosophical disquietudes that language provokes is a tendency to confuse surface grammar with depth grammar. This confusion involves identifying language with words, signs and symbols as opposed to understanding it in terms of the practices (»language games«), which confer meaning upon those words, signs and symbols. It is a perspective consistent with Krausian practice but foreign to Kraus' writings on language. Indeed, at just the point where Kraus appeals to the mystical »Ursprung« of language the mature Wittgenstein de-mythologizes *die Sache selbst* by demanding that we take a good look at practice, quoting Goethe all the while: »Im Anfang war die Tat« (*OC*, 402). So philosophical analysis as Wittgenstein would understand it is in fact a sort of gesturing that aims at helping us to see what is always before our eyes. The fact that our conventional view of the world is drilled into us until it has become second nature makes it devilishly difficult to redirect our attention. Thus the need for a technique to remind us of what it is to be an animal that speaks, something that is as important for such a creature as it is easy to forget.

Thus Wittgenstein is emphatic in insisting that philosophers are engaged in a battle with language (C+V, 13). Here there is an interesting passage reminiscent of Kraus that deserves to be mentioned:

Kraus writes,

> When I don't make any progress, I have bumped my head against the wall of language. Then I draw back with a bloody head. And would like to go on.[141]

Wittgenstein writes,

> The results of philosophy are the uncovering of one or another piece of plain nonsense and bumps that the understanding has got by running its head up against the limits of language. These bumps make us see the value of the discovery (PI, I, 119).

Here we have a hint of Kraus at a crucial junction in Wittgenstein's own discussion of his »work of clarification«.

Wittgenstein's philosophical strategy is dictated to him by the inherent capacity of language to seduce us into metaphysical forms of thinking that lead us to disregard what is normally before our eyes. In effect, Wittgenstein must re-seduce philosophers away from those outer forms of language. So it is no wonder that his strategy for restoring philosophers' orientation to the everyday *must be strange* as, indeed, his curious way of writing philosophy is. Wittgenstein must continually surprise us in order to lead us to insight into how language functions. Thus despite the fact that Wittgenstein insists that the description must replace explanation in philosophy, we find virtually nothing that corresponds to a straight-forward description, be it phenomenological or empiricist, in Wittgenstein. Instead we find gestures in the form of thought experiments, questions, aphorisms and reflections, often of a most peculiar character. Should there be any doubt of this; one need merely consider once more the fact that in the *Philosophical Investigations* Wittgenstein poses 784 questions. He answers but 110 of them and then 70 intentionally false.[142] His questions typically surprise us by catching us off balance as it were. They too are gestures that direct us away from our accustomed way of looking at things.

Furthermore as we have already seen in connection with Schopenhauer a curious kind of humor plays a definite role in Wittgenstein's strategy, one which is also dictated by the need to get straight about our natural history. As we have already seen in other contexts Wittgenstein suggests that »in philosophy it is significant that such-and-such a sentence makes no sense; but also that it sounds funny« (Z, 328). So there is clearly room for humor in his philosophizing even if it is not typical of him. It is worth repeating some examples here:

> So he is having real pain and it is the possession of this by somebody else that he feels doubt of. – But how does he do this? – It is as if I were told: Here is a chair. Can you see it clearly? – Good, – now translate it into French! (Z, 547).
> or
> »A rose has no teeth.« This ... is obviously true! It is even surer than that a goose has none. – And yet it is not so clear. For where should a rose's teeth have been? (*PI*, II, xi, 221)

These questions are less to be answered than to be thought through by Wittgenstein's reader. That these questions seem to verge on the absurd is intentional: We speak of red hot or white hot but we do not speak of brown hot or gray hot? (*OCL*, I, 34) Why do we speak of brown rather than reddish green? (*OCL*, 11).

Strange questions that should provoke a smirk, if not a sense of wonder.

Like the servant girl who laughed at Thales when he fell into the well while observing an eclipse, Wittgenstein suggests that normal people will find the kinds of that claims that analytic philosophers make to be simply mad:

> I am sitting with a philosopher in the garden. He says repeatedly, »I know that is a tree«, as he points to one nearby. A third person comes along and hears that. I tell him, »this man is not crazy: we are only doing philosophy. (*OC*, 467)

His thoughts thus have to be ways of thinking that are crazier than those of the philosophers if he is to dissolve their problems. He does this by creating fictive natural histories that illuminate our actual one. Thus his questions about what would have to be different about us (i.e., our natural history) for us to prefer calling a color »reddish green« rather than »brown« have to seem silly. It is in this sense that Wittgenstein insists that philosophy can only really be written as fiction (*C+V*, 28) or as jokes (he once suggested in conversation that he could imagine a work of philosophy entirely composed of jokes).[143] This should not be entirely surprising if his aim is really to teach us what is in essence the Russellian lesson, »to pass from a piece of disguised nonsense to something that is plain nonsense.« (*PI*, I, 164) In fact, if I negate the seemingly straightforward, but in fact wholly nonsensical, report, »I know that is a tree«, the result is pure nonsense: »I do not know that is a tree«. This move is as old as philosophy itself but sometimes such things escape even clever analytic philosophers.[144] It should hardly seem curious to suggest that Wittgenstein's wit

6. KARL KRAUS ...

and perspicacity here owe something to Kraus. Moreover, we forget at our peril that Wittgenstein cultivated a collection of nonsense for his personal edification.[145]

Yet, it is not beside the point to ask how these factors became crucial for Wittgenstein's mature philosophical »work of clarification«. That story turns out to be surprising indeed, for it ultimately leads us back to the absolute centrality of Gottlob Frege in Wittgenstein's philosophical development and it is precisely at a juncture where we would have least expected him. Let us begin by recapitulating the role of wit in our story up to this point. The teenaged Wittgenstein was drawn to Boltzmann – and repelled by Mach – on the basis *inter alia* of his style. It has been more or less overlooked in the literature on Wittgenstein that Boltzmann was celebrated for his wit. As we have seen earlier, Schopenhauer found a definite place for wit in philosophy appending a chapter on the absurd character of what we would today term category mistakes to his *chef d'ouvre The World as Will and Representation*. Frege, as we have seen ruthlessly exploited the resources of wit in defending his radically new conception of mathematics. What turns out to be astonishing is the parallels between how the two, Frege and Kraus, influenced Wittgenstein's mature notion of philosophical method. Indeed, they are so trenchant that it seems safe to conjecture that Wittgenstein found his way to Kraus from Frege – and, paradoxically, the way beyond Frege in Kraus.

Let us examine some of these parallels. The first is the indirect character of the influence each exerted upon Wittgenstein's overall development, receding ever deeper into the background without being any the less important for all that. Second, it was the practice of both Frege and Kraus to take their opponents at their word only to proceed to show that their conventional, seemingly sensible view of a given matter was anything but that. Third, Krausian moral analysis aimed at reaching

159

moral objectivity behind duplicitous, hypocritical assertions by laying bare the precise nature of the difference between what was being said and what was really meant. Briefly, for all their differences, Kraus' moral critique of the language of Viennese civil society exactly paralleled Frege's quest to understand mathematics objectively. Fourth, both Kraus and Frege each in their own way had to develop means of gesturing at what needed to be shown but could not be said in their respective spheres of interest (*cf.* the famous Fregean »Wink« that we have already had occasion to mention). Fifth, style is of paramount importance to each of them in his own way as it became for Wittgenstein himself. Sixth, Frege, every bit as much as Kraus, albeit in a context that bore little surface similarity to the one in which Kraus operated, was, from his own point of view, an isolated figure every bit as much involved in a battle to set an »inverted« world upon its feet again. Finally, as would become crystal clear in the course of World War I, the world has been turned upside down because the human imagination has gone wild: people are no longer capable of distinguishing between reality and fantasy because *they don't want to*. Already before the War this thought dominated his polemics against the feuilleton, that literary form which systematically obliterated the distinction between fact and fiction.[146] It would be the axis around which he would construct his »Martian« satire upon the War, *Die letzten Tage der Menschheit*. The War is happening because, having abolished the line separating the two, we are no longer capable of imagining it.[147] The point could hardly be lost on a Fregean, who saw some of the War's heaviest fighting.[148] Little wonder that he would come to see both logic and ethics apocalyptically in the *Tractatus*. More than that, the mature Wittgenstein can well be considered to be engaged in an equally monumental struggle against the philosophical imagination gone wild in its search for certainty.

6. KARL KRAUS ...

Be that as it may, for all Frege's importance for Wittgenstein, we cannot minimize Russell's role of in showing Wittgenstein how it is that language so clothes thought as to disguise its true character. This idea, which runs in a different direction from the sort of Fregean considerations we have just mentioned in connection with Kraus' polemic against war-mongering, is crucial because, despite all temptations, it attributes the confusions of philosophers, not simply to ignorance or overt prejudice, but to certain quasi-transcendental features of language. These lines of thought converge to influence Wittgenstein profoundly in all of his later developments. Be that as it may, if his commitment to Frege's concept of objectivity showed Wittgenstein the way to Kraus via Russell, the confrontation with Kraus began the process of transforming the heritage he bore from Frege into something that the master in Jena himself, like Russell in his Introduction to the *Tractatus*, would no longer recognize. Thus he had to find very style of the *Tractatus* strange[149] And this takes us back to Kraus.

Wittgenstein was most certainly at one with Kraus with respect to the idea that, »language is the mother, not the handmaiden of thought«[150], however differently they might have construed that notion. The constitution of morality in language was a favorite theme of Kraus, which parallels Wittgenstein's conviction that human knowledge, indeed, human existence itself, is constituted through language. Moreover, both were entirely convinced that understanding morality or meaning was a matter of investigating tell-tale nuances. Thus, when Kraus came to pillory Maximilian Harden the polemic would turn *inter alia* upon Harden's falsely construing a dative as a genitive[151]; whereas Wittgenstein would ponder the differences implied by prefacing a thought variously: what differences to it make to begin »one might say...«, »Could one say ...«, One could can ...«, »can one say ...«[152] That conviction would shape their respective style as satirist and philosopher. For Kraus it would lead to an absolute morality based upon style: »That one is a murderer does not necessarily prove anything against his style. However, his style can prove that he is a murderer.«[153] So he would take his opponent at his word literally and extract all that was dubious about him from the nuances of his typical mode of expression. This way of concentrating upon exact quotation was Kraus' method of setting an inverted world on its feet again. It doubtless played a role in Wittgenstein's realization that philosophy must do something similar in helping us to »see the world aright« by aiding us to acknowledge the limits of language in the *Tractatus*. Later, sensitivity to style in the form of singling out the very strange, peculiar character of traditional philosopher's seemingly reasonable, but actually »insane«, claims about the world will be central to Wittgenstein's philosophical mission. Moreover, that same sensitivity to style suggests a way of waking philosophers up to those simple and familiar things that are the foundations of their inquiries but, nevertheless, fail to strike them in everyday life precisely because they are so familiar. (*PI* I, 129) His task, then, was the paradoxical one of bringing that which is always before us to our consciousness powerfully and strikingly. No wonder that the task required special stylistic tactics. Is it absurd to suggest that his early readings of Kraus' satires and polemics presented him both with a parallel problem about seeing what is morally before us rightly and insight into how we must understand language if we are to cope with the deep disquietudes that tempt us to misunderstand it? Hardly. Parallel to Kraus' relationship to language, Wittgenstein in his philosophical »work of clarification« was obliged to turn the prostitute of everyday »impure reason« into a virgin again. Adolf Loos and Otto Weininger would offer him further insight into how that must be done.

CHAPTER 7

Adolf Loos: Craftsmanship

[Philosophy for Wittgenstein] was a craft, a discipline ... and its value consisted in its being well done. So one should do it well and not preach about it: ... showing not saying was important. Like all crafts, its exercise at its highest produces beauty, a beauty which requires an intellectual effort to grasp ...
Brian McGuinness[154]

APART FROM PIERO SRAFFA, about whose relationship to Wittgenstein virtually nothing is known, Adolf Loos is the most mysterious figure on Wittgenstein's list. He insisted that Ludwig Boltzmann, Heinrich Hertz, Arthur Schopenhauer, Gottlob Frege, Bertrand Russell, Karl Kraus; Adolf Loos, Otto Weininger, Oswald Spengler and Piero Sraffa were the figures who influenced his philosophical work of clarification but he hardly said anything about *how* any of these figures had an impact upon him. In the case of Loos we know even less than in the others. Further, it is unclear where we should even begin our investigation: in the realm architecture or in the realm of social criticism? Certainly, Paul Engelmann, allegedly Loos' favorite pupil and Wittgenstein's most important interlocutor between 1916 and 1929[155], reports that Loos said upon meeting Wittgenstein »you are me!«[156] but we do not have the slightest documentary evidence *why* he said so. It is a safe bet that they shared similar tastes in the matter of design but even that is speculation. Moreover, when Wittgenstein took over the project of building a house for his sister from Engelmann, who had been entrusted with it, he produced an elegant stately home, the Palais Stonborough, which has often been compared with the work of Loos in its undecorated magnificence. However, upon close scrutiny the house has less to do with Loos than meets the untutored eye. For, example, despite the smooth, unadorned, »modern« façade, the progression of the windows is absolutely classical and not at all modern; whereas anyone with the slightest knowledge of the architecture of Adolf Loos will note that there, at best, but a trace of the Loosian atrium principle with its interlocking levels in the Palais Stonborough and then only on the lower floors.[157] Yet, we know that, if Wittgenstein put Loos onto his list beside Kraus and Weininger in the first place, he must have contributed to Wittgenstein's mature concept of philosophy in an important and original way. But that is not much help either, except as a reminder of the scope of our problem here.

The best thing that we can do in this situation is to examine Loos' lifework as closely as we can with a view to extrapolating what it *might have been* that would have tempted Wittgenstein to list him along with the other nine. This is no small task because we have even less to go on here than in the case of Kraus. In what follows we have chosen to begin with Loos' social criticism, proceed to an account of his view of architecture as a craft including his view of what architectural education is all about and end with an account of his notion of the relationship between architecture and art. With that behind us we can then consider how such ideas may have made an impact upon the author of the *Philosophical Investigations*.

In the witty, satirical manner of Karl Kraus, Loos, whose social criticism in fact antedates that of Kraus, polemicized against the clichés about taste prevalent in Old Vienna.[158] For a time he edited a periodical, *Das Andere* (The Other), which was dedicated to the »introduction of western culture« into Austria. Nearly all of his cultural criticism is directed against the Vienna Secession. Like Kraus, Loos exploited all the possibilities of irony in his efforts to bring Austrian society to its senses regarding matters of taste and design. »For the epoch, its proper art; for art its proper freedom« was the Secession's motto. Loos would turn that motto against Viennese modernism (*die Wiener Moderne*[159]) with a vengeance. The motto suggests a certain historicism, which is, indeed, related to Viennese modernism's search for a sense of style appropriate to the life of modern man. Nowhere was this more evident than in architecture. The rebellion of the sons of the entrepreneurs who industrialized the Dual Monarchy took an aesthetic rather than a political form. The fathers had endeavored to legitimate their vision of a liberal society on the basis of an eclectic, historicist architecture. Their buildings symbolized their relationship to a past more imaginary than real as Carl Schorske has pointed out in his brilliant essay on Ringstrasse architecture.[160] Thus the Burgtheater was built in a neo-Renaissance style to commemorate the first mingling of the bourgeoisie in the theater at that time, the city hall was a neo-Gothic building that celebrated the spirit of the medieval burgesses, parliament a Greek temple to commemorate the ancient origins of modern liberalism and so-on around the Ring. To the next generation, people born around 1880 and coming to maturity just after the turn of the century and thus sometimes known as the Generation of 1905[161], eclectic historicism seemed to be no style at all. The search for a truly modern style thus originated in a rejection of historicism (and, indeed, history itself, if we are to believe Prof. Schorske) as irrelevant to the conditions of modern life, above all, its nervous energy: Hermann Bahr, the standard-bearer of *die Wiener Moderne*, had defined that movement in 1891 as a »Romanticism of Nerves«.[162] Part of its histrionics was a desperate search for a coherent way of building. Loos found this whole project nonsensical for two reasons: first, because the highly ornate Viennese *art nouveau* or *Jugendstil*, as it was known in Vienna, which allegedly filled the stylistic gap, definitely subordinated functionality to ornamentation; second because there was, indeed, an indigenous, harmonious Austrian style that had got lost in the shuffle, The *Biedermeier*, whose potential for fulfilling what was not merely fantasy in the dream of a truly modern style was anything but exhausted:

> The second half of the 19th century was filled by the cry of an uncultivated people: »We don't have a building style! How wrong, how incorrect! Precisely this era had a more strongly accentuated, more differentiated style than any previous epoch. It was a vicissitude without precedent in cultural history. However, since false prophets only recognize a product on the basis of variously composed ornaments, ornamentation became a fetish for them. They foisted this, the enchanted child of our times upon us by calling it style. We had already had true style but we did not possess ornament. If I could knock all of the ornaments off our old and new buildings such that only naked walls would remain, it would certainly be difficult to distinguish a 15th century building from a 17th century building. However, the buildings of the 19th century could be identified by a layman at a glance. We did not have ornamentation and they complained that we did not have a style. Then they copied past ornamentation until they themselves found it ridiculous and when that could go no further they invented new ornaments, which means they had sunk as deep as they could

culturally. Then they rejoiced that they had found a style for the 20th century.[163]

Paradoxically, the values which informed the tradition that his Viennese contemporaries had lost sight of had been incorporated into the work of architects principally in England and America in Loos' day. Thus Loos set out to distinguish the genuine historicism from its counterfeit. That entailed a massive attack upon the role of ornamentation in *Jugendstil* art. But his project was even bigger than that.

In fact, Loos, like Kraus, campaigned to restore a lost (some might prefer to say missing) integrity to Austrian public life.[164] For Loos the introduction of truly modern, truly, functional architecture into Vienna demanded a rigorous critique of Viennese »good taste« starting with such simple matters as table manners and fashion, subjects that he instructed at the first girl's Gymnasium in Vienna, which had been founded by the progressive Eugenie Schwarzwald. It was to this end he produced the periodical, *The Other*, whose purpose was to remind the Austrian public that the first quality of good design and, indeed, good taste, is its unobtrusive character: it makes life simpler, not more complicated, more natural, not more elaborate. If the challenge was great, the goal was simple in the words of Kraus:

> Adolf Loos and I – he literally and I grammatically – have done nothing else than to show that there is a distinction between an urn and a chamber pot and that it is this distinction above all which provides culture with elbow room. The others, who fail to make this distinction, are divided into those who use the urn as a chamber pot and those who use the chamber pot as urn.[165]

In a culture so fascinated by ornamental »beauty« that it sought to embellish a butter knife by turning it into a Turkish dagger, an ash tray into a Prussian helmet and a thermometer into a pistol, and in which every material tried to look like more than it was[166], Loos fought desperately to demonstrate that there is a fundamental distinction between art and utility, between functionality and fantasy, that we ignore at the price of our incapacity to understand anything at all except superficially. In this spirit Kraus would later insist that World War I was happening precisely because we could not imagine it.[167] Viennese aestheticism in its fascination with decoration was on the verge of criminality in its disavowal of fundamental values and in the end rationality and objectivity itself. Thus Loos would insist »cultural evolution is equivalent to the removal of ornament from articles in daily use«.[168] Thus Loos proclaimed a revolution against revolution, not because he was a counter-revolutionary, but because the very term »revolution« had been co-opted into the mainstream of Viennese *Jugendstil* conventionality. In his writing, as in his building, Loos demanded that scrupulous attention be paid to precisely that solid craftsmanship that conventional Viennese »good taste« tended to ignore or ever suppress.

The dazzling character of Loos' polemical essay, »Ornament and Crime«, which the MIT architecture historian, Stanford Anderson, insists is highly unreliable as a guide to Loos' architecture[169], has tended to obscure his emphasis upon the paramount role of craftsmanship in building. He summarized his views succinctly in a manifesto which originally was published in the *Jahrbuch der Schwarzwald'schen Schulanstalten* in Vienna and later reprinted by Ludwig von Ficker in *Der Brenner* in Innsbruck that is brief enough to be cited here in its entirety:

7. ADOLF LOOS ...

Rules for Building in the Mountains

Don't build colorfully. Leave that to the walls, the mountains and the sun. He who dresses colorfully isn't colorful but simply a clown.

Build as well as you can. Not better. Don't be presumptuous. Not worse either. Don't express yourself intentionally at a lower level than the one your birth and education place you upon. That applies to your mountain walks as well. Talk to the peasants in your own language. The Viennese lawyer who speaks to peasants in bumpkin stage dialect[170] has to be exterminated.

Pay attention to the forms that peasants employ when building. For their content runs replete with ancestral wisdom. But seek out the reason for the form. If technical progress has made it possible to improve on the form, this improvement should always be employed. The threshing flail is replaced by the threshing machine.

Plains require structuring buildings vertically; mountains horizontally. The work of man should not compete with the work of God. Hapsburg watchtowers disturb the chain of the Vienna Woods, but the Hussars' Temple melts harmoniously into them.

Don't think of the roof, rather think of the rain and the snow. That's how the peasant thinks and thus he builds the flattest roof that his technical expertise permits in the mountains. In the mountains the snow should not slide off when *it* wants to, but rather when the peasant wants it to. For that reason he has to be able to climb up onto the roof in order to remove the snow. So we too have to produce the flattest roof that our technical expertise allows.

Be true! Nature only suffers truth. Iron reinforced bridges fit well into Her, but She rejects Gothic arches with ramparts and firing slits

Don't be afraid of being chided as unmodern. Radical departures from the old ways of building are only allowed if they clearly mean improvement. Otherwise stick with the old ways. For truth, even if it is hundreds of years old has a more immediate relationship to us than the lie that strides alongside us.[171]

This text is of particular interest for the remarkable way that it presents all of the themes near and dear to Loos' heart in an extraordinarily succinct, entirely concrete way: the campaign again ornament, the demand for integrity, the sense of tradition and the subordination of technological development to it, contextualism, the importance of Nature, the architectural concept of truth and, finally, the *courage* to be »old fashioned« when being modern. Above all, it is a clear statement of Loos' fundamental belief that practice as incorporated in living tradition is the only reliable guide to building.

His own architectural principles, he insisted, were Roman rather than Greek. What impressed him was the fact that the Romans, unlike the Greeks, constructed buildings from the inside out.

It is no accident that the Romans were not able to invent a new order of columns, a new ornament. They had progressed too far for that. They took everything that they could from the Greeks and adapted it to their own purposes.

7. ADOLF LOOS ...

> The Greeks were individualists. Each building has to have its own profile, its own ornamentation. The Romans thought socially. The Greeks were hardly in a position to govern their cities, the Romans could govern the entire earth. The Greeks wasted their powers of invention in the orders of columns; the Romans concentrated them on the floor plan. And those who can solve he problem of the large-scale floor plan do not have to think about new profiles.[172]

A leading authority on Central European architecture of the period, Ákos Moravánsky, comments upon what Loos learned from the Romans' atrium principle with respect to the infamous *Haus am Michaelerplatz*, which so scandalized old Emperor Francis Joseph that he never used the main entrance to his palace opposite it again, as follows:

> The interior of the department store in the Looshaus was developed around the spatial cage of the stairs. Loos' idea, the *Raumplan*, the interlacing, continuous structure of interior space, is the important result of his critical attack against surface decoration. The destruction of the traditional tectonics of the house, replaced by an isomorphous spatial grid or by cubist folded forms was a process in which all the major Central European architects of early modernism participated, but others did not make its spatial results a conceptual goal. Loos was proud that photographs could not capture his interiors, that he destroyed the »picture« character of the home.[173]

The idea that interior space is continuous and interlacing across the storeys of a building, then, is the fundamental principle of Loosian architecture. It explains how Loos could claim that he was building the house from the inside out and at the same time it explains his aversion to decorated facades, for the very act of decorating requires structuring the building from the outside and ultimately subordinating function to ornament. On his view the façade is more or less irrelevant to the structure of the building. In all this it is important to point out that the very building whose unadorned simplicity so scandalized the old Emperor was entirely traditional inasmuch as it strictly separated public, business space from private living space even with respect to its façade.[174]

In describing how the Adolf Loos *Bauschule* functioned, Loos gives us further important clues about the distinguishing features of his way of building. The three principles around which he oriented the education of his students were *style*, *form* and *material*. So his pupils studied interior consolidation, art history, and what we would today call materials science. Moreover, their education was oriented around project work so that they might learn from one another how to grapple with the problems presented by the challenge of building from the inside outwards. Learning to build that way meant considering the floor plan of a house as a three dimensional cube, whose distribution of axes, i.e., floors and ceilings, presented the young would-be architect with no small difficulty. The overall aim was to capture a particular *mood*; the *je ne sais quoi* of what Wittgenstein terms a form of life, its ephemeral defining quality. On Loos' view, capturing that mood is only possible on the basis of a knowledge of traditional forms of building practice, i.e., of those who had previously been successful in creating the desired mood. Tradition should be a continual source of inspiration for architects, at once a source if ideas and a kind of limit within which truly functional architecture must move (one important point which distinguishes Loos from the Bauhaus, with which he is perennially confused). Thus tradition can mean many things. For Loos it was clear that architecture went wrong when architects ceased to pay attention to craftsmen and began to put their trust in books.[175] Then drawing ceased to be a mere means to an end. The result was that the architect lost his relation to the practice of building and, ultimately, became an artist. There is a noteworthy affinity with Arnold Schoenberg's concluding remark to the first chapter of his *Theory of Harmony*: »... I would be proud ... if I could say I have taken a bad aesthetics away from students of composition and given them a solid set of teachings about skill«[176]. That could just as well have been written by, Loos – or Wittgenstein. (Indeed, the idea of becoming degraded to the status of an artist echoes a theme in both Weininger and Nietzsche[177] but it would take us too far a field to explore that topic.)

Decadence had set in. Loos' task was to fight it tooth and nail. It was not that there was merely a single error at work a whole constellation of values that had come to be identified to what is modern were at stake in the issue of the relationship between art and architecture. The focus of the debate for Loos was the private house:

> The house has to please everybody. In contrast to the work of art that does not have to please anybody. The work of art is the artist's private affair. The work of art is put into the world without any need for it. The house is the response to a necessity. The work of art is not responsible to anybody, the house to everybody. The work of art aims at wrenching people out of their ease. The house serves the purpose of making them comfortable. The work of art is revolutionary, the house conservative. The work of art shows humanity new paths and thinks of the future. The house thinks in the present. People love everything that serves their comfort. They hate everything that wrenches them from the secure position they have won for themselves. Thus people love houses and hate art.

> *So has the house nothing whatsoever to do with art and is architecture not to be considered an art? That's the way it is.* Only a small part of architecture belongs to art: the tombstone and the statue. Everything else that belongs to the sphere of the purposeful should be excluded from that of art.[178]

Art is a matter of individual creative intelligence, building a social affair, a utilitarian task of an entirely different order. So it is a corollary of his view that the architect is fundamentally a craftsman that architecture is not art. These spheres remain integral only as long as long as they are rigorously separated.[79] Ornamented facades are masks that paradoxically conceal the identity of those who live in such houses from everybody, including themselves – and the architects who construct them. Thus there is powerful Socratic thrust in Loos' insistence that architecture and art have to be kept apart.

How can this help us to understand Wittgenstein's mature concept of philosophical method? It is not an easy question to answer. In order to venture a response let us begin by considering Wittgenstein's views about architecture and philosophy, proceed to examine his own contribution to architecture in the light of those remarks and conclude with some reflections upon the role of art and craftsmanship in his understanding of what philosophy is all about.

In *Culture and Value* he writes in a Socratic vein that is not entirely foreign to Loos, »Working in philosophy – like work in architecture in many respects – is really more a working on oneself. On one's own conceptions of things. On one's way of seeing things. (And of what one expects of them.).«(16) Wittgenstein agrees with Loos[180] that the period in which he works, however, drastically limits an architect's ability to do good work and continually tempts him to inferior solutions for his problems. (*C+V*, 5) The architect – and presumably the

7. ADOLF LOOS ...

philosopher – is at the mercy of the predominant values of their epoch – a notion that we also find in Spengler, who seems himself to be profoundly influenced by Loos in his discussions of architecture. He must be continually on guard to defend the integrity of his subject, which is for that reason inherently polemical. So there can be little doubt that Wittgenstein saw a parallel between philosophy and architecture as an activity of clarification.

It will do well to remind ourselves here of how Paul Wijdeveld's trenchant analysis of Wittgenstein's achievement in the construction of the house for his sister provides us with a clear example of how Wittgenstein understood clarification in architecture. Paul Engelmann, who made the original drawings, was principally acting as a draftsman, rather than a fullfledged architect, for Gretl Stonborough. Mrs. Stonborough systematically frustrated Loos' student, Engelmann, by strictly ruling out a house designed around the Loosian conception of functionality (the so-called *Raumplanung*). Instead, she wanted to have a traditional semi-aristocratic city mansion. When Ludwig joined the project in late summer 1926 he was able to realize her wishes to build a traditional house in a modern way (it has become increasingly clear that her wishes were the decisive factor in determining the nature of the house[181]). Moravánsky contrasts Loos and Wittgenstein as follows:

> As a consequence of the *Raumplan* principle, the interior spaces of Loos strike the visitor as negative volumes, carved out of a building mass. Their niche-like enclosedness, emphasized by lower ceilings, contributed to the intimacy of house as »home«. The interior of the Wittgenstein house appears more generous and transparent because it is not compartmentalized. The structural columns are always freestanding, while Loos always ties them to a parapet, a stair or built-in furniture, to underline the direction of spatial movement.[182]

Only the smooth, unadorned façade is modern. The classical progression of the windows, as we have seen, betrays the architect's traditionalism. As for the interior, Wijdeveld suggests that it is an effort to purify, to clarify, the essence of classical monumental architecture. So Wittgenstein would employ the *stucco lustro*, the favored material for churches and palaces since the baroque. The stone slabs of the floor, the unadorned pillars, the naked light bulbs and the two winged doors all reflect what we might consider Wittgenstein's Hertzian alternative realization of the traditional city mansion reflected in the concerns of an engineer and ultimately a craftsman.

The lack of ornamentation and the austerity of exterior and interior did not result from the need to create a new architectural aesthetic form from the technical and constructional developments in the late 19th and early 20th centuries, but from the wish to clarify the roots of traditional monumental architecture as exemplified by the work of Johann Bernhard Fischer von Erlach, whom he greatly admired.[183]

In effect, Wijdeveld has shown how Wittgenstein, despite working in a different architectural idiom from Loos, was entirely consistent with Loos' demand to »knock all of the ornaments off our old and new buildings such that only naked walls would remain«. His house, for all its un-Loosian character, bears that out. However, this runs exactly parallel to his sketch for a Foreword to the *Philosophical Remarks* printed in *Culture and Value* (7) where he says, »I am not interested in constructing a building, so much as having a synoptic view of the foundations of possible buildings«. He took this to be what distinguished him from modern scientists (and a-fortiori scientific philosophers of his day, i.e., the Vienna Circle).

Yet, like Loos and unlike so many opponents of »scientific« philosophy in the so-called Continental tradition from Nietzsche through Heidegger to Derrida his alternative was

7. ADOLF LOOS ...

not an »artistic« philosophy. Wittgenstein considered that his philosophizing stood a definite relationship to art but was, nevertheless, to be distinguished from art. In 1930 Wittgenstein wrote:

> »Now it seems to me that there is another way of capturing the world *sub specie aeterni* apart from the work of the artist ... thought ... can fly over the world as it were and the leaves it as it is – observing it from above in flight.
> (C+V, 7)

Clearly philosophy is not art, even if it should have a strong resemblance to art. It might even have a certain »poetic« character without being poetry. This assertion might seem to fly in the face of Wittgenstein's aphorism, »Philosophie dürfte man eigentlich nur *dichten*« (C+V, 28) but only if one identifies *Dichtung* in a Romantic vein with lyric poetry (as opposed simply to fiction) and only if one neglects to consider the profound role that skill plays in literary production. Moreover, his philosophy should be businesslike; it should get a job done.[184] In order to present a Hertzian synoptic view of the workings of language, which turn out to bear principally upon use and, ultimately tradition, Wittgenstein strove in the manner of a craftsman to develop a set of philosophical techniques for reminding us of all those incredibly important things, whose very simplicity and familiarity (*PI*, I, 129) prevent us from seeing them. These techniques amounted to a curious way of writing fiction with a view to reminding us of striking facts that the surface grammar of language seduces us into passing over – e.g., the plurality of activities that correspond to the innumerable modes of »thinking.« This is why his philosophy must be a sort of analysis without being what is usually thought of as analytic philosophy. The result was, indeed, great beauty which could only be grasped in the basis of great intellectual effort but is was the beauty of craftwork not art.

We can see this if we return to Wittgenstein's work in architecture again for a moment. We have already noted that Wittgenstein's own concern for craftsmanship is most clearly evident in the metal doors, door handles and window latches, which reflect the skill of the mechanical engineer. In short, the »beauty« in Wittgenstein architecture is the result of his consummate craftsmanship. It has rightly been compared with the kind of simple elegant beauty produced by American Shaker furniture makers.[185] Those doors and windows are dramatic examples of the way Wittgenstein's »aesthetics« are determined on the basis of skill rather than art.[186] The same holds true of his »philosophical work of clarification«. As such both are continuous with the work of Loos both as architect and as cultural critic. How is that true?

By the time that Loos had become important for him Wittgenstein had already learned from Russell that the surface grammar of language can tempt even the most insightful philosopher to pose loaded questions to himself, questions whose answers provoke us into formulating covertly nonsensical propositions as the answer to profoundly puzzling questions. Like Russell, the critic of metaphysics has to be armed with a *technique* for showing how we have smuggled confusion into our own thinking by formulating the questions that we do about the nature of thinking or the essence of language in philosophy. The most fruitful application of this approach to philosophical problems in the *Tractatus* was the invention of truth tables, which enabled him to solve Frege's problem about the nature, number and properties of logical axioms. However, solve is the wrong word for truth tables turn out to be a mechanical technique for showing with absolute clarity what propositions are tautologies belonging to logic and distinguishing them from impossible propositions (i.e., contradictions) and empirical propositions. That technique of representation made the whole debate over axioms superfluous – and obviously so. In effect, Russell (and Hertz) had shown him the way to understanding things that were in Frege in a more profound way than Frege, who clearly envisaged the concept of the truth table himself did not. The point is that, if Russell showed Wittgenstein the importance of technique (Wittgenstein would have already a solid sense of its importance in science from Boltzmann) in philosophy, Loos showed him *how that technique was part of a craft*.

In Wittgenstein's mature philosophy, as we have had frequent occasion to reiterate, no single technique is sufficient for disabusing us of our tendency to ask for the meaning independently of considering how terms are used in language. In fact, the notion that we obtain philosophical insight by considering use is clearly present in the *Tractatus* at 6.211 in the parenthetical statement: »In philosophy the question, 'What do we actually use this word or this proposition for?' repeatedly leads to valuable insights.)«. In fact, the notion of practice around which his mature thought revolves is already present there *in nuce*. The point is clearly continuous with what we have seen Loos insisting to be the basis of good architecture, i.e., understanding architectural practice. In the *Tractatus* the notion of use comes to play a crucial role in demarcating the various kinds of meaning that a sign can have (3.321ff). In addition, use in language shows which signs are identical with one another and which are not, which turns out to be a reason for rejecting the idea that we need propositions that assert identity. Brian McGuinness attributes Wittgenstein's notion that unnecessary units in a sign-language are superfluous as part of his heritage from Loos and as Wittgenstein's way of eliminating ornament in philosophy.[187] It is no less important that a certain understanding of use determines what counts as ornament (i.e., as metaphysical) in language.

This is all crucial here because it is precisely this constellation of concepts that develop into the core of his so-called later philosophy. Briefly, as the concept of use develops into the myriad ways of interweaving words and actions our possibilities for confusing ourselves about the nature of objective reality (now construed as use, i.e., practice itself) demands not simply mechanical techniques for disabusing us of the confusions that ensue from taking the surface grammar for the depth grammar of language but the artful use of techniques (which turns out to be identical with the »language game« method of analyzing practice) to wean us away from the seductive powers of external linguistic forms.

Enter the philosophical craftsman. His function would be to assemble reminders of what we actually do with words such that our tendencies to pose metaphysical questions about practice would disappear. So Wittgenstein would collect notes on the natural history of an animal that speaks – and even make fictive forays into natural history, to show us »what would be different if ...«. These efforts would be in aid of disabusing us of the desire to ask oversimplified questions, employ misleading examples and form crude judgments on the basis of misconstruing the logic of language. Those techniques would include examples, which were mostly fictive, aphorisms and, above all, questions, some answered, most not, several falsely answered on purpose. A very strange set of techniques indeed. In totality they hardly resemble traditional philosophy at all. But why should they? Wittgenstein aimed, as he put it himself, at putting the troubled philosophical mind to rest once and for all. That was a matter of showing traditional philosophers that their very questions rest upon a misunderstanding of the logic of language. In an early version of section 106 of part I of the

Investigations Wittgenstein writes in a vein that Hegel could approve of[188]: »One of our most important tasks is to express all false thought processes so characteristically that the other says: yes, that's just the way I meant it«.[189] He has to be put into a position where his difficulties cease to be difficulties and he finally attains peace of mind. The first step to doing so is to get the views of those he would criticize straight, then, and only then, would he be in a position to show that those views were incoherent such as the idea of a private language or that the question posed was in fact a loaded question »what is the essence of thought?«. Wittgenstein's philosophical task was to develop intellectual techniques for doing so. His questions, examples and aphorisms aim at introducing new comparisons and in so doing enabling philosophers to overcome their fixation on the idea that the essence of language is representation (or, for that matter, anything else) His intellectual craftsmanship is eminently literary without being »art« – a way of helping philosophical flies out of fly bottles. Moreover, it was precisely the craftsman's approach to philosophy that enabled a »merely reproductive« thinker like him to understand the work of others, including Hertz, Frege and Kraus, better than they did themselves (C+V, 17). Finally, dissatisfaction with his intellectual craftsmanship, rather than an inherent inability to put what he wanted to say into words, as is sometimes alleged, that led him to disparage being able to write a good book in the Preface to the *Philosophical Investigations*, a matter of finding the *mot juste*, rather than despair at being able to express himself at all.

In *Culture and Value* he would reflect upon whether he was not really demanding that we live in a different way: »I am by no means sure, that I should prefer a continuation of my work by others to a change in the way people live which would make all these questions superfluous« (C+V, 70). This surely implies that philosophers, like architects, do not get to choose the circumstances in which they ply their trade. Socio-cultural forces of the sort that Kraus had long been battling against continually threaten to drag their attention from *der Sache selbst*. Part of doing philosophy for him thus involved the prophetic role of calling philosophers gone astray back to objectivity. It entailed the courage to defy conventional ways of thinking and an inability to question the tacit assumptions of classical philosophers from Descartes to Russell. Thus Wittgenstein discovered that there was a moment of social criticism, an inherently moral dimension, to practicing philosophy as a craftsman, one that could not be said but only shown in how one did philosophy. It involved getting straight about the limits of the world and of philosophical thought. Otto Weininger would supply him with the link between philosophy, aesthetics and ethics that would at once help Wittgenstein to get straight about his own life and transform the project that he undertook for Russell into the *Tractatus* as we know it as well as inform the spirit of his later work.

CHAPTER 8

Otto Weininger: The Problem of Limits

EVEN PRIOR TO WORLD WAR I we find indications of that moral intensity in Wittgenstein, which subsequently became typical of the man and his work. Thus he informed Russell that he was reading William James's *The Varieties of Religious Experience* in 1912 in the vain hope of becoming a saint.[190] Somewhat later Wittgenstein told Russell in a midnight visit that his disturbingly silent, hour-long pacing in Russell's rooms was motivated by reflections about logic *and* his sins.[191] When the war broke out, to the dismay of his family, Wittgenstein enlisted as a buck private to put his character to the test (*GT*, 10.VIII.14). Many years afterward Norman Malcolm related that he was afraid that Wittgenstein might kill himself if he was convinced that he could no longer do philosophy.[192] Nothing in his intellectual background goes further than his encounter with Otto Weininger to account for the intimate relationship between the substance of Wittgenstein's personal values and his philosophical views at all stages of his development after 1916. All in all, Wittgenstein's intense concern with both logic *and* his sins has a distinctly Weiningerian flavor. To be sure his Schopenhauerian wrestling with the opacity of the self and his Fregean striving for objectivity in his own life are crucial aspects of the story but it is his encounter with Weininger and the problem of limits that goes farthest in explaining the characteristic moral passion that informed his philosophy and, indeed, everything that he did.

In fact we have seen exactly when Wittgenstein's personal and his philosophical concerns began to fuse.[193] It was in 1916 in the wake of the most devastating series of battles in the First World War, the Brusilov Offensive, in which he distinguished himself for valor under fire, he writes,

> Colossal strain in the last month. Have reflected much about everything but curiously incapable of producing the connection with my mathematical trains of thought. However, the connection will be produced! What cannot be said *cannot* be said! (*GT*, 6–7.VII.16).

He had attained clarity about his problems relating to logic in terms of an Hertzian alternative representation of propositions on truth tables according to a suggestion from Frege's *Begriffschrift*. Now he was determined to take the same, approach, ultimately inspired by Frege's anti-psychologistic notion of objectivity, to his existential problems. The problems of life must »dissolve« of themselves on the basis of a way of living (*GT*, 26.XI,14; cf. *C+V*, 27) that could be described as objective in the sense that it conformed to his actual situation rather than his fantasies. It is precisely at the point where Wittgenstein began to »produce« that connection, as he put it, that Otto Weininger began to be philosophically important to him. Wittgenstein's reference to the parallel between the solutions to his mathematical and his existential problems would indicate the imperative to produce that connection seems to have originated with Frege. Moreover, the similarities between Wittgenstein and »Continental philosophers«[194] such as Friedrich Nietzsche, Søren Kierkegaard, and Martin Heidegger, with their roots in his early encounter with Schopenhauer become more pronounced at this turn in his thinking.

Thus, curiously, in a way that is without precedent in the history of analytical philosophy, Wittgenstein struggled to produce a common solution to *both* his existential problems and his philosophical problems. Heinrich Hertz had taught him that »showing« is the only strict way to resolve philosophical problems, i.e., by dissolving them on the basis of an alternative representation of the problematic matter. Schopenhauer challenged him to get straight about the relationship between the self – himself – and the world: the first set of questions about these topics, which appear so dramatically in his early *Notebooks* on the 1st (or 4th) of July (misdated in the printed edition as 11.6.16[195]): »what do I know about God and the sense of life? etc.« are framed in Schopenhauer's terms. Thus he would employ a few pages in Weininger's *Über die letzten Dinge*[196] to answer the existential questions about God and the sense of life that he had inherited from Schopenhauer but which Frege's demand to transcend mere subjectivity and arbitrariness had *pressed* upon him in a very peculiar way. (To be sure, James and Tolstoy also played a role in that most crucial chapter in his philosophical biography but it was a secondary one.) Weininger would ultimately help him attain the clarity he sought here.

G. H. von Wright has called attention to Wittgenstein's profound interest in the section of Weininger's *Über die letzten Dinge* called, »Animal Psychology« already referred to in connection with »the mystical« in the *Tractatus*.[197] It is only now that we understand Wittgenstein's relation to Hertz, Schopenhauer and Frege that we can appreciate the full importance of this aspect of Weininger's work for his development. Inter-textual evidence indicates that the breakthrough of July 1916 was connected to reading Weininger's curious fragment on animal psychology. How did that text come to have such great importance for him?

The following passages introduce the concerns that deeply disturbed the man and the philosopher at that time: »What is it to be happy?« »What is it to live without fear and hope?« (14.VII.16); »How is the subject a limit of the world?« (2.VIII.16; 2.IX.16); »Man is the microcosm« (12.X.16); »The spirit of animals is your spirit« 14.X.16); »I have to judge the world« (2.IX.16). Furthermore, all of these matters were intimately linked to the problem of solipsism posed by Schopenhauer's philosophy in Wittgenstein's eyes.[198]

David Pears has produced an insightful account of how the confrontation with solipsism as the limit of language forms an axis around which all of Wittgenstein's thinking revolves,[199] which is particularly relevant to grasping what he took over from Weininger. Beginning from his encounter with Russell's views about solipsism in 1913 (which doubtless complimented deep personal concerns), where Russell observes that my experience of any given object is somehow more than that object because it is my object, Wittgenstein became increasingly fascinated by the mysterious way in which the self is a correlative of the world. However, in the course of the War there was a radical transformation in Wittgenstein's attitude to this problem connected to the way the world and the self mutually limit one another that is foreign to Russell but became increasingly important for Wittgenstein. Indeed, Russell's way of conceiving the problem of the relation between the Self and the world could hardly inspire the sort of »obsession with limits«[200] that we find in his *Notebooks* and would characterize all of his future philosophizing. Neglecting Weininger, Pears ascribes that transition to the influence Schopenhauer,

8. OTTO WEININGER ...

who transformed Wittgenstein's thinking about the matter as well as the intensity with which he pursued the issue. In this context Schopenhauer gave Wittgenstein a complex picture of the self according to which it was at once 1) the seat of representation and thinking but at the same time, 2) a nebulous set of pre-rational urges that I am, the Will. This twofold notion of the self had profound implications inasmuch as it helps to establish 3) a metaphysical significance for art as a release from willing and a way of contemplating the world as a whole. Schopenhauer posed the questions, he set the scene as it were; Weininger would not simply provide the answer (it was not that kind of question to begin with) but a scenario for living objectively. Both the testimony of his colleagues and intertextual evidence point to the centrality of Weininger at this crucial stage in his development.

It seems that in his description of The Criminal Weininger gave him something philosophically vivid that he could ruminate upon with his entire personal intensity. How, then, did Weininger further help Wittgenstein in his effort to let the problems of life dissolve of themselves? The answer is not, as we have said, that Weininger provided him with a solution to his problems but that he gave him a Hertzian striking alternative picture of the relationship between the Self and the world, the Will and the facts to the conventional one. Moreover, it was less the »truth« of Weininger's ideas than their power to grip him intellectually, i.e., to help him restate his problem so that it »dissolved« that was crucial.[201] Ultimately, it would help him get on with the business of living in a situation where his life could come to an end at any moment. How does the picture of the self with which Weininger presented Wittgenstein look? How did Wittgenstein use it?

To begin with, we must grasp that Weininger is not concerned with making empirical generalizations about the mentality of actual people, rather, he is producing a thought experiment about the nature of immorality with a view to establishing by implication what genuine moral behavior is. The point of producing this quasi-phenomenological description is to move the reader to reflect upon what it really is to be happy and to lead a good life by giving us the negative example of their opposites. Weininger's criminal is that person who lives as though there were no limits upon him. In developing this picture Weininger in fact describes the polar opposite of Kant's autonomous human being – and the Christian notion of doing unto others as you would have them do unto you. Thus Weininger takes Criminality to be a continuation of original sin. The criminal's sin, like original sin, is nothing other than selfishness, the will to self-assertion, the pursuit of happiness at any cost, the refusal to acknowledge any authority outside of one's self. Ultimately immorality, here termed criminality, is to be understood in terms of successfully living without limits, i.e., possessing wonderful things without having worked for them. It is nothing other than the vulgar concept of »happiness«. To this end the Criminal will manipulate anything that he can get hold of. Indeed, he views everything as an extension of himself, subject to his Will and existing for his pleasure. On this view human life there is no room for guilt whatsoever. Yet, unbeknownst to himself the Criminal is in fact the »unhappiest man« because he has encapsulated himself solipsistically in his »earthly« existence by virtue of his very successes.

The Criminal world is psychologically egoistic, morally nihilistic and ontologically accidental. It has no principle of inner unity. The reality of things is a function of the criminal's ego. It is only coherent as long as the criminal is successful, in failure everything falls nightmarishly to pieces. In all situations he is master or slave, possessor or possessed. The criminal wants to destroy everything that he cannot possess – or be destroyed by it. There is a certain flip-flop in his character, whereby greed and fatalism are two sides of single coin, for he is a fatalist with respect what he cannot have or has lost. Thus he goes to the gallows without feelings of guilt or remorse but, nevertheless, resigned that it is simply his lot. Being dominated is entirely consistent with the desire to possess; it is simply its obverse: being possessed by Fate.

The Criminal's world is the opposite of that of the Nietzschean *Übermensch*, who affirms the order in the world and its suffering as he finds it. Since the principle of reality is the fulfillment of the Criminal's wishes, the Criminal World is a curious kind of expressionistic dream world, in which fear and hope reign supreme (adding boredom to the constellation, you get a scenario not unlike Kierkegaard's analysis of Don Juan in *Either/Or* or his discussion of selfhood and possession *The Sickness unto Death*). The past and the present are uninteresting to him. Only the prospect of future self-aggrandizement interests him. He is essentially anti-social because he is incapable of recognizing the intrinsic worth of the Other, who, as Other, is a limit upon him. He can never be a comrade, for he enters relationship with a view to exploiting the Other. Thus the sexual exploitation that Don Juan embodies is a paradigm case of criminality inasmuch as the Don can never relate to the other as an »I« to a »Thou«. Weininger goes so far as to insist that Don Juan's exploitation of women is morally equivalent to murder. Beyond that, it certainly would not have been lost on Wittgenstein, that Weininger's Criminal is compulsively talkative,[202] always chattering to somebody, even when he is alone. However, his words are never true, but only a function of his wishful thinking. Like the alcoholic who despises drunkards, he experiences anxiety and disgust when confronted with his own self-image. He cannot bear to be alone. Thus he has no real life of his own, which is reflected in his lack of respect for others. Being spiritually dead, he is capable of killing the Other without compunction. Finally, and perhaps most significantly in connection with Wittgenstein, his very attitude to knowledge is determined by wishful thinking:

> his drive to know is never pure, hopeful, needy, longing, never directed against insanity, never an inner need for self preservation, rather he wants to force things and also to know. The idea that something should be impossible for him contradicts his absolute functionalist mentality that will join itself to everything and everything to itself. Therefore, he finds the idea of bounds or limits, *even of knowledge* (my emphasis AJ), intolerable.[203]

It is precisely here that Wittgenstein found the common solution to both his existential and his intellectual problems. Henceforth they both must be solved in the only rigorous way, i.e., on the basis of drawing limits from within (*F*, Letter 23, undated).

This is a completely different approach to the problem of solipsism from the one that we find in Russell's reflections in »On the Nature of Acquaintance« which are purely epistemological. However, Wittgenstein seems to have sought and found a connection between them in the acknowledgement that the Self is mysteriously linked to the limits of language: »It is true: Man is the microcosm. I am my world« (*N*, 12.X.16). Precisely this notion of man as microcosm seemed to provide him with a key to both his philosophical and his existential problems.

The notion of the microcosm would seem to be exactly Wittgenstein's »mystical« point of departure in the discussion that appears so abruptly in the notebooks of 1916 about God and the meaning of life. His remarks proceed from the (curious) notion that despite its independence of the world my will penetrates the world, without being able to change any of the facts – a view which is clearly continuous with Weininger's concerns in »Animal Psychology«. In fact, Wittgenstein's emphasis that my Will is independent of the facts is the exact obverse of the Weiningerian criminal who wallows in his own causality as it were. All of Wittgenstein's questions and remarks in the 1916 notebook can profitably be read against the background of Weininger's view of the »functionalist« Criminal who refuses to recognize any ethical or logical limits to his action.

In this scenario logic and ethics are *both* »transcendental«, i.e., conditions of the world as I find it, precisely because the Will or the Self at once penetrates the world (as good or evil, happy or unhappy) and constitutes the facts that are its substance in the application of logic. Just as logic must take care of itself, the problems of life must be solved in the living and not in a set of beliefs about it or expectations from it. In both instances the problems must disappear (*N*, 6.VII.16). Happiness is a matter of learning that I can only master the world (the facts) by making myself independent of them, Wittgenstein claims in a Spinozistic turn (here again the project character of the enterprise is emphasized) that independence is a matter of taking a position with respect to the world (»eine Stellungnahme zur Welt« *N*, 4.11.16[204]). Wittgenstein insists with Weininger that »I must judge the world, measure things« (*N*, 2.9.16) – this is neither Schopenhauer nor Russell nor Tolstoy but it is Weininger: »judging is a phenomenon of the will; the Criminal does not judge [things]«.[205] To will is not merely to wish but to act, to live fully in the present without fear and hope. Fear and hope, it should be noted, presuppose that I identify myself with what I possess or what I want to possess – in the most extreme case with life itself considered as something which I have, as opposed to something which I *am*. Fear and hope presuppose loss and gain as well as a past and a future in which said loss or gain can transpire. When I abandon the idea that life is a possession to be hoarded, the problem of life disappears. I have nothing more to fear. Thus it would seem that an evil life would be one in which I expected to be rewarded for my actions. In the end the happy life is a life in which our actions are by their nature rewarding because they are »harmonious«. Thus the Spinozistic element is transformed with the help of Frege and Weininger into an Aristotelian point here as ethics and aesthetics become one in a profound sense. Such a happy life is an active one, dedicated to living in the present and to work in the form of the pursuit of knowledge, i.e., exactly what those »Secret Diaries« show him striving for.

Yet, it is certainly not accidental that one of the only propositions from the logical part of *Tractatus* to be found in the »Secret Diaries« is proposition six which states that simultaneous negation is the general form of the proposition (*GT*, 21.VIII.14) – nor is it accidental that that proposition should also be reflected upon in the 1916 notebook (*N*, 13.VII.16) in the middle of his ruminations about God and the world. Logic exists only in its application, which determines a state of affairs in the world. Ethics too is a matter of recognizing in action that the self or the will and the world mutually limit one another. The »I« (the Self or the Will) is a limit of the world: the facts of themselves, neither happy nor unhappy, limit what I am. It seems as though the application of the Sheffer stroke »p | q« (neither p nor q), simultaneous negation somehow provided Wittgenstein with the key to understanding both logic and ethics. On the one hand, when simultaneous negation is given truth and falsity and therefore the condition of the possibility, as it were, of all other truth functions is also given, i.e., all possible propositions are given. On the other, the vain attempt to deny that the world is neither a happy nor unhappy world produces insight into the experience that the world is always *my* world. Its substance always has a »mood«, as Heidegger puts it.[206] Simultaneous negation »shows« both the general form of the proposition, i.e., as truth function, but is also capable of illuminating that inarticulable relationship between the Self and the world that we first find in Schopenhauer and that Heidegger attempts to capture in the phrase the »Jemeinigkeit der Welt«.[207] Indeed, this seems to be the difference between the mere facts and »the world« for Wittgenstein. Everything that bears upon the world as my world and the form of the world as such must take care of itself. Problems with both logic and ethics must be solved in action, i.e. in application. The application of logic shows us the nature of the world as it confers form upon it. Furthermore, the act of applying logic shows us an aspect of reality which we know with moral certainty without being able to describe in propositions, namely, the self that we are. The prominent reference to Heidegger in Wittgenstein's conversations with Schlick more that 10 years later is a clear indication that we are not amiss to refer to parallels between him and Wittgenstein here.[208] Moreover, Russell's way of playing fast and loose with axioms in logic is clear evidence that it is not absurd to consider the subject from the moral point of view.

How is this reflected in the *later* Wittgenstein? To answer that question we should consider the fact that at roughly the same time that Wittgenstein came under the influence of Weininger he also realized that the problems of philosophy were rooted in a quasi-transcendental source, namely, our tendency to misunderstand the logic of language. This is one of the important features that unite the two Wittgensteins, early and late. Moreover, the idea that philosophical problems rest upon misconstruing the logic of language, which he attributes to Paul Ernst[209], is intimately related to the task of showing the limits of language from within. This is a point where we ought to feel Weininger's influence as well; for the whole point of Weininger's philosophizing was to demonstrate that there is within human nature something like a transcendental source of self-deception (which his theory of bisexuality could *inter alia* explain).[210]

With that in mind let us look at Wittgenstein's mature view of philosophy. By now the terrain that we must cover has become familiar. What do we find of Weininger's notion of limits there? In fact, the question amounts to asking »what is left of the mystical in the later philosophy?« for the concept of the limits of language provided the grounds for introducing it in the first place. There are at least five interrelated points of continuity that should be discussed here. First, there is the rejection of theory in philosophy. Second, we have the notion of pragmatic contradiction according to which we must recognize conceptual limits. Third, is the idea that the complexity of language prevents its being systematically and comprehensively treated as an object of knowledge. Fourth, the notion that humans are animals must be recognized, even in logic. Finally, Wittgenstein emphasizes the unpolitical, unheroic character of philosophy. This quietist dimension to his thought is the converse of his view that it is not ideas but a different way of living that we need to solve philosophical problems, i.e., we must dissolve them.

As far as theory goes, what is most striking at first glance is Wittgenstein's notion of philosophy as an activity directed against traditional philosophy in all its forms, not only its metaphysical (i.e., Scholastic or Cartesian) and transcendental (Hegelian or Kantian) forms, but also its traditional empiricist and conventional analytic forms.[211] In this respect his mature program is continuous with his early thought. Here Wittgenstein resembles William James inasmuch as both of them ask traditional philosophers whether their theories really make any difference to the practice of science, or, for that matter, to art or religion or anything whatever. Wittgenstein fully rejected the idea that philosophy could actually produce theories, not simply because he wanted to reform it, but on the grounds that the very notion of a philosophical theory is a curious kind of self-deception on the part of philosophers, which involves trespassing a conceptual limit. In fact Wittgenstein had shown on the basis of truth tables in the *Tractatus* that there were only two types of propositions, contingent, empirical propositions informing us about the world, and tautologies, necessary but insubstantial truths. This implies that all theories are as such on the same level: none are privileged in the sense of being any deeper than the others. Where there is theory, there is science, regardless of what it calls itself. Try as we might, we can never succeed in producing a genuinely philosophical theory any more than we can succeed in producing a private language. However, in rejecting the idea that philosophy could be a science, Wittgenstein was not prepared to dismiss the problems which troubled philosophers as mere pseudo-problems. On the contrary, for him the roots of the confusing conundrums of philosophy, has we have seen on several occasions in the course of these inquiries, are »deep disquietudes« *(tiefe Beunruhigungen)* or torments, which are rooted in language itself inasmuch as we do not have a direct grasp of its workings (*PI*, I, 111). Thus they are subject for profound reflection but the results of that reflection will not be a theory.

It cannot be exaggerated how radically his later conception of language as a plurality of game-like activities deviates from the standard views of philosophers and linguists.[212] For

Wittgenstein, language is not merely a matter of words, sign, symbols and sentences, but of how they are interwoven into gestures to form meaning. One of several functions of the game analogy is to emphasize what a small role semiotics and syntax play in it. It is what we do with words that counts. Indeed, apart from instinctive behavior such as that of the baby, which pulls its hand immediately from the fire,[213] all human action is constituted through language inasmuch as nobody ever learns anything, including how to walk, without someone talking to them. However, what is said in the course of teaching a child to walk has more to do with encouragement than it does with information. For lacking the ability to speak and thus to understand, words can only function as cues in guiding the child to grasp what we want it to *do*. Thus the notion that play is the first vehicle through which we come to understand how experience hangs together is another important and often neglected aspect of the idea that language is constituted as we play with words. On Wittgenstein's view we all learn the most basic things we know through experience, but not our own experience. Be that as it may, the point is that if we only look at words, signs, symbols and sentences, the pragmatics of meaning, the activities through which the significance of those units is constituted, will be wholly opaque to us. This is his point in wanting us to ponder the interactions of a group of builders who only use the words »block,« »pillar,« and »beam« as a complete primitive language (*PI*, I, 2); he wants to emphasize how much linguistic theorists from Plato to Chomsky have *left out* of their accounts of language. However, it is not a matter of mere ignorance: the very prominent role of referring expressions in language continually tempts us to reduce meaning to semantics and/or syntactics at the expense of pragmatics.

Given the predominant role of representational expressions (i.e., nouns and verbs) in language as it is normally understood, we are tempted reify them, i.e., to forget that the representational function is but one of many linguistic acts and a highly developed one that rests upon more primitive functions such as, say, ordering (cf. the »builders«). It is not that the forms of language themselves are essentially deceptive, but that they *tempt* us to see language and ourselves wrongly. Here, as in the *Tractatus*, the point of philosophy is to help us see the world aright, i.e., to recognize the order in the apparent chaos of everyday language. Philosophical problems originate when words like »know,« »judge,« and »thought« as well as »language« itself are confusedly taken to refer to things in the way that words like »cat,« »fork,« or »bicycle« do, i.e. such that we are inclined to understand them in the same ways. Thus we tend to look for specific things corresponding to them, rather than for a number of loosely related activities linked to each other on the basis of various sorts of analogies. However, the danger of reification is only part of the problem for Wittgenstein, because what we must learn to see is that there is in fact something corresponding to such words, but not one thing. Instead, we must learn to see the plurality of loosely related referents as a family of more and less closely related members rather than members of a single species capable of being defined by genus and specific difference.

Let us consider how the word »know« epitomizes this point. Typically nurses, golfers, and opera singers have little facility in articulating what they know in their proper functions as nurses, golfers, and opera singers. However, Socrates was wrong to infer from that that they did not know anything at all. Rather, their kind of knowledge, unlike, geometry and physics, does not lend itself directly to verbal expression. As Saint Augustine pointed out with respect to the concept of time, there are many things that I clearly grasp in practice so long as I am not asked to explain the matter (*PI*, I 89).[214] As we have seen Wittgenstein strove to develop techniques for coping with the situation by assembling reminders of the multiplicity and nuances of those particular activities and, above all, to dissuade us from invidious comparisons; in this case from equating all knowledge with, say, theoretical physics as the logical positivists did. His task in his own eyes was a literary effort to remind us of striking facts that the very nature of language tends to tempt us to pass over – e.g., the plurality of activities that correspond to the many modes of »thinking.« This is why he would insist that philosophy must be analytic without its being what is conventionally understood under the rubric analytical philosophy.

Moreover it is precisely here that the notion of the limits of language – the influence of Otto Weininger – enters into Wittgenstein's mature philosophy. Wittgenstein's celebrated rejection of the coherence of the notion of private language rests upon the notion that there are concepts that seem normal to us but in fact involve what we here term pragmatic contradictions, i.e., because they entail something which we cannot succeed in doing no matter how cleaver we are or how hard we try. Our example is not from Wittgenstein but it illustrates his point dramatically. Consider the case of someone who proposes to commit adultery with his own wife. If this is more than a metaphor, then we would have to insist that either the person in question does not understand the English language or that the person had lost his mind. In normal circumstances – like pornography, difficult to define but nevertheless clearly recognizable to the critical eye – we would hardly be able to take such a person seriously. We would think he had gone mad – which is precisely what Wittgenstein insists with respect to philosophers in *On Certainty*.

There are indeed limits of language that we ignore at our peril. These limits are, however, pragmatic and not semantic or syntactic in nature as one has, for the most part, hitherto believed. It is not that one cannot produce well-formed sentences or that these sentences are substantially incomprehensible but that they cannot do what the people that utter them would like to do with them. Just as we can sit before the chess board moving, say, the knight three squares right or left as we play. Both the figures and the board as well as the concept of »game« permit that, however, the concept of chess does not. To play such a game under the rubric chess is merely to imagine that you are playing chess, i.e., a form of self-deception. The limits of language, then, are neither syntactically nor semantically but pragmatically determined. This explains why we refer to them in speaking and even discuss the problems involved in transgressing them. The fact that we can always use words metaphorically makes the matter even more difficult: I might deliberate about sacking Troy, N.Y. or there might be a sense in which »committing adultery« with one's own wife could be meaningful in an unconventional sense, i.e., as involving a certain kind of gratifying fantasy. However, given the state of our language, a man who asserts that he wanted to commit adultery in the normal sense of the term with his own wife would be saying something nonsensical.

This brings us to our third point about the limits of knowledge in the mature Wittgenstein: language cannot be the subject of scientific study. The logic of language, the regularities that underlie it, is not a matter not formal rules but examples that we employ as canonical, i.e., paradigm cases, in learning. Learning language and, indeed, everything else is not something that can be systematized because following a rule in this sense is essentially open-textured. There will always be open questions about the relationship between rules and exceptions and new ways of following an established rule. In short, there is a tacit dimension that does not permit articulation in terms of propositions (we shall discuss it more fully in the next chapter). Our knowledge of language is necessarily a matter of reflection upon what we do when we learn to use words, signs and symbols. Moreover, since we are enmeshed in language it is extraordinarily difficult to bring ourselves into the position to reflect properly.

Thus Wittgenstein sought to develop a technique for reflection upon the games that we play when we learn and employ language that would introduce clarity into the question of, say, what it is to »know« such that the question would simply cease to bother us. Gaining insight into the natural history of an animal that speaks, our propensity to pose philosophical questions should dissolve. However, it became increasingly clear to him that a single technique could never suffice to show us how language works; for it is as complex as the human organism itself, as he had always insisted. He would assemble reminders of the complexity and nuances of human knowing and acting in aid of disabusing us of the desire to ask oversimplified questions, employ misleading examples and form crude judgments on the basis of misconstruing the logic of language.

Thus, strange as it may seem, philosophy ends up being a matter of coming to grips with our own animality as the prerequisite for understanding language – and its limits. Wittgenstein's reaction to Weininger here was not simply to affirm his view but, as Rhees has suggested with respect to Judaism, he used the striking example that Weininger presented to him to get straight about just how the animal is »in« human nature.[215] In effect Weininger (later assisted massively by Spengler, as we shall see in Chapter 9) helped him to rehabilitate the old Aristotelian view of the human being as the ζωον λόγον εχον, which, after the later Wittgenstein, might be translated »rule following animal«. Here we see the personal and the philosophical coming together in Wittgenstein's work across the decades. Significantly, his point bears upon the role of limits in his thought early and mature.

In 1916 we find him making the following crucial observation about himself in battle remarking almost despairingly,

> From time to time I become an animal. Then I think of nothing other than eating, drinking, sleeping. Dreadful! And then I also suffer like an animal without the possibility of inner rescue GT, 29.VII.16).

It seems that this thought is the remote ancestor § 475 of *On Certainty*:

> I want to regard man here as an animal; as a primitive being to which one grants instinct but not the power to reason. As a being in a primitive condition. Any logic good enough for a primitive means of communication needs no apology from us.

Moreover, in *On Certainty* Wittgenstein finds himself all but compelled to assert that this »animal logic«, if you will, cannot be described (in the way that description is conventionally understood by analytical philosophers).

> Am I not getting ever closer to saying that in the end logic cannot be described? You have to look at the practice of language, then you see it (*OC*, § 501).

Here we find ourselves running up against the limits of language in thoughts that are among Wittgenstein's last philosophical reflections. Wittgenstein would remind us that we never entirely cease to be an animal and that it is sometimes necessary for the philosopher to pay close attention to the beast in us. This is how logic ends up taking care of itself.

Wittgenstein's great achievement turns on his showing us how the logic that confers systematicity (*OC*, § 410) upon human activity and therefore underlies experience is not formal logic. Wittgenstein's position follows upon the central insight in his mature epistemology namely the idea of following a rule where no formal rule is present. The most primitive sort of human knowledge is constituted in practice alone, without recourse to explicit rules (*OC*, § 95). Thus, Wittgenstein could refer to the picture of the world immanent in a particular mode of rule-following as a »kind of mythology« *(OC*, § 475). It is fundamental to this mythology that our very participation in the myth hinders us from forming an accurate account of the practical basis of knowing. Formal (i.e., propositional) knowledge is a matter of representation. Yet, in the very context of the everyday this is a considerably more complex procedure than we tend to believe. Further, the ability to form representations is learned only after we have mastered a number of other tasks principally that of executing commands. Representation already assumes other practical abilities that have to be drilled into us (*abgerichtet*). Such dressage issues in what we might call »knowing in the body«, rather than »in the mind«. Thus when required to explain certain things that we perfectly well know in practice, we find ourselves in a similar position to St. Augustine confronted with the question, »What is time?«. The question perplexes us precisely because we are tempted into thinking that what we need is a theory to penetrate its depths when the solution in fact can be read on the very surface of our conduct. Thus Wittgenstein must remind us of any number of things that we normally accept without question concerning the world and ourselves but that limit us as knowers.

Philosophers have a way of regularly overlooking precisely those aspects of practical knowledge and learning that are the

8. OTTO WEININGER ...

key to understanding why the questions that they pose are misconceived. Their need for clarity concerning those misconceptions is linked to a fundamental misapprehension of the logic of language. Thus the clarity Wittgenstein strives for differs radically from that of the formal logician. It is a matter of seeing a certain subject rightly and realizing that there is really nothing more to question: the practice can take care of itself. Be that as it may, that difference dictates Wittgenstein's philosophical strategy. It accounts for the reason why aphorisms, questions (often unanswered), and thought experiments are so central to his way of doing philosophy. The task is, then, to dissolve philosophical problems by gesturing convincingly at practice, thereby showing us why there is really no need for inquiry. It is not a matter of analysis but of looking at the practice. Anthony Kenny has rightly argued that this notion of philosophizing bears principally upon the *will* rather than the intellect.[216]

Our inclination to be dazzled by the surface grammar of language has roots as deep as language itself. It can only be countered by *doing* something that traditional philosophical education excludes, namely, to take a look at those roots, i.e., at what we normally do and how we normally do it. The very familiarity of the practical foundations of knowing we discover explains why Wittgenstein's reminders have to be striking in character and also why they are often examples in the form of fictive natural histories. They should show us clearly and incontrovertibly how human experience hangs together and by demonstrating what would be the case, say, with respect to meaning if we were differently endowed by nature concerning our fundamental modes of learning.

Thus we arrive at the point where Weininger's influence upon Wittgenstein is at its profoundest. For both of them, philosophical problems can only be eliminated on the basis of what Pascal calls a change of heart, i.e., a change in our comportment:

> Difficulty of philosophy, not the intellectual difficulty of science but the difficulty of a conversion. Resistance of the will has to be overcome (MS 213, Big Typescript, 406, *BEE*, my translation).

The requisite transition from a theoretical to a practical point of view – for Weininger in ethics, for Wittgenstein in metaphysics and epistemology – is little less than a transformation. It is certainly not merely an intellectual matter. The source of temptation to confusion lies in a way of life that Wittgenstein considered is dubious. Weininger helped to guide him to this insight be presenting him with a striking alternative to that life style on the basis of the recognition of transcendental limits to thought and action that Wittgenstein transformed into the problem of the limits of *language*. Thus philosophy in its traditional form became a sort of intellectual tragedy with the philosopher's *hubris* leading him to destroy the very human reality he thought he was rescuing.

CHAPTER 9

Oswald Spengler: The Physiognomical Turn

DISCOMBOBULATING AS IT MAY seem in the light of logical positivism's intense animosity towards *Der Untergang des Abendlandes*, it is hardly possible to exaggerate the extent to which Oswald Spengler influenced Wittgenstein's mature philosophy.[217] The publication of *Culture and Value* both documents and exemplifies Spengler's influence upon Wittgenstein in its tone as well as its substance. Spengler, Wittgenstein says, was one of those 10 figures from whom he »enthusiastically snatched up« elements for his philosophical work of clarification. It is surely significant that Spengler was one of the original list of four that was later extended to ten mentioned as having influenced him.[218] Rudolf Haller has rightly insisted that the mature Wittgenstein's philosophical method i.e., what Wittgenstein himself took to be his main contribution to philosophy, was decisively influenced by Spengler's notion of descriptive morphology but Haller wrongly restricts Spengler's influence exclusively to the matter of method.[219] In fact Spengler influenced the substance of Wittgenstein's mature philosophy profoundly. Rafael Ferber has made an important step towards correcting Haller's view by showing how the very conception of language in the *Philosophical Investigations* bears profound traces of Spengler.[220] However, Ferber too has not got to the bottom of the matter, for, apart from numerous allusions to Spenglerian ideas there and elsewhere in his later works, Wittgenstein's most radical *epistemological* claim in the *Philosophical Investigations* is clearly anticipated by Spengler, namely, the idea that there is genuine knowledge that is not propositional in character. That claim, in turn, is conceptually linked to his anti-essentialist concept of knowledge and determines his approach to philosophizing. In what follows I propose to 1) begin from a consideration of Wittgenstein's view of what is sometimes termed »tacit knowing« in the phrase of Michael Polanyi, 2) proceed to a reconsideration of the questions that Haller and Ferber have raised as well as 3) adumbrating some of the most obvious points at which we find Spenglerian notions in Wittgenstein's mature writings and 4) close with some reflections upon Spengler's place in Wittgenstein's philosophical development.

That Wittgenstein considered there was a kind of genuine knowledge that was non-propositional is clear from the following often-cited passage from the *Philosophical Investigations*, II, xi:

> Is there »expert« judgment about the authenticity of expressions of feeling? – Even here there are people with »better« and »worse« judgment.
>
> Generally, more correct prognoses proceed from the judgment of those with a better knowledge of human nature [*Menschenkenntnis*].
>
> Can knowledge of human nature be learnt? Yes, Some people can learn it. But not from a course of instruction, rather through »experience«. – Can another person be a teacher in this matter? Certainly, From time to time he gives him the right *tip*. This is what »learning« and »teaching« look like here. – What one learns is not a technique;

9. OSWALD SPENGLER ...

one learns correct judgments. There are rules also but they do not form a system, and only people with experience can apply them correctly. Unlike the rules of calculation.

Wittgenstein terms the basis of judgment in personal matters such as the authenticity of feelings »imponderable« (*unwägbare*) evidence, i.e., evidence which cannot be systematically subjected to detached assessment. Learning to make judgments on its grounds is a subjective matter of getting a knack for something, for example, »having an eye« for painting (the German here is »Blick«, the same word that Spengler uses to characterize such knowledge (1112), whereas Miss Anscombe's translation »getting a nose« transfers the metaphor to the olfactory sense but the point remains the same). This is tantamount to recognizing the significance of glances, gestures and tone of voice as stimuli to and indices of understanding another's feelings. Thus Wittgenstein clearly endorses a notion with significant similarities to Michael Polanyi's idea of tacit knowing, a more primitive, personal form of knowledge than propositional knowledge.

As we have already mentioned, it has been the service of the Norwegian philosopher Kjell S. Johannessen in his numerous explorations into the interrelations between epistemology and aesthetics in Wittgenstein's mature philosophy to articulate how it is that this intransitive form of knowledge, as Wittgenstein calls it, that we normally term experience is a matter of following a rule where no explicit, formal rules are available, only examples to be imitated.

Moreover, the text about *Menschenkenntnis* under consideration, not only builds upon the idea of following a rule developed in *PI*, I, 199ff. but is also itself embedded in *PI*, II, xi, which has clearly demonstrable links to *On Certainty* (»the earth has existed for millions of years«), the *Lectures of Aesthetics* (the emphasis upon the significance of nuances, aspects, fine shades of behavior etc. in appreciating art) and *Culture and Value* (the relationship between philosophical and aesthetic investigations); so there can be no question of its centrality to Wittgenstein's mature thought.

Be that as it may, it is precisely in defending the primacy of practical knowledge over theoretical knowledge that Wittgenstein bids farewell to Logical Positivism and analytic philosophy as conventionally understood (including the »new Wittgensteinians«, who do not seem interested in such matters). The dramatic character of that break cannot be overestimated. As it turns out there is indeed in Wittgenstein's most mature philosophizing a kind of genuine knowledge that cannot be said in the language of the *Tractatus* but only shown in what we do. He would ask himself rhetorically in *On Certainty* whether or not he was getting closer and closer to the idea that logic cannot be described. You simply must look at the practice of language (*OC*, §501). In philosophy we can at best use language to gesture at the role of action in determining meaning.

The speech acts Wittgenstein employs to communicate what we know here typically have the form of aphorisms (which by their very nature are orders of sorts[221]), thought experiments (i.e., imaginary language games) and questions (frequently unanswered or even falsely answered), whose purpose it is to direct our attention, and thus permit us to see something for ourselves, rather than reports on observations or conventional arguments. Thus, the limits of propositional language are encountered in a form of knowledge that is irreducibly personal but for all that teachable and therefore genuine knowledge.

However, Wittgenstein's indebtedness to Spengler here is no less profound than his break with conventional analytic philosophy is dramatic, for in fact the »tacit« character of knowledge of human nature is a central theme in *Der Untergang des Abendlandes*.

Scattered throughout Spengler's *chef d'oeuvre* from beginning to end we find a discussion of the kind of knowledge typically possessed by statesmen (577, 111), experienced animal lovers (1112), people who know each other intimately such as long married couples, (721) gamblers (1112) and, astonishingly, but nevertheless credibly, under certain circumstances, even animals (713), which involves a profound sensitivity to the idiosyncrasies of individuals and an intuitive recognition of the meanings of situations (584, 611). Spengler characterizes knowledge of people as a »deep wordless understanding« (75) arising from our experience of people as opposed to nature. A mere glance suffices someone who really understands people to size up what is going on. A *Menschenkenner* has a firm grasp of what Spengler terms the *Takt des Werdens*, literally the (musical) measure of becoming, the pulse of developments as it were. Where another sees a random succession of happenings, the *Menschenkenner* sees the Gestalt or in Spengler's terms, the *physiognomy* of a situation in all its uniqueness. *Menschenkenner* are adept at perceiving crucial differences, especially as regarding the *timing* of their interventions in the world (1014). Moreover, it is typical of those who lack *Menschenkenntnis* that they generalize too quickly (584). Finally, *Menschenkenner* do not explicitly »know« what they know in the sense of being able to given an account of it but that does not hinder them from acting with certainty and security (577). The comparison between Spengler's *Menschenkenner* and Aristotle's *phronimos* or man of practical wisdom suggests itself here.[222] For example, it does not seem unlikely in view of Spengler's that *Menschenkenntnis* is the intellectual basis of statesmanship that he was entirely ignorant of Aristotle's notion that knowing what is appropriate to situations is the basic characteristic of statesmanship.[223]

In sum there is little doubt that Wittgenstein's discussion of *Menschenkenntnis* is heavily indebted to Spengler. However, we can get yet a better purchase upon the importance of this connection if we examine the context in which Wittgenstein makes the remark, *PI*, II, xi more closely. This is the famous discussion of aspect seeing which employs Jastrow's duck-rabbit as an example i.e., the part of Wittgenstein's later work which has proven most interesting to so-called Continental philosophers. We shall do well to reconsider some of its central elements, for they will also lead us back to Spengler.

Strangely enough it is not the perspectivism, so fashionable in post-Nietzschean philosophy, that fascinates Wittgenstein with respect to aspect seeing but the *difference* between our relationships to the two aspects, old and new, as a new one dawns upon us. The aspect that we are used to is something we can simply report upon; whereas the aspect that dawns upon us *surprises* us and in doing so educes an exclamation from us almost involuntarily. In a passage reminiscent of Spengler Wittgenstein says that seeing the new aspect is a matter of *physiognomy*: we suddenly *recognize* a new intelligible unity (a »face«) where we previously *perceived* a commonplace object. The surprised reaction is a primitive one in that involves instinctive behavior but, as a matter of sudden recognition, it clearly involves thinking, as opposed to mere perception, and as such for Wittgenstein is a matter of using language in a peculiar way. The point is that we refer to the two aspects we can see in different speech acts, the one we usually see is perceived and reported upon; whereas the aspect that dawns upon us more or less forces an exclamation out of us upon recognition of the surprising form. That exclamation is attendant upon the novel *thought* that the second aspect presents. It is not simply a report but an expression of *feeling* associated with the surprise. The sudden thought of a rabbit where I only have previously seen a duck has done something unusual to me and I express that by exclaiming »a rabbit!« A form of thinking which is not »logical« is involved; for there are no surprises in logic as Wittgenstein says in the *Tractatus* (6.1251, 6.1261). Be that as it may, Wittgenstein points here to the similarity between the expression of surprise and the expression of pain which it the utterance »I am in pain« (*PI*, I, 244f). Neither are reports pure and simple. The point is that not one but two functions of language are involved in aspect seeing: reporting upon perception and expression of a surprise. This in turn brings us to the heart of Wittgenstein's mature conception of language: the idea that it is not words alone that convey meaning but the ways that they are interwoven into our actions. In this analysis the distinction between language games of reporting and language games of expression is of paramount importance. It is a distinction that has a prominent parallel in Spengler.

Wittgenstein's point here is parallel to, but not identical with, a distinction that is at the very center of Spengler's view of language, his distinction between language as expression (*Ausdruck*) and language as communication (*Mitteilung*). We shall have more to say about the significance of the *differences* between Wittgenstein and Spengler later. For Spengler human beings have a kind of animal need for self-affirmation as living beings and a social need to communicate with others that have to be distinguished sharply from one another. Expressive language is a direct reaction to our experience of consciously being alive. It is a matter of gesturing in words by calling attention to ourselves. This, according to Spengler, is ultimately the basis of art and religion. In a Schopenhauerian vein we could say that the language of expression is the individual's response to experiencing nature in himself. Communicative language, on the other hand, presupposes the Other, the »Thou«, as the object of communicative utterance (717). Expressive language is a form of display *before* others; whereas communicative language involves an exchange *with* them.

It is central to Spengler that these two forms of language cannot be precisely demarcated from one another (691f, 722). This is turn confers a certain opacity on language. Moreover, we can confuse ourselves, as primitives do, by thinking that there must be a personal object of expressive language. Thus all the surrounding objects that make an impression upon the expressive »I« are »divine« and »Thous«. On the other hand, Spengler insists that in the course of becoming civilized practice becomes swallowed up by theory: culture, in the literal sense of what has grown up organically, becomes »paralyzed« (143, 452). A technocratic, formalistic, mandarin mentality emerges that conceives the whole of reality mechanistically. Thus language ceases to be a means of communication and becomes an ornament or fetish (248). In Saussure's terms *langue* is increasingly detached from *parole*. Schools and churches institutionalize the fetish. The effect is to make language as it is used incomprehensible to speakers. Only the mandarins can now understand it. They systematically forget the more primitive expressive function of words: they come to worship »truth« as the basis of communication. This dichotomy, which seems to owe a great deal to Schopenhauer's dichotomy between the world as will and the world as representation, is a far cry from anything we find in Wittgenstein – except for the central claim about how the very complexity of language itself confuses us into oversimplifying it by producing philosophical theories that explain its nature, which is absolutely central to his mature concept of philosophy. In the end Wittgenstein agrees that in the process of becoming civilized we have lost sight of the primitive functions of language that underlie our sophisticated techniques of representation:

9. OSWALD SPENGLER ...

I want to regard humans here as animals; as a primitive being to which we grant instinct but not reasoning. As a creature in a primitive state. Any logic good enough a primitive means of communication suffices, we do not need to be ashamed of it. Language did not emerge from a reasoning process. (*OC*, §475)

This has to be strange stuff to a Logical Positivist but it is absolutely central to Spengler, who believed that our humanity has in fact been grafted onto our animal nature. But let us turn to Spengler's view of language.

In a passage that Ferber has rightly highlighted in Spengler's account of language he writes:

> Whoever wants to penetrate the essence of language should ignore scholars' investigations of words, rather, he should look at how a hunter speaks with his dog. The dog follows a finger which has been stretched out before it. It listens attentively to the sounds of words and shakes his head. He does not understand this kind of human language at all. Then he produces a few sentences in order to indicate *its* conception, it stands still and barks. That is a sentence in its language, which contains the question whether the master his meant perhaps this. Then there follows the joy, similarly expressed in dog language, if it grasps that it understood rightly. If a country parson explains something to a peasant woman, he takes a hard looks at her and involuntarily puts everything that she cannot understand in the church's mode of expression he has to say into his gestures. Today's word languages all together can only lead to communication in connection with other forms of language. (713)

Thus Spengler believes that there is a common behavioral language that underlies all communication between people and even between people and animals that is somehow implicit in spoken language; whereas Wittgenstein will speak of the common behavior of mankind as the »common human form of acting as the frame of reference by means of which we interpret a foreign language« (*PI*, I, 206). Here again, there is an important difference: Wittgenstein employs the example of what people, as opposed dogs, do continually in the *Philosophical Investigations* to *differentiate* between the kind of meaningful human action appropriate to animals that speak and the behavior of animals that do not. Thus he asks rhetorically whether a dog is too honest to be able to stimulate pain (*PI*, I, 250). Be that as it may, in the passage in question Spengler emphasizes that a child speaks this common behavioral language before it has mastered its first word (713); whereas Wittgenstein will insist that, although we learn the most fundamental things from experience, we do not learn them from our own experience but from that of others (*OC*, §275). Moreover, Wittgenstein emphasizes that we first learn language by playing (*PI*, I, 7); whereas Spengler insists that children discover what »truth« means by playing (582). For Wittgenstein that playing has the character of »Abrichtung«, which is a term usually associated with training animals *PI*, I, 5). In addition, this practical mode of learning by being disciplined determines that we do not explicitly »know« what we know. Thus Wittgenstein writes in *On Certainty*.

> I did not get my picture of the world by satisfying myself of its correctness; nor do I have it because I am satisfied of its correctness. No. it is the inherited background against which I judge between true and false.
> The propositions describing this world-picture might be part of a kind of mythology. And their role is like that of

rules of a game; and the game can be learned purely practically, without learning any explicit rules. (*OC*, §94-5)

This lack of explicit knowledge is what determines the indirect character of Wittgenstein's philosophical method – but that is to run ahead. Indeed, Baker and Hacker insist that Wittgenstein's notion of language builds upon the Spenglerian notion of a »homogeneous, spiritualized, well-ordered *Weltbild*« that comprehends the totality of knowledge, In fact Wittgenstein is describing the point where nature grows into culture – something that is clearly continuous with Spengler. Baker and Hacker go so far as to suggest that Wittgenstein owes the much discussed notion that meaning is to be explained ultimately in terms »forms of life« to Spengler.[224]

On Spengler's view the »civilized« spirit of formalizing, mechanizing and systematizing everything has a way of blinding us to the behavioral origins of knowing as written language becomes a fetish. Thus dazzled by the fetish the sophisticated systematic philosopher seeks things that correspond to word, thereby overlooking the possibility that one word can stand for many (related but hardly identical) things. Thus Spengler will insist that there should really be a discussion of three Aristotles, the Greek, the Arabic and the Gothic, to do justice to all the historical phenomena that fall under the rubric »Aristotle« (622). For Spengler as for Wittgenstein a single term can refer to many different things. In order to see language in all its complexity from within »civilization« we have to develop a method for inducing skepticism about the comfortable certainties upon which modern thought is based, including the idea that there is such a *thing* as language. For Spengler this means doing battle with the mechanistic spirit of systematic thought: the tendency to generalization and the pursuit of causal explanations (Spengler polemicizes in a Schopenhauerian vein in several places against casual explanation in philosophy – 152ff. et *passim*).

Spengler calls his antidote to systematic philosophy, which is based upon the principle of causality, *physiognomy*. His aim is to justice to human history on the basis of a »strict and clear physiognomy that is completely conscious of its resources and limits« (142). Its method, attributed to Goethe's botanical studies, is that of comparative morphology. In fact, physiognomy is a matter of describing analogies. Its perspective originates in sensitivity to style and form in the individual and the analogies which bind together things that are similar but not identical (4). Moreover, the physiognomic perspective is a developmental one: the physiognomist is ever sensitive to the *Takt des Werdens* as we have seen: »movement is only an embarrassment to the thinking man, it is something obvious to somebody who takes a look« (500). So with respect to language physiognomic knowledge proceeds from the melodies rhythms, emphasis, color tone and gesture that is part and parcel of language in use (694). To employ terms that are not Spengler's, but nonetheless appropriate for all that, physiognomic understanding is much more a grasp of pragmatics than it is of semantics or syntax. Understanding language is grasping usage and not a set of formal structures underlying it. As such physiognomic understanding is historical and differentiating.

The explicitly skeptical dimension of Spengler's physiognomy attaches to his battle against the spirit of the system. The skepticism that Stanley Cavell and others have attributed to Wittgenstein is largely a matter of his Spenglerian heritage – something that is also true of the historicism that is clearly present as sub-text but never quite comes to the surface in the mature Wittgenstein's view of meaning. Both Wittgenstein and Spengler want to undermine systematic philosophy's universalistic a-historical claims about knowledge and society on the basis of a comparative perspective which shows that the systematizer's claims to universality are unfounded on the basis of culturally given multiplicity. The aim of Spengler's physiognomy is to remind us about the importance of nuances and minutiae that in fact amount to big differences when we are trying to understand human reality. Thus Spengler will compare his task to that of a portrait painter: »describing, fashioning physiognomy is the art of portraiture carried over into the realm of the intellectual (*das Geistige* – 136)«. It is therefore a profoundly *descriptive* rather than an explanatory enterprise. A certain similarity with Wittgenstein's self-description as a landscape artist in the introduction to the *Philosophical Investigations* suggests itself here. Moreover, Spengler insists that the »Ursymbole«, determining the collective ideals that distinguish cultures from one another are determined by a collective experience of space in the form of landscape (244).

With that notion we reach the point where a smooth transition of a discussion of Wittgenstein mature concept of philosophy is possible. The step from the discussion of physiognomy in the *Untergang des Abendlandes* to the discussion of the task of philosophy in the *Philosophical Investigations* is a short one indeed. After Spengler, Wittgenstein's central assertion that description must replace explanation and the seemingly scandalous idea that philosophy simply describes the world and leaves everything as it is fit into place. The same is true of the notion that we simply need to take a look at how things stand but that we are tempted to speculate rather than look is no less part of the story for both of them. Indeed, the whole enterprise of philosophizing against the spirit of the system as Wittgenstein does is perfectly sensible for a Spenglerian – it has been the burden of the previous discussion of understanding people, language and physiognomy to show that Wittgenstein did accept central Spenglerian notions in his mature thought.

More than Spengler Wittgenstein is convinced that the very opacity of language makes taking a look à la Spengler very difficult indeed. Thus Wittgenstein emphasizes the curious character of philosophical perplexity in a way that Spengler does not but, nevertheless, by opening his discussion with a favorite text of Spengler's The quotation from St. Augustine with which the so-called philosophy chapter of the *Philosophical Investigations* opens with (PI, I 89) is one that Spengler characterizes as (162) as the only »deep and respectful characterization of time« that he has ever come across. Much more than Spengler, who was content to fall back on Goethe here, Wittgenstein is convinced that he must develop a new method adequate to unraveling the »deep« sources of philosophical conundrums. Thus he writes:

> It is a main source of our incapacity to understand that we do not have the ability to grasp the use of words *at a glance*. Our grammar lacks a synoptic character. A synoptic view conveys an understanding, which consists in our ability to »see contexts«. Thus the importance of finding and discovering connecting links.
> The concept of the synoptic view is of fundamental significance for us. It characterizes our form of presentation, the way we see things. (Is this a 'Weltanschauung'?). (*PI*, I, 122)

In the *Big Typescript* version of that text there follows the word »Spengler« (*BEE* MS 213, 417) and, Indeed Spengler characterizes a »Weltanschauung« precisely that way: a way of seeing things together (74f.) meaningfully (216) that is a feeling for from (224f.). So, despite their differences in style and emphasis the influence of Spengler is clearly central in the account of what philosophy is in the *Philosophical Investigations*: while Wittgenstein owes the idea of the synoptic view as a technique

9. OSWALD SPENGLER ...

for dissolving philosophical problems on the basis of alternative representations to Heinrich Hertz, the notion that we must cultivate a way of thinking to do so successfully in philosophy is what he owes to Spengler here.

Indeed, against the background of these similarities a number of other points of similarity take on greater significance than they otherwise might. Consider the curious parenthetical remark at *PI*, I 109: »Die pneumatischen Auffassung des Denkens«), which we find already in the *Urfassung* of the text from 1936. Miss Anscombe has rendered it »the conception of thought as a gaseous medium«. However, it is not at all clear what we are to understand by that phrase. However, if we know that Spengler uses the word in connection with the concept of *pneuma* in Neo-Platonism and Gnosticism, the so-called Magian (we would say, Semitic) cultures, with their belief in the *ratio superior* that gives us access to »higher truth« and ultimately the divine, which is itself divine or even magical (390 *et passim*), the phrase becomes both clear and fitting in the context. In effect Wittgenstein uses it to describe the dazzling notion that thought, i.e., philosophy, can correct our preconceived notions because it has access to a higher realm of truth, which makes perfectly good sense in the context.

Not even Wittgenstein's philosophy of mathematics remains unscathed by his encounter with Spengler – which is not to say that it is derived from Spengler but that his thinking about mathematics was certainly reinforced by his encounter with Spengler. For example, the thrust of the mature Wittgenstein's rejection of logicism is an important point of agreement with Spengler. The word »mathematics« for Wittgenstein circumscribes a large number of heterogeneous activities: Mathematics is a *heterogeneous mixture* (*buntes Gemisch*) of techniques of proof – And upon this is based its manifold applicability« (p. 176). Thus Wittgenstein's aim is to explain that heterogeneity (182). It echoes Spengler's view loudly: *Es gibt keine Mathematik, es gibt nur Mathematiken* (There is no such thing as mathematics, only ways of doing mathematics, 82). Moreover, Spengler enthusiastically cites Weierstrass view that nobody can really be a mathematician without at the same time being a poet. Wittgenstein echoes this thought by saying: »The mathematician is an inventor, not a discoverer« (99). There is doubtless much more to explore here.

The same holds true for his aesthetics. the basic characterization of aesthetic experience itself seems to owe a great deal to him. In fact aesthetics itself is based upon expression: »Perhaps the most important thing in connection with aesthetics is what may be called aesthetic reactions, e.g. discontent, disgust, discomfort. The expression of discontent is not the same as the expression of discomfort.« (*L+C*, 13 § 10). In the end aesthetics for Wittgenstein turns out to be the search for the reasons why we are discontented, disgusted or made uncomfortable as the result of encountering a particular object – or the opposite of these reactions. In any case the notion is clearly Spenglerian and it is absolutely central to Wittgenstein mature philosophy. The point is intimately connected with the idea of aspect seeing in *Philosophical Investigations* II xi. However, this is by no means the only trace of Spengler in his discussion of aesthetics.

In Section 32 of the *Lectures and Conversations on Aesthetics* Wittgenstein suddenly and inexplicably turns to discuss »the Darwin upheaval« which polarized intellectuals for decades after the appearance of the *Origin of Species*. He wants to illustrate how it could be that people could be certain that Darwin either was or was not right without themselves being in an informed position to verify or falsify the theory (*L+C*, 26f). The example would seem to be yet another veiled reference to Spengler. In the *Untergang des Abendlandes* Darwin and

9. OSWALD SPENGLER ...

above all Darwinism is presented as the epitome of the »civilized« tendency to produce mechanistic systems of explanation. Spengler is a paradigm case of an anti-Darwinian. He misses no opportunity to denounce the decadence Darwin and Darwinism as a causal system of nature, as mechanistic (203), as materialist (284) as socialist (48), as English (474, 590), as Manchestrian, (475) as Malthusian (474), as a superficial caricature of the true understanding of race in history (774) and above as anti-Goethean. An enthusiastic reader of Spengler could not but be struck by the acrimony with which he rejects everything connected with Darwin. Wittgenstein discussion is surely related to Spengler diatribe.

At the more anecdotal level we have the following: in a remark that so deeply impressed Stephen Toulmin that he could distinctively remember John Wisdom telling him about it twenty five years later Wittgenstein once said, »Poor [C. D.] Broad thinks of philosophy as the physics of the abstract«.[226] It exactly parallels an observation of Spengler's on the attitude of psychologists in his day:

> Wanting to hang on to an »exact knowledge« of the eternally mysterious soul, is senseless, however, the ...drive to think abstractly compels the »physicists of the inner world« nevertheless to explain an illusory world of representations and concepts on the basis of newer and newer representation and concepts (384).

Whatever differences of content and context the point of the assertion in each case is to criticize illusions within the academic community and the blind worship of physics in a community with little real understanding of the subject *as practiced*.

However, it might be objected in my search for the »influence« that Spengler exerted upon Wittgenstein that I have fallen into a kind of reductionist encyclopedism that would deny any originality to Wittgenstein at all. After all, hardly anybody takes his claim seriously that he was merely a »reproductive«, »Jewish« thinker as he asserts in the passage in *Culture and Value*, where he mentions who influenced his philosophical work of clarification. However this is to overlook a very important part of the passage towards the end of the entry in which he so describes himself: »It is typical of a Jewish mind that it understands the other better that he understand himself«. (C+V, 41). Thus Wittgenstein could see far *more* in the Hertzian criterion that models be »appropriate« (*Zweckmäßig*) than Hertz did himself or more in Frege's notion of objectivity than Frege himself did – or that he would find more depth in Spengler's distinction between expressive and communicative language than Spengler himself did. In any case, Wittgenstein is much less modest in that entry than meets the eye: what he has conceded at the beginning, he takes back with a vengeance at the end.

It remains now to examine how Spengler fits into Wittgenstein's list of »influences«, i.e., to establish how his influence converges with those that precede him. Just as Boltzmann was absolutely convinced that metaphysics has its root in the tendency of the human mind to overshoot the mark by overgeneralizing from our models, Spengler's attacks the spirit of systematic philosophy for the same reason. Like Hertz, Spengler would correct that on the basis of striking alternatives to our conventional ways of representing things but would insist that what was involved was »Weltanschauung«. With Schopenhauer (and parallel to the Heidegger of *Sein und Zeit*) Spengler wants to emphasize that there are two basic ways of seeing any object, the systematic and the physiognomic. The former sees the object in isolation, in the abstract as it were; whereas the latter perceive the object in all is particular-

9. OSWALD SPENGLER ...

ity and concreteness, dynamically as it develops. Moreover, the profound influence of trio, Boltzmann, Schopenhauer and Spengler upon Wittgenstein helps to explain the strong similarities between his mature philosophy and Goethe's concept of knowledge: Boltzmann was a classicist through and through, who dedicated his *Popular Scientific Lectures*, in which there are copious allusions to Goethe, to the spirit of Schiller, Schopenhauer, for his part, quotes Goethe copiously in the *Aphorisms For Living Wisely*, which Wittgenstein was known to respect. In effect, the influence of Goethe upon Wittgenstein is mediated by all three, Like Loos, Spengler considers that the »civilized« world is one in which the spirit of formalism transforms dynamic things like language into fetishes. They are epitomized in the notion of the ornament. Therefore, Spengler, like Kraus and Loos finds himself engaged in mortal combat with the forces of progress and »civilization«. As a disciple of both Wittgenstein would write *Culture and Value* which is deeply influenced by both but distinctly written in the spirit and, above all, the tone of the author of *Der Untergang des Abendlandes*. Like Weininger, Spengler is deeply concerned with the notion that there are limits to what we can scientifically analyze that we ignore at our peril. In short, Wittgenstein's encounters with all of these thinkers paved the way for his encounter with Spengler: he could be so taken by him because he was already deeply under their influence. However, being under their influence does not mean that he simply picked up things from them unreflectively, for on his own account he was helping himself from their ideas but, nevertheless, had a way of finding more in those ideas than the figures who influenced him did themselves. In short, all of the 8 figures that influenced Wittgenstein before Spengler made a contribution to making him the central figure in the development of the *Philosophical Investigations*. However, there he does not mention Spengler but Sraffa. Spengler paves the way for Sraffa to exert a powerful influence upon Wittgenstein. Ferber has shown that the single idea that Wittgenstein is known with certainty to have attributed to Sraffa, the notion of the so-called Neapolitan gesture, is something that we in fact find in Spengler in the first place. Spengler's views about money may also have been a bridge to Sraffa. However, the exact nature of Sraffa's influence upon Wittgenstein remains a mystery and a matter for speculation until today. If anything is sure it is that in the light of Spengler's enormous influence upon the later Wittgenstein Sraffa's impact must have been no less great. So there is a topic of immense significance to be investigated here.

Endnotes

1. Allan Janik, »Culture and Society: Creativity and the Creative Milieu,« *Europa im Zeitalter Mozarts*, eds. Moritz Csáky & Walter Pass (Vienna: Böhlau, 1995), 15-20.
2. Paul Wijdeveld, »Engelmann and Wittgenstein: The Relevance of the Palais Stonborough to Contemporary Architectural Discussion«, *Architecture, Language, Critique: Around Paul Engelmann*, eds. J. Bakacsy, A.V. Munch, A.L. Sommer (»Studien zur österreichischen Philosophie« vol. XXXI; Amsterdam-Atlanta: Rodopi: 2000), 112.
3. *Ludwig Boltzmann His Later Life and Philosophy, 1900-1906*, ed. John Blackmore (»Boston Studies in Philosophy of Science No. 174«; 2 vols; Dordrecht: Kluwer, 1995), I, 136.
4. *Loc. cit.*
5. This point has been made by several Wittgenstein scholars, notably the Norwegian philosopher Kjell S. Johannessen, *Wittgensteins senfilosofi* (2nd ed. rev. Filosofisk institutt stensilserie, no. 42; Bergen, 1994) cf. Johannessen, *Praxis och tyst kunnande* (Stockholm: Dialoger, 1999).
6. Brian McGuinness, *Wittgenstein, A Life: Young Ludwig* (London: Duckworth, 1988), 54.
7. On this matter see Susan G. Sterrett, *Wittgenstein Flies a Kite: A Story of Models of Wings and Models of the World* (New York: Pi Press, 2006).
8. Ludwig Boltzmann, *Populäre Schriften* (Leipzig: Johann Ambrosius Barth, 1905). Most of the relevant articles in these

lectures have been translated in Ludwig Boltzmann, *Theoretical Physics and Philosophical Problems*, ed. Brian McGuinness, trans. Paul Foulkes (»Vienna Circle Collection Vol. 5; Dordrecht: Reidel, 1974). I shall refer to Boltzmann from these editions parenthetically in the text with the reference to the English translation first and that to the German original following. I have occasionally emended the translation.

9   Boltzmann's answer is perhaps most succinctly summed up in the essay »On the Indispensability of Atomism in Natural Science«, *op cit.*, 40–53; 141–157.

10 David Pears, *The False Prison: A Study in the Development of Wittgenstein's Philosophy* (2 Vols.; Oxford: Clarendon Press, 1987–88).

11 Cf. »It seems to me that to call this logic [the idea that anything at all should exist or change] would be like someone putting on a long pleated garment to make mountain hike in, in which his feet would be continually entangled and he would fall down already with his first steps on the plain«. (164; 352–3)

12 »Grau, teurer Freund, ist alle Theorie, und grün des Lebens goldner Baum«, J. W. von Goethe, *Faust*, I, Studienzimmer.

13 Blaise Pascal, »Préface pour le traité du vide, *Œuvres complètes*, ed. J. Chevalier (Paris: Gallimard, 1954), 529–35; cf. Albin Krailsheimer, *Pascal* (Oxford: Oxford University Press, 1980), 23.

14 The idea is reminiscent of Pierre Duhem, a believing Catholic, like Boltzmann, who wanted to make room for both science and belief. It is unclear if Boltzmann was aware of Duhem's work in this area. John Blackmore has pointed out to me that, as an anti-atomist, Duhem was no friend of Boltzmann's.

15 On the use and abuse of the concept of »influence« see Allan Janik, »Wie hat Schopenhauer Wittgenstein beeinflußt?« *Schopenhauer Jahrbuch*, 73, (1992), 75–6.

16 Cf. note. 4.

17 See Allan Janik, »«Philosophy Between Science and Religion«, *Miscellanea Bulgarica*, 13 (Vienna, 1999), 43–50.

18 Brian McGuinness, »Wittgenstein and the Unsayable: A Genetic Account««. Unpublished lecture at the University of Sienna, Spring 1999. I am grateful to Prof. McGuinness for putting his typescript at my disposal. A version of the lecture is reprinted in his *Approaches to Wittgenstein: Collected Papers*

(London: Routledge, 2002), 160–176. The printed version is different from that which forms that basis of this chapter.

19 On the transition from the »early« to the »later« Wittgenstein see, Anthony Kenny, *Wittgenstein* (Harmondsworth: Penguin, 1973) Ch. 6, 103–119.

20 Ray Monk, *Ludwig Wittgenstein: The Duty of Genius* (London: Penguin, 1990), 260–1.

21 Thus Wittgenstein remained true to Boltzmann's injunction to eschew explanation by coming to eschew theory in philosophy. On the matter of what is required to describe how human thought is rooted in natural history Wittgenstein would go far beyond anything concretely conceived by Boltzmann – without contradicting his method in any fundamental ways – insisting that it was absolutely necessary to invent *fictional* natural histories to grasp our actual one.

22 The remarks on levers, mechanisms and super-mechanisms that precede are also suggestive of Boltzmann, 16ff.

23 M. O'C Drury, »A Symposium: Assessments of the Man and the Philosopher«, *Ludwig Wittgenstein: The Man and His Philosophy*, ed. K. T. Fann (New York: Delta, 1967), 69.

24 Cf. Allan Janik, »Wittgenstein on Madness and Mistakes, Metaphysics and Method«, *Wittgenstein's Vienna Revisited* (Piscataway, NJ: Transaction Publishers, 2001), 213–224.

25 An important part of the problem here bears upon the fact that the successors of Mach, i.e., Logical Positivism in its various forms, claimed *exclusive* rights to title of »scientific« philosophy uniting hitherto disparate figures like Mach, Hertz and Boltzmann under one banner. As a student of Hertz and Boltzmann Wittgenstein was not faced with a choice between »scientific philosophy« and something else; for the very idea of a scientific philosophy, i.e., a comprehensive »theoretical« account of reality, was a contradiction in his eyes from the very start. Thus he could concern himself with the limits of knowledge without embracing irrationalism.

26 K.T. Fann, *Wittgenstein's Conception of Philosophy* (Berkeley: University of California Press, 1969), 109.

27 Heinrich Hertz, *Die Prinzipien der Mechanik in neuem Zusammenhange dargestellt* (Leipzig: J.A. Barth, 1894), 9. Hereafter referred to parenthetically in the text as *PM* with

the appropriate page number). Translations are my own unless otherwise noted.

28 Professor G. H. von Wright emphasized this to me in conversation in 1966; cf. von Wright, *Wittgenstein*, trans. J. Schulte, (Frankfurt/Main: Suhrkamp, 1982), 29. Brian McGuinness emphasizes how it was the boldness of Hertz (and Boltzmann), as opposed to Mach's less daring way of thinking – and of presenting his thoughts – that impressed Wittgenstein so deeply, *Young Ludwig*, 39; whereas Ray Monk writes, »throughout his life, Wittgenstein regarded Hertz's solution to the problem [of force in Newtonian physics] as a perfect model of how philosophical confusion should be dispelled«, *op. cit.*, 446. Monk sees Hertzian element in Wittgenstein's wartime suggestion to the doctors with whom he worked at Guy's Hospital that they always write the word »shock« with a line drawn through it to remind themselves of how many different things it was used to refer to and thus of its dubious classificatory value.

29 G. P. Baker & P. M. S. Hacker, *Wittgenstein: Understanding and Meaning* (Oxford: Basil Blackwell, 1980), 16.

30 Ernst Cassirer, *The Problem of Knowledge*, trans. W. Woglom and C. Hendel (New York and London: Yale University Press, 1950), 85 *et passim*. See Ernst Mach, *The Analysis of Sensations*, trans. C.M. Williams (New York: Dover, 1959); *The Science of Mechanics*, trans. T.J. McCormack (LaSalle, Ill.: Open Court, 1960); *Erkenntnis und Irrtum* (Leipzig, J.A. Barth, 1905); cf. A. Janik and S. Toulmin, *Wittgenstein's Vienna* (New York: Simon & Schuster, 1973), 132–45.

31 Lesek Kolakowski, *The Alienation of Reason: A History of Positivist Thought*, trans. N. Guterman (Garden City: Doubleday, 1969), 102; 120.

32 Mach, *The Science of Mechanics*, 577.

33 »A sign or *representamen* is something which stands to somebody for something in some respect or capacity« C. S. Peirce, »Logic as Semiotic: The Theory of Signs«, *Philosophical Writings of Peirce*, ed. J. Buchler (New York: Dover, 1955), 99. It follows from this definition that we never know the meaning of a sign till we understand it in the sense of the person or persons for whom it functions as a sign.

ENDNOTES

34 On these relations see, Michael Heidelberger, »From Helmholtz's Philosophy of Science to Hertz's Picture Theory,« *Heinrich Hertz: Classical Physicist, Modern Philosopher*, eds. Davis Baird, R.I.G. Hughes & Alfred Nordmann (»Boston Studies in Philosophy of Science Vol. 198; Dordrecht: Kluwer, 1998), 9–24. Various other contributions in this indispensable volume also treat the relationships in question.

35 Robert S. Cohen, »Hertz's Philosophy of Science: An Introductory Essay« in Hertz, *The Principles of Mechanics Presented in a New Form*, trans. D.E. Jones & J.T. Walley (New York: Dover, 1956), section 4 (unpaginated).

36 I have benefited from conversation with Kelley Hamilton on Hertz generally and particularly on the question of how successful Hertz's program for axiomatizing mechanics really is.

37 Immanuel Kant, *Prolegomena zu jener künftigen Metaphysik, Werke*, (3 Vols.; Berlin: Knauer, n.d.), II, 353.

38 William Shakespeare, *King Lear*, I, 4, 88. Cf. Baker & Hacker, *op. cit.*, 17

39 On Wittgenstein's relationship to Freud see Brian McGuinness' excellent »Freud and Wittgenstein«, *Wittgenstein and His Times*, ed. B.F. McGuinness (Chicago: University of Chicago Press, 1982), 27–43; cf. my »Wittgenstein on Madness etc.«, n. 24.

40 Kenny, *op. cit.*, 33.

41 See John Passmore, *A Hundred Years of Philosophy* (London, Duckworth, 1957) 154.

42 In a sense the difference between Wittgenstein and Frege with respect to clarity could be formulated as a difference of opinion with respect to the value axiomatization as an aspect of the permissibility or appropriateness of a theory. In any case both of them could have appealed to aspects of Hertz in defending their particular notions of clarity. However, »philosophical thinking *began* for him with 'painful contradictions' (and not with the Russellian [and Fregean] desire for *certain* knowledge),« Ray Monk, *op. cit.*, 26. Moreover, it is altogether too little recognized that the truth table method of showing the distinction between empirical propositions and tautologies is for Wittgenstein simply a way of getting clear about things that we already know in practice, i.e., with respect to things

that »show themselves« in practice: in the *Tractatus* emphasizes that the mark of a tautology is that you can do anything with it in reasoning, nothing with a contradiction. Everybody knows this. The problem is that we cannot always distinguish between the different types of propositions. Thus the value of the truth table method of representing them, *T*, 6. 1262.

43 Kenny, *op. cit.*, 42.
44 The similarities between Wittgenstein's mature concept of philosophy and R.G. Collingwood's view of metaphysics as the analysis of the unquestioned elements in scientific inquiries, i.e., their »absolute presuppositions«, are particularly striking. See my *Style, Politics and the Future of Philosophy* (»Boston Studies in the Philosophy of Science«, Vol. 114; Dordrecht: Kluwer, 1989), xiii *et passim*.
45 On Heidegger see my »Carl Dallago und Martin Heidegger: Über Anfang und Ende des Brenner«, *Untersuchungen zum Brenner: Festschrift für Ignaz Zangerle*, eds. W. Methlagl, E. Sauermannn & S.P. Scheichl (Salzburg: Otto Müller, 1981), 28–9.
46 Alois Pichler, »Wittgensteins spätere Manuskripte: einige Bemerkungen zu Stil und Schreiben«, *Mitteilungen aus dem Brenner Archiv* 12 (1993), 8–26.
47 Jörg Zimmermann has brilliantly explored the hermeneutic moment in Wittgenstein in *Wittgensteins Sprachphilosophische Hermeneutik* (Frankfurt/Main: Klostermann, 1975). The fact that Prof. Zimmermann was long a practicing geologist perhaps accounts for his perspicacity here.
48 For example Hans-Georg Gadamer only reluctantly and very late (thanks to the persuasive efforts of Patrick Heelan) came to see that natural science was relevant to hermeneutics and vice versa. See Gadamer, »Naturwissenschaft und Hermeneutik«, *Filosofi och Kultur* 3 (Lund, Sweden, 1986), 39–70. The standard works on hermeneutics barely mention natural science at all except as a stalking horse.
49 Maurice O'C. Drury, *The Danger of Words* (London: Routledge & Keegan Paul, 1973), ix
50 K.T. Fann, *Wittgenstein's Conception of Philosophy*, 42–3.
51 Maurice Drury, »Some Notes on Conversations with Wittgenstein« *Ludwig Wittgenstein: Personal Recollections*, ed. Rush Rhees (Totowa: Rowman & Littlefield, 1981).

ENDNOTES

52 G.E.M. Anscombe, *An Introduction to Wittgenstein's Tractatus* (London: Hutchison, 1959), 11–12.
53 Bertrand Russell, Introduction, *Tractatus Logico-Philosophicus*, trans. D.F. Pears & B.F. McGuinness, (London: Routledge & Kegan Paul, 1961), p. xxi.
54 Arthur Schopenhauer, *Sämtliche Werke*, ed. Wolfgang Freiherr von Löhneysen (5 Vols.; Frankfurt: Suhrkamp, 1986), *Über die vierfache Wurzel des Satzs vom zureichenden Grund*, Werke, III, 55.
55 Schopenhauer II, 256. I cite Schopenhauer by volume and page number in parenthesis in the text.
56 McGuinness, *Young Ludwig*, 180, cf. 265.
57 See chapter 8 below.
58 This is very close to the view that Stephen Toulmin and I presented in *Wittgenstein's Vienna*. The question that must be posed to commentators like Haller & Röd who would deny that Wittgenstein is a Kantian or transcendental philosopher is »transcendental as opposed to what?« We have to ask what hangs on the question: Most of the original claims of this sort were intended to drive a wedge between Wittgenstein and Hume by comparing him with Kant. Nobody to my knowledge ever claimed that Wittgenstein was Kant as Haller and Röd seem to think, only that his work bore significant similarities with a Kantian as opposed to a Humean or Leibnizian approach to philosophy, for example, in its emphasis upon the scientist as an inventor rather than a discoverer: Rudolf Haller, »War Wittgenstein ein Neu-Kantianer«, *Fragen zu Wittgenstein* (»Studien zur österreichischen Philosophie, Vol. 10; Amsterdam: Rodopi, 1986), 155–69; Wolfgang Röd, »Enthält Wittgensteins Tractatus transcendentalphilosophische Ansätze?«, *Wittgenstein – Aesthetics and Transcendental Philosophy*, eds. Kjell S. Johannessen & Tore Nordenstam (Vienna: Hölder-Pichler-Tempsky 1981), 43–53 (Haller's article is also reprinted in that volume). It is significant that those who deny that Wittgenstein is a transcendental philosopher do not consider the arguments in favor of that view advanced by, say, Erik Stenius, *Wittgenstein's Tractatus* (Oxford: Blackwell, 1964), 214–226.
59 David Pears, *op.cit.* (n. 10).
60 I owe this apposite phrase to Kjell S. Johannessen.

61 Personal Communication from Rudolf Koder, Vienna 1969.
62 See Brian McGuinness, »In Praise of Nonsense« in the forthcoming Festschrift for Rosaria Egidi for an account of that collection and Wittgenstein's preoccupation with the subject generally.
63 Drury, *op. cit.*, 96.
64 Brian McGuinness, *Approaches*, 161.
65 See Anthony Kenny, *op. cit.*, Ch. 2 »The Legacy of Frege and Russell,« 19–42. The crucial issue here bears upon the role of axioms in logic. Wittgenstein showed by means of truth tables that all tautologies had the same logical status.
66 See my »Weininger and the Two Wittgensteins«, *Wittgenstein Reads Weininger*, eds. David Stern and Bela Szabados (Cambridge: Cambridge University Press, 2004).
67 Ludwig Wittgenstein, *Vermischte Bemerkungen*, ed. G.H. von Wright und Alois Pichler (2nd ed.; Frankfurt/Main: Suhrkamp, 1994), 167.
68 See *The New Wittgenstein*, eds. Alice Creary and Rupert Read (London: Routledge, 2000).
69 Brian McGuinness, *Young Ludwig*, 79
70 Gottlob Frege, *Die Grundlagen der Arithmetik: Eine logisch mathematische Untersuchung über den Begriff der Zahl* (Stuttgart: Reclam, 1987), 23.
71 See Hans Sluga, *Gottlob Frege* (London: Routledge & Kegan Paul, 1980) 105–7 *et passim*
72 *Ibid.*, 56–9.
73 Sluga argues for a Kantian view of Frege's objectivism against Michael Dummett's more Platonic view of it. However, this Kantian variation is hardly identical with the historical Kant. See n. 71. Sluga's view of Fregean objectivity tends to co-incide with ours as Dummett's does not.
74 Gottlob Frege, *Grundgesetze der Arithmetik, begriffschriftlich abgeleitet* (2 Vols.; Darmstadt: Wissenschaftliche Buchgesellschaft, 1962), Vorwort, I, XV.
75 For example, it is possible to consider Wittgenstein's search of a way of living that would make his fear of death vanish during World War I (see above Chapter 2) as an existential exercise in separating the subjective, psychological aspects of

his situation as an ideal target for enemy fire operating his searchlight on the Goplana from its objective »logical« reality. As we have shown in our discussion of Hertz, Wittgenstein endeavored to solve his existential problem in exactly the same way that he had solved his mathematical ones, i.e., on the basis of ideas taken over from Frege whose whole significance the master had not recognized. At that point the respective »influences« of Frege and Hertz merge completely.

76 Rudolf Haller, »Justification and Praxeological Foundationalism,« *Inquiry* 31, 335-45

77 See my »Myth and Certainty«, in Janik, *Style, Politics and the Future of Philosophy* (»Boston Studies in Philosophy of Sciences, vol. 114; Dordrecht: Kluwer, 1989), 159-71.

78 This is partly explicable by the fact that the earliest consideration that went into *On Certainty* date from the early 30s, i.e., from the time that he was giving lots of thought to Frege. I am indebted to Alois Pichler for information about the genesis of the text of *On Certainty*.

79 See Sterrett, *op. cit.*, 99f.; cf. McGuinness, *Young Ludwig*, 92ff.
80 Frege, *Grundlagen*, 28.
81 Sluga, *Frege*, 194.
82 Frege, *Grundgesetze*, I, XIVff.
83 *Ibid.*, VIII
84 *Ibid.*, VII.
85 Frege, *Grundgesetze*, I, XVI.
86 Frege, *Grundlagen*, 39.
87 *Ibid.*, 30.
88 *Ibid.*, 64.
89 *Ibid.*, 35.
90 Frege, *Grundgesetze*, I, XII.
91 *Ibid.*, I, XXVI.
92 *Ibid.*, I, VII.
93 McGuinness, *Young Ludwig*, 73ff. See n. 5
94 Frege, *Grundlagen*, 25ff.
95 Frege, *Grundgesetze*, I,XII.
96 Gottlob Frege, *Begriffschrift*, ed. I. Angellelli (Darmstadt: Wissenschaftliche Buchgesellschaft, 1964), § 9; cf. *Routledge*

Encyclopedia of Philosophy, (10 Vols.; London: Routledge, 1998) 3, 771.
97 McGuinness, *Approaches*, 133-4 (n. 1).
98 Frege *Grundgesetze* I, XI.
99 See Brian McGuinness, *Approaches*, 161-74 (n.1) and my discussion of Russell in the next chapter.
100 Kenny, *Wittgenstein*, 35.
101 Bertrand Russell, »On Denoting« *Mind* 1905 reprinted in *Logic and Knowledge: Essays 1901-1950*, ed, R. C. Marsh (London: Allen & Unwin, 1956).
102 I have discussed this matter profitably with the Russell scholar Prof. Alejandro Garciadiego of the National Autonomous University of Mexico.
103 Passmore, *op. cit.*, 209.
104 Noam Chomsky, *Aspects of the Theory of Syntax* (Cambridge [Mass.]: The MIT Press, 1965), 136, 198, 199; cf. Chomsky, *Cartesian Linguistics: A Chapter in the History of Rationalist Thought* (New York: Harper & Row, 1966), 31-51.
105 McGuinness, *Young Ludwig*, 89.
106 *Ibid.*, 89-91.
107 *Ibid.*, 79-86,
108 Bertrand Russell, *My Philosophical Development* (London, Allen & Unwin, 1959), 261f; cf. Wittgenstein, *Z*, 456.
109 McGuinness, *op. cit.* 89-91.
110 Ludwig Wittgenstein, *Prototractatus: An Early Version of the Tractatus Logico-Philosophicus*, eds. B.F. McGuinness, et al. (London: Routledge, 1971) In facsimile, 71.
111 McGuinness, »Wittgenstein & the Unsayable« (typescript of an unpublished lecture at the University of Siena 1999), 9-10. I am grateful to Prof. McGuinness for putting his text at my disposal. McGuinness, *Approaches*, 160-76 is a revised version of the Siena lecture in which the text cited here does not appear.
112 Ludwig Wittgenstein , *Philosophical Investigations*, II, xi, p. 227e. This has been the subject of innumerable articles and lectures by the Norwegian Wittgenstein scholar Kjell S. Johannessen. See, for example, his »Art. Philosophy and Intransitive Understanding«, *Wittgenstein: Towards a*

Re-Evaluation eds. Rudolf Haller & Johannes Brandl (3 vols.; Vienna: Hölder-Pichler-Tempsky, 1990), 323–33.
113 Otto Weininger, *Über die letzten Dinge* (München: Matthes & Seitz, 1980), 7–54.
114 Cf. Allan Janik, »Weininger, Ibsen and Viennese Critical Modernism«, *Wittgenstein's Vienna Revisited* (New Brunswick, N.J.: Transaction, 2001), 171–184.
115 Bertrand Russell, *The Problems of Philosophy* (Mineola, N.Y: Dover Books, 1999), 117.
116 McGuinness, *Young Ludwig*, 103.
117 *Ibid.*, 37.
118 Personal communication from the late Rudolf Koder.
119 Georg Henrik von Wright, »Wittgenstein in Relation to His Times«, *Wittgenstein and His Times*, ed. Brian McGuinness (Chicago: University of Chicago, Press, 1982), 116.
120 McGuinness, *op. cit.* 37.
121 Paul Engelmann, Letters from *Wittgenstein with a Memoir*, trans. L. Furtmüller (Oxford: Basil Blackwell, 1967), »Memoir«, 123.
122 Engelmann's account seems to reflect his own views as much as it documents Wittgensteins. See Christoph Leitgeb, »Engelmann erinnert sich nicht nur an Wittgenstein: Nationalitätenkampf, Assimilation und Philosophie in Olmütz nach dem ersten Weltkrieg«, *Mitteilungen aus dem Brenner Archiv* No. 17 (1998), 32–46.
123 Timms, *Karl Kraus, Apocalyptic Satirist: Culture and Catastrophe in Habsburg Vienna* (New Haven and London: Yale University Press, 1986), 206 (n. 4).
124 Kraus, »Grimassen über Kultur und Bühne«; »Lob der verkehrten Lebensweise«, *Die chinesische Mauer, Schtiften* II, 141–156; 167–170
125 *Ibid.*, 51.
126 Cf. »Die weiße Kultur oder Warum in die Ferne schweifen«, *Die chinesische Mauer, Schriften*, II, 211–214.
127 eine Welt idyllischer Naturhaftigkeit und reiner Geistigkeit, Sigurd Paul Scheichl, »Politik und Ursprung« *Wort und Wahrheit*, XXVII (1972) 45).
128 The translation is that of Timms, see Timms (n. 124), 232–3.

129 Cf. my »Engelmann's Role in Wittgenstein's Philosophical Development,« *Architecture, Language, Critique: Around Paul Engelmann*, eds. J. Bakacsy, A. V. Munch + A.L. Sommer (Amsterdam: Rodopi, 2000) 40–58.
130 Cf. Jean Lafond (ed.) *Les formes brèves de la prose et le discours discontenu (XVIe –XVIIe siècles)* (Paris: J. Vrin, 1984). Cf. my »From Montaigne to Diderot: Pascal, Jansenism and the Dialectics of Inner Theater«, in *Skill, Technology and Education: On Practical Philosophy*, ed. B. Göranzon (London: Springer, 1995), 57–74.
131 J.P. Stern, *Lichtenberg: A Doctrine of Scattered Occasions* (Bloomington: University of Indiana Press, 1959), 191–220.
132 Kraus, »Sprüche und Widersprüche«, *Sprüche und Widersprüche, Schriften*, 8, 161.
133 Wittgenstein, *BEE* Ms 110, 18.1.1931.
134 Kraus, »Stimmungen, Worte«, *Spruche und Widersprüche, Schriften* 8, 155.
135 Kraus, »Sprüche und Widerspruche«, *Spruche und Widersprüche, Schriften* 8, 179.
136 Kraus, »Von der Gesellschaft«, *Pro domo et mundo, Schriften* 8, 193
137 *Die Fackel*, 331–332, 30.9.1911, 57.
138 Joseph Owens, *A History of Ancient Western Philosophy* (New York: Appleton Century Crofts, 1959), 38.
139 Cf. Johan Huizinga, *Homo Ludens* (Boston: Beacon Press, 1955), 115–17.
140 Cf. Allan Janik, »On Edification and Cultural Conversation: A Critique of Rorty«, *Style, Politics and the Future of Philosophy*, 80–92.
141 Kraus, »Kunst«, *Nachts, Schriften* 8, 326
142 K.T. Fann, *Wittgenstein's Conception of Philosophy*, 109. The similarity of the *tone* in Wittgenstein's questioning to that of St Augustine in his *Confessions* is as striking as it is generally unobserved the literature on Wittgenstein.
143 Norman Malcolm, *Ludwig Wittgenstein, A Memoir* (Oxford University Press, 1958), 29.
144 Normal Malcolm assured me in conversation that the example was a real one bearing upon one of Wittgenstein's conversations with Moore

145 See n. 62.
146 Allan Janik and Stephen Toulmin, *Wittgenstein's Vienna* (2nd. ed rev., Chicago: Ivan Dee, 1996), 79f.
147 Timms, *op. cit.*, 273ff.
148 On Wittgenstein's war experiences see, McGuinness, *Young Ludwig* (n.1), 204–266.
149 Frege to Wittgenstein 16.9.19. »Gottlob Frege: Briefe an Ludwig Wittgenstein«, eds., Allan Janik & C.P. Berger, *Grazer Philosophische Studien*, Vol. 33/34 (1989), 3–33.
150 Kraus, »Vom Künstler«, *Pro domo et mundo, Schriften* 8, 235.
151 Kraus, »Maximilian Harden,« *Die chinesische Mauer, Schriften* 2, 58
152 See Alois Pichler, *op. cit.*, 8–26.
153 Kraus, *op. cit.*, 55.
154 Brian McGuinness *Young Ludwig*, 77.
155 See *Paul Engelmann: Architektur, Judentum; Wiener Moderne*, ed. Ursula A. Schneider (Wien & Bozen: Folio, 1999).
156 Paul Engelmann, *op. cit.*, 127.
157 Brian McGuinness *Approaches*, 20f.
158 The most important study of Loos to date is Anders V. Munch, *Den stilløse Stil – Adolf Loos* (København: Kunstakademiets Arkitektskoles Forlag 2002).
159 On the vagaries of this expression see my *Wittgenstein's Vienna Revisited*, 261, n. 1.
160 Carl E. Schorske, *Fin de siècle Vienna: Politics and Culture* (New York, Random House; 1981), 24–115.
161 See David Luft, *Eros and Inwardness in Vienna* (Chicago & London: University of Chicago Press, 2003), 6 *et passim*.
162 Hermann Bahr, »Die Décadence ,« *Die Wiener Moderne*, ed. Gotthart Wunberg (Stuttgart: Reclam, 1981), 226.
163 Loos, »Architektur«, *Sämtliche Schriften*, (2 Vols.; Vienna: Herold, 1962), I, 102.
164 On this dimension of Loos see Ludwig Munz & Gustav Künstler, *Adolf Loos: Pioneer of Modern Architecture* (New York: Praeger, 1966).
165 Kraus, *Schriften*, ed. C. Wagenknecht (12 Vols.; Frankfurt: Suhrkamp, 1987) 8, 341.

166 The locus classicus for the description of Viennese »good taste« is Egon Friedell, *Kulturgeschichte der Neuzeit*, (2 Vols.; München: dtv, 1976), II, 130ff., »Der Stil der Stillosigkeit«.
167 Kraus, »In dieser großen Zeit«, *Die Fackel* (1914) No. 404, 1
168 Adolf Loos, »Ornament und Verbrechen«, *Sämtliche Schriften*, I, 277
169 In a lecture on Loos and Alois Riegl at the conference on canons and conventions at the American Academy of Science in May 1982.
170 Literally »Steinklopferhans dialect«. The reference is to a bumpkin in Ludwig Anzengruber's play *Der Kreuzelschreiber*. It is, in fact, this character, who utters the pharase that so deeply struck Wittgenstein that he would it mention centrally in his famous Lecture on Ethics in 1929: »Nix kann dir geschen«, »nothin' kin happen ta ya«. *Cf.* Allan Janik & Hans Veigl *Wittgenstein in Wien* (Vienna: Springer, 1998), 164.
171 Adolf Loos, «Regeln für den, der in den Gebirgen baut,« *Der Brenner* IV, I (1 Okt., 1913), 40–1. My translation.
172 Loos, »Architektur«, 110.
173 Ákos Moravánsky, *Competing Visions: Aesthetic Invention and Social Imagination in Central European Architecture 1867–1918* (Cambridge and London: MIT Press, 1998), 314–6.
174 Timms, *op. cit.*, 124ff.
175 Loos, »Architektur«, 97ff.
176 ... ich wäre stolz, wenn ich ... sagen dürfte: 'Ich habe den Kompositionsschülern eine schlechte *Ästhetik genommen*, ihnen dafür aber eine gute *Handwerkslehre gegeben*', Arnold Schoenberg, *Harmonielehre* (Vienna: Universal Edition, 1911), viii.
177 See my, »The »Dionysian« Element in Kant or How Friedrich Nietzsche Influenced Otto Weininger,« *Nietzsche and Austrian Culture*, ed. J. Golomb (Vienna: WUV, 2004), 220–243.
178 *Ibid.*, 107.
179 See Paul Engelmann, *op. cit.*, 131 f.
180 Loos, »Architektur«, 96ff.
181 Cf. Ursula Prokop; *Margret Stonborough-Wittgenstein: Bauherrin, Intellektuelle, Mäzenin* (Wien, Köln, Weimar: Böhlau, 2003).

182 Moravánsky, *op. cit.*, 329-30.
183 Paul Wijdeveld, »Engelmann and Wittgenstein«, *Architecture, Language, Critique*, 112.
184 See the contribution of M. O' C Drury to Fann *Ludwig Wittgenstein: The Man and His Philosophy* (n. 22), 69.
185 Elisabeth Veit, *La Maison de Wittgenstein*. Unpublished Dissertation. (»Unité Pédagogique d'Architecture no. 6«; Paris, 1984), 335-40.
186 See Paul Wijdeveld, *Ludwig Wittgenstein, Architekt*, trans. Ulrike Kremsmair and Martina Heilingsetzer (Basel: Wiese Verlag, 1994) and »Engelmann and Wittgenstein«, 105-113 (n.31).
187 McGuinness, *Approaches*, 162-3.
188 G. W. F. Hegel, *Phänomemologie des Geistes* (Frankfurt/Main: Suhrkamp, 1973), Vorrede, 27f.
189 Ludwig Wittgenstein, *Philosophische Untersuchungen: Frühversion 1937-1938*, eds. G.H. von Wright & H. Nyman (Helsinki: privatly printed, 1979); I, 106.
190 Wittgenstein to Russell 22.VI.12, *RKM*, R, 2.
191 Ray Monk, *op. cit.*, 64.
192 Norman Malcolm, *Ludwig Wittgenstein: A Memoir* (London: Oxford University Press), 1962, 66-7.
193 Cf. Allan Janik and Stephen Toulmin, *Wittgenstein's Vienna* (2nd ed.), 32.
194 The term is a complete misnomer with little more than a polemic sense, as William Barrett pointed out in an (unpublished) address to the American Philosophical Association in the early 1980s. For example, what is normally understood as »Continental philosophy« has precious little to do with philosophy in such countries as Portugal, Poland, Holland, Belgium, Austria, Sweden, Norway, Finland etc. »Analytic« philosophy is equally confusing for reasons partly explained below.
195 Cf. McGuinness, *Young Ludwig*, 244n.
196 Otto Weininger, *Über die letzten Dinge* (Vienna: Braumüller, 1904), 115-21. This work in now available in English as *On Last Things. A Translation of Weininger's Über die letzten Dinge (1904/19079*, trans. Steven Burns (»Studies in German

Language and Literature,« Vol. 28; Lewiston, NY et al: The Edwin Mellen Press, 2001).
197 Personal communication from G.H. von Wright in Philadelphia, 1966; cf. his »Biographical Sketch« in Malcolm, *op. cit.*, (n.7), 21.
198 Brian McGuinness, *Approaches,* 133–6.
199 David Pears, *op. cit.* (n. 10).
200 I owe this apposite phrase to Kjell S. Johannessen.
201 This is why he could agree with Moore that Weininger was »fantastic« but nevertheless »great and fantastic« *RKM, M,* 17 (23.VIII.31).
202 This text certainly bears examination in the light of Wittgenstein's injunction to silence at the end of the *Tractatus* and vice versa.
203 Weininger, *op. cit.*, 119.
204 At this point, as well as several others, Miss Anscombe's translation is misleading: »Stellungnahme« refers to a position, taking a stand, making a commitment. »Attitude« only catches part of the word's sense. Similarly, »das erlösende Wort« is more than merely »the key word«, »the redeeming word« or the »saving word« would be closer.
205 Weininger, »Tierpsychologie«, *Über die letzten Dinge,* 116.
206 Martin Heidegger, *Sein und Zeit* (Tübingen: Max Niemeyer Verlag, 1967), § 29, 134–40 *et passim.* Wittgenstein's similarities with Heidegger and Nietzsche stem partly from his reading of Weininger and through him from the so-called South-West German School of Neo-Kantianism – as well as Schopenhauer and Spengler. On the South-West German School in general, see Lucien Goldmann, *Lukács et Heidegger* (Paris: Denöel, 1973).
207 *Ibid.*, § 9, 42–3 *passim.*
208 Friederich Waismann, *Wittgenstein und der Wiener Kreis,* hrsg. B. F. McGuinness (Oxford: Blackwell, 1967), 68–9.
209 »If my book is ever published the preface must contain a reference to the foreword to Paul Ernst's edition of Grimm's fairy tales which I should have mentioned in the *Logische-philosophischen Abhandlung* as the source of the expression »misunderstanding the logic of language«, (*Philosophische Bemerkungen,* 184, *BEE,* my translation).
210 Janik, *Wittgenstein's Vienna Revisited,* 52–3.

ENDNOTES

211 Anthony Kenny, »Wittgenstein on the Nature of Philosophy«, *Wittgenstein and His Times* (n. 38), 13.
212 See my »Wittgensteins revolutionäre Auffassung der Sprache«, *Wissenschaftliche Nachrichten* 80 (Vienna, April, 1989), 5–7.
213 Norman Malcolm, »Wittgenstein: The Relation of Language to Instinctive Behavior« *Philosophical Investigations* 5, I (1982), 3–22.
214 Cf. St. Augustine, *Confessions*, trans. Rex Warner (New York, 1963), 1963, 14.
215 This is the explicit subject of Weininger's essay, »Über Henrik Ibsen und seine Dichtung *Peer Gynt*« in *Über die letzten Dinge*, to which the fragment on animal psychology is an appendage. See *On Last Things* (n. 196 above), 1–40 and my *Wittgenstein's Vienna Revisited*, Chs. 3 and 8.
216 Kenny *op. cit.*, 26
217 I cite Spengler from Oswald Spengler, *Der Untergang des Abendlands: Umrisse einer Morphologie der Weltgeschichte* (Munich: DTV, 1972) by page number in parenthesis in the text.
218 Wittgenstein, *Vermischte Bemerkungen*, 41, cf. 167, n. 8.
219 Rudolf Haller, »War Wittgenstein von Spengler beeinflusst?« *Fragen zu Wittgenstein und Aufsätze zur österreichischen Philosophie*, (»Studien zur österreichischen Philosophie«, Bd. 10, Amsterdam: Rodopi, 1986), 155–69.
220 Rafael Ferber, »Wittgenstein und Spengler«, *Archiv für die Geschichte der Philosophie Bd. 73, 2 (1991)*, 188–207.
221 See my review of Elazar Benyoëtz, *Die Zukunft liegt uns am Nacken, Mitteilungen aus dem Brenner Archiv* 19 (2001), 94–8 for a discussion of the commanding character of aphorisms.
222 See Pierre Aubenque, *La prudence chez Aristôte* (Paris: Presses Universitaire de France, 1963).
223 Aristotle, *Poetics*, trans. Malcolm Heath (London: Penguin, 1996), 50b.
224 G.P. Baker & P.M.S. Hacker, *Wittgenstein: Understanding and Meaning* (Oxford: Basil Blackwell, 1980), 136. The term »Lebensform« does in fact occur in Spengler, for example, see 794.
225 See Allan Janik and Stephen Toulmin, *Wittgenstein's Vienna*, 258.

Index

A

Anderson, Stanford 168
Anna O. 15
Anscombe, G E M 73, 120, 207, 219
Archimedes
 Archimedean 149
Aristotle 138, 209, 215, 241
 Aristotelian 20, 192, 200

B

Bahr, Hermann 165
Baker, G. P. 215
Baumann 107, 111
Bohr, Niels 26
Boltzmann, Ludwig 11, 12, 18, 19, 23–43, 45, 47, 48, 53, 74, 75, 84, 86, 93, 98, 109, 110, 113–116, 127, 159, 163, 179, 222, 223
Bolzano, Bernhard 101
Breuer, Joseph 12, 14, 15
Broad, C. D. 221

C

Carnap, Rudolf 28, 55, 82
Cavell, Stanley 216
Cezanne, Paul 58
Chagall, Marc 14
Chomsky, Noam 126, 196
Columbus, Christopher 24, 25
Continental philosophers 184, 210

D

Darwin, Charles 35, 114, 220, 221
 Darwinism 27, 115, 221
Derrida, Jacques 176
Descartes, René 182
 Cartesian 54, 107, 194
Dilthey, Wilhelm 46, 68
Don Juan 189
Drobil, Michael 12, 17
Drury, Maurice 69, 73, 92
Duhem, Pierre 60

E

Einstein, Albert 14
Engelmann, Paul 97, 132, 147, 150, 163, 164, 175
Erdmann, Benno 107
Ernst, Paul 194

F

Fann, K. T. 32, 69
Faraday, Michael 24, 54
Ferber, Rafael 205, 206, 213, 224
Ficker, Ludwig von 63, 64, 168
Fischer von Erlach, Johann Bernhard 17, 176
Fleck, Ludwik 14
Foucault, Michel 73
Francis Joseph, Emperor 171
Frege, Gottlob 11, 12, 18, 19, 34–36, 41, 43, 62–64, 71, 73–75, 79–81, 91, 94, 97–120, 123, 124, 127, 129, 130–132, 134, 136–139, 141, 143, 146, 147, 149, 154, 159, 160, 161, 163, 178, 179, 181, 184, 185, 192, 222
    Fregean 62, 85, 98, 102, 115, 118, 137, 160, 161, 183
Freud, Sigmund 12, 14, 15, 20, 59

G

Gadamer, Hans-Georg 46, 68
Galileo, Galilei 31
Goethe, Johann Wolfgang von 31, 99, 151, 155, 216, 218, 223

H

Hacker, P. M. S. 215
Haller, Rudolf 102, 205, 206
Harden, Maximilian 161
Hegel, Friedrich 41, 93, 181
    Hegelian 194
Heidegger, Martin 14, 46, 66, 73, 154, 176, 185, 193, 222
Helmholtz, Hermann von 51, 56
Herder, Johann Gottfried 149
Hertz, Heinrich 11, 12, 15, 18, 19, 26, 33–35, 41, 43, 45–48, 50–61, 63, 64, 66, 68, 70, 71, 74, 75, 78, 116, 130, 134, 136, 140, 163, 179, 181, 185, 219, 222

Hertzian 26, 33, 60, 62, 64, 65, 67–69, 71, 116, 136, 176, 177, 184, 187, 222
Hilbert, David 65, 97
Husserl, Edmund 14, 81

I

Ibsen, Henrik 139, 148

J

James, William 20, 183, 185, 195
Jastrow, Joseph 210
Johannessen, Kjell S. 207
Joyce, James 124

K

Kant, Immanuel 29, 30, 41, 50, 56, 83, 85, 93, 95, 101, 107, 110, 111, 140, 188
    Kantian 62, 86, 101, 118, 194
Kenny, Anthony 203
Kierkegaard, Søren 19, 71, 185, 189
Kraus, Karl 11, 12, 18, 35, 43, 71, 74, 91, 92, 110, 111, 119, 145–156, 159–165, 167, 168, 181, 182, 223
    Krausian 147, 149, 150, 153, 155, 159

L

Lakatos, Imre 26
Leibniz, Gottfried 132
Lichtenberg, Georg Christoph 20, 71, 149, 151
logical positivism 198, 205, 208
Loos, Adolf 11, 12, 18, 43, 74, 146, 162–168, 170–176, 178, 179, 223
    Bauschule 172

M

Mach, Ernst 25, 26, 31, 33, 48–55, 64, 68, 159

INDEX

Malcolm, Norman 183
Mauthner, Fritz 123
Maxwell, James Clerk 15, 25, 51, 54
Mayer, J. Robert 24
McGuinness, Brian 21, 23, 24, 35, 95, 103, 117, 130, 131, 133, 134, 145, 148, 163, 179
Mill, John Stuart 107
Moore, George Edward 20, 125
moralists, French 151
Moravánsky, Ákos 171, 175
Morrell, Lady Ottoline 129

N

Neurath, Otto 20, 61
Newton, Isaac 43, 48, 49, 53, 55, 56, 57, 130
  Principia Mathematica 77, 81, 131
Nietzsche, Friedrich 39, 73, 151, 176, 185, 189

O

Ostwald, Wilhelm 55

P

Pascal, Blaise 81, 151, 204
Pears, David 28, 83, 84, 88, 186
Peirce, C. S. 127
Pichler, Alois 18, 66
Plato 101, 196
  Platonic 49, 154
Polanyi, Michael 206, 207
Popper, Karl 25, 27
positivism 71, 81, 149
Proust, Marcel 14
Pythagorean 154

Q

Quine, W. V. O. 61, 130

R

Ramsey, Frank 20

Rhees, Rush 200
Rochefoucauld, François de La 151
Romantics, the 149
Russell, Bertrand 11, 12, 18, 19, 27, 31, 34–36, 40, 43, 46, 64, 73– 75, 77, 81, 84, 86, 87, 99, 103, 119, 121, 123–126, 128–134, 138–141, 143, 146, 154, 161, 163, 178, 179, 182, 183, 186, 190, 191, 193
Russellian 82, 85, 158
Ryle, Gilbert 90, 110

S

Saint Augustine 19, 81, 197, 202, 218
Saussure, Ferdinand de 212
Schlick, Moritz 64, 87, 193
Schlömilch, Oskar 107
Schoenberg, Arnold 173
Scholastic 194
Schopenhauer, Arthur 11, 12, 18, 19, 32–34, 36, 41, 43, 73–95, 99, 109, 110, 115, 117–119, 141, 151, 157, 159, 163, 183, 185–187, 191, 193, 212, 215, 222, 223
  Schopenhauerian 73, 78, 80–82, 85–91, 114, 117, 118, 211
Schorske, Carl 165
Schröder, Ernst 107
Schubert 41
Schwarzwald, Eugenie 167, 168
Shaker 178
Siegfried 129
Socrates 26, 151, 152, 174, 197
Spengler, Oswald 11, 12, 18, 19, 43, 71, 73, 74, 76, 92, 106, 119, 163, 175, 200, 205–224
Spinoza, Baruch 137, 138, 191, 192
Sraffa, Piero 11, 12, 18, 19, 36, 43, 69, 163, 224
Stern, J. P. 151
Sterrett, Susan 103
Stonborough, Gretl 175

245

T

Tagore, Rabindranath 148
Thales 158
Timms, Edward 148
Tolstoy, Leo 20, 71, 78, 185, 191
Toulmin, Stephen 26, 221
Trakl, Georg 148

V

Vaihinger, Hans 100
Vienna
  modernism, Viennese 165
  Vienna Circle 20, 64, 133, 176
  Vienna Secession 165
von Wright, Georg Henrik 23, 95, 146, 185
Weierstrass, Karl 220
Weininger, Otto 11, 12, 18, 20, 34, 43, 71, 74, 76, 79, 81, 92, 115, 118, 138, 139, 147, 162–164, 173, 182–189, 191–194, 198, 200, 203, 204, 223
Wijdeveld, Paul 17, 175, 176
Wisdom, John 221
Wotan 129

If you liked *Assembling Reminders* you may also be interested in the following titels from Santérus Academic Press:

The Power of Example
Tore Nordenstam

All understanding is example-based. Examples are not just appendages of understanding, illustrations or pedagogical devices, they are the cornerstones of understanding. These are some of the most important ideas in this book. The author demonstrates the fundamental role that examples play in concept formation and cultural understanding by using examples from art, literature, ethics and law.

The Practical Intellect
Bo Göranzon

The epistemology of professional knowledge is a research field that occupies itself with the development and maintenance of professional knowledge at both an individual and working group level, but also at a community level. One of its major aims is to illustrate the effect of information technology on professional knowledge and to create the basis for a sound social and productive implementation of new technology in the workplace.

The Rise of Management-Speak
Björn Rombach, Patrik Zapata (ed)

Essays about why people who speak the language »management-speak« always seem to win arguments, not because they know more, but because they speak the right language.

Standardizing Civil Society
Ola Segnestam Larsson

This book focuses on empirical phenomenon of organizational development, which seems to be trusted as the solution to many problems in civil society and the key to 'the good society'. But can organizational development fulfil such expectations?

www.santerus.se